Rabbit Lane

Memoir of a Country Road

Rabbit Lane

Memoir of a Country Road

By

Roger Evans Baker

Contents

Introduction

Rabbit Lane: *Memoir of a Country Road* tells the story of a humble country dirt road, of its human history, of its natural beauty, and of its ability to bring insight, understanding, transformation, and healing to those who mindfully walk it. The book contains stories and poems, music and nature observations that will amuse and inspire. *Rabbit Lane* helps us to slow down and pay attention to the beauty around us and within us. The prefatory poem, *Silent Spring*, honors the vision and hope of Rachel Carson, author of the 1962 classic book by the same name, for a world filled with the music and beauty of nature. Enjoy each of the many chapters, stories, poems, and songs as you walk with me on Rabbit Lane.

SILENT SPRING

Spring,
Rachel:
not silent quite.
I hear,
distinctly:
the growing hum
of humankind.

First Walk

Never betray inspiration with hesitation.

Sleepily down Church Road I walked, past an unmarked dirt lane traveled most often by farmers on tractors. Somehow I had tumbled out of bed and out the door. I would much rather have continued my slumber under warm covers. Crisp darkness and the ripe fragrance of dew upon cut hay greeted me as I stepped onto the covered porch. I could see only silhouettes in the lingering darkness: old trees planted by farmers perhaps a century ago; the Oquirrh mountain range; cattle chewing mechanically on coarse grass.

I blamed Angie. It was because of her that I began to walk on Rabbit Lane.

"I intend to live a long, full life, and I want you to live it with me," she confronted me where I lay on the bed staring despondently to the south through the big window, over fields of tall, brown grass. "I'm afraid that if you don't change something, you won't be there with me, and I don't want to be alone in my old age."

Early the next morning I arose, quietly, so as not to awaken her, not out of consideration so much as pride, out of not wanting her to know that she had motivated me to escape the perpetual pull of sleep, to move beyond my miserable comfort. As yet I was unwilling to confess it.

I walked toward the highway, the dog baying at my back, begging me to take him along. *No, Tank. This is for me.* Sensing my resolve, he set to a mournful howling, like a lonely wolf under a full moon. I shuddered at the neighbors' unheard curses.

Past Harvey's log-clad trailer I lumbered, past Ron's house dressed shabbily in fake red-brick asphalt shingling, past Shirley's once-neat bungalow with peeling white paint and rotting wood soffit, past Lucille's brown two-room clapboard shack with the outhouse thirty feet from the front door. Past fields of golden oats and purple-flowered alfalfa ready to cut, dry, bale, and stack.

Directly above the entrance to the dirt road, leaves suddenly rustled high in a Cottonwood tree, as if from the sharp release of a branch pulled back taut. I looked quickly up to see the gray shape of a great owl flying powerfully with wide, deep wing beats, but making no sound at all in its flight. It screeched suddenly, high and hoarse, as if to say, *How ignorantly you interrupt my repose!* The owl flew eastward toward the mountains, behind which a faint pink light steadily grew in anticipation of sunrise.

My encounter with the owl felt personal, even miraculous, as if a gentle reward from some nature-spirit pleased that I had summoned the strength to venture forth into her marvelous but fleeting realm of early morning stillness.

The soft lowing of cattle began to give way to an irksome highway hum that grew to a buzz, and, as I approached the intersection, to a morning rush-hour roar that pressed against me as if it were the gale of a howling hurricane. Reaching the highway, I turned and recoiled as the force of the terrific noise pushed me away, back to the interior of the farmland. This hurried human commotion had quickly usurped the magical peace of my meeting the owl, had compelled me to reverse course and walk toward home, my back to the noisy artery. I determined never to approach the intersection on foot again.

Half-a-mile from the highway, I began to hear again the faint sounds of water trickling idly through an irrigation ditch. In the new light of morning, a muskrat splashed its startling alarm and dove to streak back to its burrow in the bank.

Here, at the ditch, begins Rabbit Lane, a narrow dirt road that follows the natural terrain between farms. Rabbit Lane marks the county's zero longitude line on the Salt Lake Base and Meridian survey system: everything east is east; everything west is west. Ancient cottonwood trees form a shaded canopy where the road begins, like the shrouded entrance to a magical green world. The irrigation ditch, overgrown with Cattail reeds, Watercress, and Russian Olive trees, follows along one side of the lane. Pink-blossomed Milkweed lines the road edges where the county grader has pushed up a slight berm. Repelled by the memory of the highway's howl, I turned north onto the hard-packed dirt, and found myself forever changed.

Russian Olive tree

COME WALK WITH ME

Come walk with me
down Rabbit Lane.
Come walk with me,
my child.
Tell me your troubles.
Tell me your fears.
Tell me your joys and your dreams.
Tell me everything,
while we walk,
past racing horses and cudding cattle,
past the llama guarding thick-wooled sheep,
past deep-green alfalfa and wispy golden grain,
past the skittish muskrat diving to its ditch-bank burrow,
past Monarch caterpillars poised on pink, perfumed milkweed.
Come walk with me,
my child,
just you and me.
Come walk with me
down Rabbit Lane.

To the Country

You deserve a palace made of gold.
(But even a gold palace needs to be kept clean.)
(Dad to Erin-8)

We moved to the country in the Spring of 1998. Our new home offered so much room for the children to explore and play and run around. They tromped through the tall, tan field grass making twisting paths that were not even visible from the house. Once the children entered the grass they could not see out (or be seen from without). They were pioneers, blazing new trails in the wilderness, whacking at the grass with stick swords.

A sudden shrieking, flapping sound frightened the children and sent them running and shrieking themselves to the safety of home. A large bird had sprung up from its hiding place in the grass, flying off with loud whirring strokes of its short wings. They found me on the porch and told me about their terrifying encounter. A moment later we heard the guttural "Er-Er!" of a cock Ring-necked Pheasant, earning its name from the bright red head and white collar around its neck. They had been too scared to notice its beauty. Pheasants like the tall grass in which to hide from feral cats, skunks, raccoons, and sword-wielding children.

Darkness prevailed on the first occasion when we took the children to see the soon-to-be-ours country house with the big porch. No moon. No city street lights. No cars. Just the twinkling stars, much brighter than seen from our house in the city, and the lights from the sparse neighbors' windows.

A strange sound started up across the street, a deep grunting that rose to a loud, rough bellow. Soon dozens of similar bellows started up, all at different times, deafening, dissonant, and frightening. Laura (2) started to cry, and still cried even after I picked her up and explained to her that the racket was just a bunch of cows mooing in the neighbor's farm. She was not convinced or set at ease. Black cows unseen against the black earth under the black sky. Even I wished for the morning light.

Laura felt happy the next time we came, during the day, when she could see the herd of black cows slowly munching their grass, lazily wandering around the pasture, and mooing peacefully.

"Just a bunch of black cows," she said in a matter-of-fact, confident, but relieved toddler voice.

Hawk

In the presence of goodness, good people rejoice.

My boots crunch loudly on the loose and frozen gravel, rousing common House Sparrows from their cold roosts in the Willow and Wild Rose. Despite being leafless in December, the bushes seem an impenetrable tangle of twigs and dead leaves. I hear, rather than see, the birds fluttering and tweeting within. I have bundled myself against the bitter cold, and wonder how these almost weightless creatures survive Winter. I imagine them huddled in their houses, mostly protected from the wind, their feathers puffed out to gather insulating air, with temperatures sinking to just above zero. I marvel that these birds constantly peep and sing, fluttering about with the energy of jubilation. I envy them their unconditional happiness. I have come to appreciate their enthusiasm, to rely upon their unassailable cheerfulness.

A short distance down Rabbit Lane, in the gray of pre-dawn, a sizable lump slightly darker than the dark road began to show itself

100 yards ahead. I slowed my pace for fear of encountering a skunk, but the lump stayed uncharacteristically still. Charcoal darkness lifted subtly to steel gray even as I approached the object lying in the middle of the lane. It remained unmoving. Now within ten yards, I could see that the lump was a bird, a large bird. Stepping nearer, I nudged the dead form with my toe, then bent to examine it more closely. The bird was a mature Red-tailed Hawk, its body still warm and supple. Its head lolled loosely on what appeared to be a broken neck. I struggled to deduce what had caused its death. No trees or power poles lined Rabbit Lane in this location. Cars were rare at this time of day, and usually drove slowly for the pot holes. Had the hawk collided with another raptor, perhaps an owl, in aerial combat? Or had it expired suddenly on the wing and landed fortuitously in my path?

Lifting the bird, I found it surprisingly light for its bulk, and cradled it in the crook of my arm like a child that needed comforting, stroking its feathers as I turned toward home without finishing my walk. I laid the hawk on my work bench to examine it more closely: ferrous tail feathers; long primaries; incisor beak. What struck me most were the ebony-black talons, two inches long each, four on each yellow foot. I spread the talons to tuck in a tennis ball, and the talons held it firmly, three talons in front, one in back. I thought for a moment of harvesting the talons and some feathers. I hungered for a token of my encounter with the great bird, to keep it with me in some tangible way. The taloned feet would make impressive trophies. But I knew that harvesting from the hawk was not only illegal, it would also make a hollow trophy, an empty souvenir, like an artifact stolen from a museum to gather dust in some necessary but forgotten hiding place. Keeping any physical part of the hawk would dishonor the bird as well as plague me with guilt and the fear of being caught. The hawk deserved better, and so did I.

After consulting with a game warden friend, I prepared to bury the hawk. My children accompanied me, admiring the hawk as I had. At the edge of my garden plot, I placed the hawk on a new three-foot-long bale of hay. Stretching out the bird's wings, the feather tips hung over the edges of the bale by at least three inches on each side. Having dug a deep hole, I refolded the wings and carefully placed the regal bird into its garden grave.

I marveled that the Red-tailed Hawk had come to me, or I to it. What would have happened to the hawk had I not encountered it at that moment? It might have been obliterated by heavy truck tires, mangled by raccoons or dogs, kicked aside to become mere carrion, or desecrated. How preferable its burial beneath rows of corn and tomatoes and pumpkin vines.

My funereal reverie disturbed by a commotion to the west, I turned to see Erin (10), Laura (7), and John (5) standing on the chicken coop roof, silhouetted against the sunset, flapping their arms and letting out descending screams like the piercings of a Red-tailed Hawk.

Desert Lighthouse

Only small people seek to make other people feel small.

Our first night in the country house, the children all slept in mom's and dad's room. We offered this arrangement until they felt comfortable sleeping in their own rooms. One night several weeks after moving to her own room, Erin (5) could not sleep.

"Daddy," Erin called in a loud whisper.

"What?" I moaned groggily after a moment.

"The lightning is keeping me awake."

"What lightning?" I yawned. "I don't hear any lightning."

"No—look—there—it's flashing right now, without thunder or rain," she persisted.

I pushed myself up onto an elbow with a groan. A light flashed rhythmically through the window, reflecting off the bedroom walls and keeping Erin, and now me, awake. I expected crashing thunder, but it did not come. I expected pouring rain, but it did not come. Still the lightning kept flashing, as steady as a slowly-ticking clock.

"Oh," I said simply after a minute, finally coming to realization. "That's the lighthouse." My answer, however, did not satisfy her at all.

"A lighthouse?" Erin asked. "We live in Utah, Dad. It's mostly desert. We are whole states away from the ocean. What's a lighthouse doing here?"

By now everyone was awake and wondering at the pulsing lights. I told the children about the small airport a few miles away, and explained that the lighthouse beacon showed pilots where the runway was at night so they would not crash in the dark.

The next night, I found Erin sitting on her bed gazing westward through her bedroom window toward the little airport. We could not see the lighthouse, but we could see the light turning atop its tower. It flashed like a bright star when it pointed toward us, turning quickly away, then flashed again, then turned away again. After each white flash came a burst of green, like a giant emerald gleaming for a moment in the moonlight.

"I love lighthouses," I said quietly. "When I was sixteen or so, a friend of Grandpa and Grandma used to take me sailing off New Jersey's Atlantic Highlands in his nineteen-foot sloop. From the sea we could see the Sandy Hook lighthouse standing proud and lonesome on its sandy seaside hill. And when your mother and I celebrated our honeymoon in Cape May, we climbed more than a hundred steps on a skinny spiral staircase to the top of the lighthouse. From there, we looked out over the huge waters, where the Delaware River meets the Atlantic Ocean. We held hands and breathed the fresh, salty air and watched the seagulls ride on invisible waves of air while fishermen cast their lures into the surf."

Erin responded with her own sense of longing in her voice, "You must have been very happy holding Mamma's hand at the top of the lighthouse, so high you could see the world."

In the months that followed, I often found Erin kneeling on her bed with her arms folded on the tile windowsill, watching the desert lighthouse sparkling its steady rhythm of white and green, white and green. Growing sleepier and sleepier, she would slip away from her vigil at the window and crawl under the covers to sleep.

One day Erin said to me, "I think our lighthouse is a perfectly wonderful lighthouse. I think the sky is the ocean, a calm ocean, and the stars are ships gliding through the water, looking to the lighthouse to guide the way."

"I like that," I responded. "And are the wheat and alfalfa fields the rolling clouds?"

"No," she answered thoughtfully after a moment. "They are the flowing, waving sky, and the white morning-glory flowers are the stars."

"I like that," I said again. "Our own ocean and our own lighthouse, with us sailing together through the sky."

I rolled over in bed one night, disturbed by an indefinable presence. My eyes suddenly attuned themselves to the spectral shape of Erin (9) standing darkly at the foot of my bed, like a ghost. She stood still, saying nothing, only staring at me. I started, my heart pounding rapidly in my chest, and my whole body quivered.

"What is it, Erin?" I managed to say after catching my breath.

"I'm scared," she whispered, sounding terrified.

Me too, I thought.

"Come here," I offered, pulling her into bed between her mother and me. I stroked her face and hair and told her she would be alright, and she soon fell asleep.

Erin seemed frightened many nights, so I occasionally laid myself next to her to help her fall asleep, humming randomly, making up little stories and songs. After several weeks, a simple tune and poem distilled itself from the randomness to become Erin's own lullaby. I sang it to her and to her sisters many nights as the years ticked by.

> *Good night my dear. Sleep well my dear.*
> *Don't fret or fear: I'll be right here.*
> *If you should worry in the night,*
> *Just call my name, I'll hold you tight.*
> *You'll see: you'll be alright.*

As I walked for months and years on Rabbit Lane, I noticed words and music spontaneously forming in my mind and coming forth from my lips. I began to hum, to sing, repeating tunes and phrases over and over until I felt they were fully birthed, whole and beautiful in their own right. I quickly learned that, for them to live, I needed to honor them by immediately putting pen to paper or fingers to keyboard. At first I drew my own musical staffs, then bought notation paper. If I put off the inspiration, I lost the inspiration, and whatever life had graced me with vanished as mysteriously as it had come.

Good Night My Dear

Roger Baker

Good night my dear. Sleep well my dear. Don't fret or

fear: I'll be right here. If you should wor - ry in the night, Just

(Repeat as often as desired or until your child falls asleep.)

rallentando (slow down a lot)   *a tempo* (back to normal)

call my name, I'll hold you tight. You'll see: you'll be al - right.

RITA

The old man was kind to me,
though I offered nothing but my youthful company,
which I made pleasant, for my gratitude,
on those summer days.

How we sailed!

From Sandy Hook toward Hudson's kills,
Twin Towers rising like brother beacons
beckoning us to tack their way,
I on the rudder,
Bill on the main sheet and jib.

Oh—how we sailed!

He tethered his wife,
a cheerful lump of rheumatoid flesh,
and tossed her offhandedly overboard,
whence she giggled and squealed
for the cool and the salt, the jostling wake,
for her release from the chair.

Sailing in the salt breeze!

Ponderous thunderheads darkened abruptly,
and we hauled her in
like a troll-caught crab
and fled the flashes, knowing
how tall and conductive was the metal mast
and how helpless we would be
on the water.

Old Cottonwood

Engage your mind or others will engage it for you.

Cottonwood trees are the legacy of the departed farmer. Once mere twigs, they grew quickly to become giants of the valley landscape. The oldest Cottonwoods are slowly dying. Each Spring the emerging leaves draw in closer to the trunks, leaving more of the outstretched branches as bare as skeletons. More and more bark sloughs off, leaving the trunks to bleach in the Summer sun. Dead Cottonwood trees resemble the ruins of medieval cathedrals. The bare branches seem sculpted and shaped, like the flying buttresses that once supported a stone ceiling but that now lift up the ceiling of the sky.

In one huge dead Cottonwood, a few rickety rungs of an old wooden ladder still remain, nailed into the trunk, sloughed of bark and smooth. Remnants of a tree house platform rest inside the forks of the branching trunk. I wonder: what children played in this tree, in the tree house they built from spontaneous adventure, and then abandoned with age? Have they grown old and died, like this tree?

In another dying behemoth, a Great Horned Owl stands regally on a top branch, silhouetted black against the deep blue sky of late twilight.

Some forgotten farmer planted a Cottonwood sprig on Ron's property long ago. It has grown to enormous girth that pushes into the dirt road of Rabbit Lane. The dilapidated plank fort-fence stops on the south side and resumes on the north, with the trunk standing between. The tree's branches arc high over the road and over collapsing coops, forming a verdant tunnel through which sunlight filters green on the ground below.

I thought one day to determine the old tree's circumference. A group of people might circle the tree holding hands, but the fence blocked the way. Instead, I took a tape measure on my walk, a length of rope, and a roll of masking tape, as well as the children. Tying the roll of tape for weight to the end of the rope, I swung it in circles above my head, letting it fly toward one side of the tree. My first attempt sent the roll of tape flying straight past the tree into the cow pen. A few more attempts taught me to throw the weight in such a way that the rope would hit the tree and pull the weighted end around. On my last attempt, both roll and rope came circling around the tree to rest conveniently on a bent, rusty nail protruding from the trunk, placed there as if for the purpose. Bringing the tape end of the rope to the section of rope I was holding, I marked the place with a piece of tape, untied the roll of tape, and pulled the rope back around the tree. Holding the rope against the closed tape measure, I pulled out the measuring tape as I stretched out lengths of the tossed rope. My mark on the rope landed on the 17-foot mark. Seventeen feet around! What a tree! What stories it could tell from its long life: storms and clear skies; plantings and harvests; birthings and butcherings; arguments and celebrations; growing and struggling and flourishing; baptisms and christenings and funerals; growing old and enduring age and change.

John and Caleb with Old Cottonwood

In early Summer, the Cottonwood trees produce wispy tufts of cottony seeds. They fall soft and thick, like snow, but slower, accumulating in clumps on the ground. Occasionally they float and rise on an unperceived breeze, seeming to defy gravity. And they make people sneeze.

OLD COTTONWOOD

The old cottonwood is dead,
dead for many years.
Leaves have flown to join with new soil.
Sun-bleached bark has sloughed and fallen.
But the aspect of its reaching is preserved.
The trunk holds steady, the unseen roots entrenched.
A thousand branches reach sharply upwards,
spiny fingers feeling upwards,
still swaying, though stiffly.
Red-tailed hawk still reconnoiters from a favorite high branch.
Great-horned owl still softly calls its mate.
And kestrel now rests in its cavities.

Harvey

Small acts of kindness soften the soul.

"Let's go over to Harvey's," I suggested one Sunday afternoon soon after moving to the country house.

"Who's Harvey?" asked Brian (8).

"Harvey is our neighbor," I explained. "You'll like his place. He has lots of animals."

We walked down Church Road toward Rabbit Lane, past Russell's arena, and turned up the dirt drive to Harvey's log-sided house. No one answered my knock at the door, but I thought it would be alright if we looked around at Harvey's animals. We smelled the animals before we saw them: skunk. No doubt about it. A wrinkled, water-stained sign wired to the cage read, *Stay Away*.

We circled a wide path around the skunk cage, never catching a glimpse of the animal, then came to a big wood-and-wire cage with tall forked branches standing like trees inside and a plywood shelter box in the upper corner. Two timid eyes peaked out at us from the dark inside, followed by a black button nose, long whiskers, and a white-and-gray masked face.

"A raccoon!" Laura (3) shouted with delight.

I took the lid off a rusty can that sat next to the cage, and handed some little hard biscuits shaped like bones to the children. Erin and Laura were a little frightened, but Brian poked a biscuit through the wire into the cage. The adorable raccoon emerged from its dark box and climbed down the branch. We watched, enchanted, as the animal gently took the biscuit in its paws, moistened the biscuit in a water pail, and scuttled back to its house to nibble in peace.

The quiet, magical moment burst into excitement as all the children now poked more biscuits through the wire, coaxing, "Here, raccoon. Come on little raccoon. Come get a delicious biscuit. Here you go." To our surprise a much bigger raccoon peeked out from the darkness of the box and scrambled down the tree-branch. It grabbed a biscuit in each hand and sauntered over to the water pail, rinsing and munching while we watched.

The excitement was more than Laura could contain. "TWO RACCOONS!" she screamed, sending the larger animal scurrying back up the branch into the safety of its dark, cool box.

"Laura," Brian complained. "Don't scare him away." But he was too enthralled to really be angry.

"It's okay, sweetie," I reassured her. "He'll come out again when he's ready."

A voice called out cheerily from behind us, "Why, howdy there, youngins!"

"Harvey!" I called out in reply.

Harvey was one of the strangest looking men I had ever seen. His face was almost completely covered by a thick, white beard that hung from his hidden chin in a mess of tangled curls more than a foot long. His wispy white hair was about that long behind his head, which was shaded with a misshapen hat of rough, sweat-stained felt. The children were timid at first and stepped behind me.

I clapped Harvey on the shoulder, "Good to see you, Harv! I thought I'd bring the children over to show them your animals."

Harvey bent down and said in a gentle voice, "Hiya, kiddies. Do you like the raccoons?"

They nodded their heads shyly, staring, and not knowing what to think of my new friend.

"You kiddies come on over here," Harvey said in a soothing voice. "I want you to meet Lucinda, my favorite pet."

Harvey's small, moist, blue eyes twinkled under the brim of his old hat. Something about his voice, his eyes, and the softness of his smile told them he was safe and kind and good. They relaxed a little and cautiously stepped out from behind me to follow Harvey.

The old man led Laura and Erin slowly by the hand to the cage not far from the raccoons. I could not see anything at first except an empty box and an overturned water dish. I jumped when the dish moved.

Harvey laughed wheezily and said, "Lucinda likes to turn her water dish over onto herself and hide inside. I think she's playing hide-and-seek, with herself."

Just then a little black nose poked out from under the dish, and Harvey said, "Come on out Lucy, and meet our new friends."

As if understanding the old man's message, Lucinda waddled out from under the dish. The girls drew in their breath with sudden fear as they saw the black bushy fur and the unmistakable white stripes. Lucinda was a skunk!

"It's all right," Harvey chuckled, noticing the girls tense up. "I've raised Lucy since she was a tiny little kit. I've never de-scented her, but she's never sprayed me either."

With that explanation he reached his finger through a hole in the chicken wire and gently scratched Lucinda's furry head and upturned snout. She was obviously pleased at the attention, and made funny noises that I would have called purring if she were a cat.

Harvey gazed at the skunk with smiles of love and tenderness, as if she were his own infant child. The animal we call *skunk* was never again just a skunk to us; she was Miss Lucinda, Harvey's special friend.

Something else moved then, but not in a cage. The ring of fat on the old man's stomach suddenly shifted, and a bushy light-brown tail emerged from under his shirt. This time we all started.

"Oh," said Harvey, chuckling. "He was so quiet and content I forgot all about him."

Harvey eased a creature out from under his shirt where it had been comfortably napping against Harvey's warm body.

"What is it?" Erin asked, as much in awe of this new animal as of its resting place.

"*Who* is it," Harvey corrected. "This is my pal Charlie. He's a chocolate skunk. You've never heard of a chocolate skunk? There's lots of kinds of skunks, you know. Blacks and chocolates and albinos. All kinds. Charlie, here, can't spray, but I do not think he would even if he could. Here, child; you hold him."

Before Erin knew what was happening she was holding a skunk, a bushy, brown, chocolate skunk named Charlie. His soft paws grasped her fingers in a friendly way, the way a baby holds your finger with his whole hand. Charlie reached up to touch his cool, moist nose against hers. She giggled at the sensation, but also at the thought. Brian, Laura, and I all watched in awe, not knowing for a moment what to think.

"He likes you," Harvey announced. "Charlie is very selective. He doesn't kiss just any girl he meets—only the special ones."

Erin blushed as Brian burst out laughing. Kissed by a skunk! A skunk named Charlie, no less. I could certainly think of worse things with a skunk.

Erin said to Brian just then, "Why don't you go make friends with the skunk in the *Stay Away* pen."

Harvey took us on a tour of the rest of his place, what we came to call the "zoo," where we saw foxes, deer, goats, sheep, ferrets, rabbits, and hundreds of birds of all kinds, including pea hens and pea cocks, pigeons, jungle fowl, and loud cackling guinea hens.

"Guinea hens make better watch dogs than dogs," Harvey observed. "They make an impossible noise whenever a stranger approaches."

What a place! Harvey invited us to come back any time, even if he was not there. He operated a tannery in a cinderblock building behind his house. Rows of pelts hung from high-strung lines: cougar, wolf, fox, skunk, beaver, deer, raccoon, pronghorn, coyote, rabbit. Enormous 200-gallon vats with dark, foul-smelling liquids sat squatly and randomly around the shop. How ironic that a man who loved living animals had found himself making a meager livelihood by tanning dead hides brought to him by others.

We invited Harvey to dinner months later, on a cold November Sunday. Brian and Erin giggled at his repeated *Mmms* and *Ahhhs* as he savored Angie's meatloaf and baked potatoes. He kept thanking her for the "delightful" meal. Harvey especially enjoyed the fresh whole-wheat bread with butter and honey. He praised Angie for grinding her own wheat and making her own bread "in this pitiful day and age of bleached, processed loaves of air." After dinner Harvey told us a story of when his father, Jim, played a joke on the rural route mailman.

"I'm sure you seen it. In the country, the mailman (or the mail lady, as the case may be) drives a reg'lar car to deliver the mail, only it's not completely reg'lar 'cause the steerin' wheel is on the right side, as opposed to the left, so he can open the mailboxes and stuff the mail, convenient like, without having to lean all the way across the car and through the opposite window.

"Now, unlike you new-comers (no offense intended, of course), us old-timers all had large country mailboxes, big enough to fit several shoe boxes. So when the mailman had parcels and packages, he could just leave 'em right there in the box with the letter mail.

"One day it occurred to my old man—God rest his soul—that our mailbox could fit other largish items besides parcels and packages. Of course, we had known for a long time that the mailbox was a perfect fit for plates of goodies or a gift at Christmas time, if we liked the mailman, that is. And if we didn't like the mailman . . . well, that just never happened in the good old days.

"It just so happened that we did like Richard the mailman. My old man was especially fond of him. In fact, the mailman and him liked to play practical jokes on each other. Nothin' mean or spiteful, you understand. Just fun.

"So, about Thanksgiving time, on that fine day that he thinks of the potential for combining the Christmas gift idea with the idea of other largish objects that the mailbox could accommodate, my old man sends me to fetch one of our turkeys. Then we go and stuff all 20 pounds of her into our mailbox, real sneaky like, and head off to watch. You could set your clock by the time of Richard's arrival: 1:10 p.m. in the afternoon. So we knew when to stuff the turkey and hide.

"When Richard arrived, that turkey hen was mad as a hornet when it stings and as scared as a rattlesnake when it strikes. Just as he did every day of the year, come rain, sleet, snow, and hail, the mailman stopped at our mailbox at 1:10 p.m., rolled down the driver's side window with the mailbox only inches from his face, reached out with the mail in one hand, and pulled down the lid with the other.

"With horrible screeches and squawks, the terrified turkey shot out from the mailbox like a blast from a black powder rifle, right through the open car window and into the mailman's face and on into the car. Shrieking and flapping furiously, she flew around the car, scattering mail everywhere, and covering the upholstery, the mail, and the mailman with feathers and guano.

"We was rollin' on the ground, cryin' and laughin' so hard it hurt, and you'd a-thought we was dyin' madmen. It was a good thing the mailman left his gun in the trunk, or we mighta both been dead. Richard managed to get the turkey out of his car and drove off, shakin' his fist and cussin'. Then we got to feelin' bad. We let 'im cool off for a couple hours, then took the turkey to his house as a Thanksgiving gift. He was a good family friend, and didn't hold it against us for too long."

Harvey was laughing uproariously, tears streaming down his cheeks into his beard. We were all laughing hard ourselves. I admit to crying as much as laughing. The children giggled as much at our sobbing laughter as at Harvey's story.

"Yes siree. Them 'uz the good old days," Harvey summed it up, wiping at his small, blue eyes.

Angie sent him home with a whole loaf of warm wheat bread.

When Harvey heard I was sick with the flu, he brought over a pint jar of yellow liquid and handed it to me through the open front door.

"Drink some of this," recommended Harvey. "It'll fix you up right quick."

"What is it?" I asked somewhat suspiciously.

"It's an old country remedy called Kick-a-Poo juice," he explained. "It's my mother's recipe, made of apple cider vinegar, honey, and cayenne pepper. It'll take care of that flu. You'll see."

"Okay," I accepted, "if you say so."

If it were his mother's recipe, and if it had worked for him, I thought it might work for me. I did not think it could hurt, anyhow. So I chugged the sweet-sour-spicy pint of liquid down, in one sitting. Within minutes I was desperately ill, and wretched in the toilet. The cayenne and vinegar burned more on the way up than they had on the way down. Shivering, exhausted, and miserable, I gave up on life for the day and went to bed.

Several days later Harvey came to collect his pint jar and to inquire as to my well-being. I told him that his kick-a-poo juice had not worked, but had made me very sick, and that I had thrown the whole unpleasant mixture up.

"Well, you weren't supposed to drink the whole pint at once!" he censured. "It's medicine! You're supposed to just sip a little kick-a-poo at a time."

"Oh." I said, feeling stupid. "I didn't know."

I have not dared try Kick-a-Poo juice since.

Harvey's Kick-a-Poo Juice
2 oz. apple cider vinegar (raw, unfiltered, organic)
4 oz. distilled water
2 Tb honey (raw, unfiltered)
African red bird pepper (cayenne pepper, from a pinch
    to a teaspoon depending on your fortitude)

Turtle Lodge

How can we get closer to God?
In airplanes . . . and helicopters! Vvrroooom!
(Caleb-3 to Dad)

Harvey's property was special to the Indians. They needed a place to perform their ceremonies, where it was quiet, where animals and nature were close, and where Indians were welcome. Harvey's place fit the requirements. The Skull Valley Band of the Goshutes had established Harvey's land as an official worship site. Area Indians of several tribes set up a turtle lodge and held their sacred sweat ceremonies there. Harvey invited me repeatedly to attend a ceremony. Respecting but resisting what I did not understand, I politely put him off. One Saturday, though, I reluctantly agreed, admittedly nervous to attend. When I came home several hours later, the children found me exhausted, my hair sweaty and matted. I took a big drink and a shower, then flopped down on the couch. They begged me to tell them all about the Indians and their turtle lodge. I sighed wearily, then told them of my experience with the sweat ceremony.

"Four Indians officiated, with Harvey and some friends. Outside the lodge, Harvey had a bonfire roaring, with big rocks in the fire. The weather was very cold, as you know, with snow on the ground, but all the men changed into only shorts, and the women changed into shorts and t-shirts or loose house dresses. We huddled around the fire to keep warm while the Indians went into the lodge for a private ceremony. Harvey kept the fire hot. But the fire was not for us—it was for the rocks.

"At the entrance to the turtle lodge was an altar—a low mound of earth with sacred Indian things placed upon it. Harvey encouraged us all to leave an offering on the altar. Most left packages of tobacco for the peace pipe. Harvey gave me some tobacco to leave on the altar, since I had not known to bring anything. Then it was our turn to enter. I left my wedding ring and glasses on the altar—it was a place for safe keeping as well as for gifts.

"The turtle lodge seemed bigger inside than it looked from outside."

I explained to them that the lodge was made of flexible poles curving upward, the bottom ends anchored in the ground, the top ends pulled down and lashed together. A circle of these poles formed the lodge's round, bowl-like shape, like a turtle shell. Smaller sticks rounded the poles, tied down where they crossed. Canvas tarps draped over the lodge's shell, one on top of the other, until no outside light seeped in. A pit about two feet deep sat in the center of the lodge. The pit would hold the hot rocks.

"We all sat around the pit, with our backs against the lodge walls, full of anticipation about the ceremony that was about to take place. One by one, Harvey carried several heavy, orange-glowing rocks on the tines of a long pitch fork, placing them carefully in the lodge's pit. Then the door flap was closed and pulled tight. The lodge became completely black, and quickly grew very hot.

"'Welcome,' the Indian chief said to us in a friendly voice. 'This is our sacred ceremony, where we leave the world behind and offer our prayers and songs and offerings to the great Creator, the Creator of earth and sky, of animals and plants, of wind and water. Our Creator.'

"The chief explained that all people are their brothers and sisters, and so we were welcome to worship with them so long as we respected the ceremony and everyone participating in it. The ceremony would consist of four parts, he explained, each about one hour long, where they would offer prayers and songs. In the first hour, we would seek the Creator's blessings for ourselves, because we cannot bless others if we are not whole ourselves. The second hour would seek strength and protection for our families. The third hour would focus on the world's children, on their purity and innocence, but also on their need for special protection. In the last hour, we would pray for our communities, and for the world.

"The chief instructed us not to leave the lodge. If necessary, we could leave the lodge between hours.

"'This is not to punish the participants, but to not disrupt the ceremony,' he explained. 'Also, you must understand that in this lodge, as our bodies become weak, our spirits become strong. This is when you can hear the voice of the Creator: in you, around you, in the earth and all things.'

"He would give us water, he said, between hours because we were not accustomed to the rigors of the ceremony. We all felt a little worried, but the chief seemed to be a nice man.

"The chief began the sweat, as Harvey called it, by singing an Indian song. The other Indians immediately joined him. I couldn't understand a word they sang, but their language and music made a compelling blend of beauty and mystery. I picked up the melody and hummed with them—as we were encouraged to do. The song ended suddenly.

"One of the other Indians was tall and thin with long, straight black hair. He was blind and had facial abnormalities that made it difficult to speak clearly. But we could understand him. All the Indians spoke and prayed. But this Indian seemed particularly in tune with earth and sky that was home to himself and to generations of his ancestors. He was also very sensitive to our ignorance of their beliefs, and explained things openly, honestly, and without suspicion or resentment of us, the descendants of white men than had driven his people from their native lands, that had destroyed the fabric of tribe and community and family. I could tell he was a good man, an honorable man, and I liked him.

"I saw scars on each Indian's chest. I knew of the Sun Dance and the painful injury that left those scars. I asked the blind Indian if he would tell us more. By their silent reactions, I quickly gathered that I had asked about something sacred. But he could tell I was sincerely interested, so he explained.

"'In the Sun Dance, we worship God, the Creator, who is symbolized by the sun, the sun which gives life and brings death to all life through its rays of light and heat. From the top of a tall tree, our brothers and sisters bring ropes to each dancer. Then a brother cuts our chest and pushes strong bones through the flesh, and the ropes are tied to the bones. We dance in worship to God, seeking from Him spiritual power. Sometimes we have visions; sometimes we hear voices. These come from God and give us spiritual power. As we dance, we move away from the tree, pulling hard on the ropes. This causes great pain. Our pain is our sacrifice—it expresses the sincerity of our dance, of our search for spiritual strength. Our pain speaks of the weakness of our bodies and our desire to distance our soul from things physical and to embrace the spirit. Our pain, our dancing, our fasting: these open us to spiritual gifts from the Creator, and give us spiritual power that will stay with us throughout our lives. We dance for hours and pull against the ropes until the bones tear through the flesh. Then we are free from the rope. Then we are free from the cares of the world which tie us down to pettiness and triviality. Then we are aware of the deepness of Mother Earth, and of all creation, and of ourselves.'

"'Thank you,' I said to him, quietly, with respect and humility. What courage! These were not just scars on his chest, but emblems of his yearning to touch his Creator, the supreme being of the universe, emblems that would always be there to remind him of who he was, of what his life was about, and of the price he had paid for this understanding.

"After the blind Indian finished speaking, the chief welcomed each of us to join them in singing, as well as we could, and by offering our prayers as we went one by one around the dark circle. Each prayer ended with the Indian affirmation, 'Aho,' similar to the Christian *Amen*, meaning, roughly, *The words from your mouth echoed in our hearts. We agree.* I prayed silently for my own strength and wisdom: to grow from the afflictions life brings; to withstand destructive forces; to be a force of creation and contribution in the world. The chief offered a summary prayer, we all whispered 'Aho,' and the first hour ended with the opening of the turtle lodge door flaps."

I told them how January's frigid air had provided welcome relief from the intense heat, which the chief explained was between 120 and 130 degrees F. We sipped gratefully from the water he dipped and passed to us. The cooled air was blissful, and I sat with a smile until Harvey brought a new bunch of glowing boulders and the darkness shrouded us again.

"As we sang and prayed and talked, and sat in silence, my back and neck and buttocks began to ache. The third hour was more difficult. I reached up and pulled on the poles to stretch and straighten my spine. The heat sapped my strength. There was enough room in the lodge that I managed to lie down, curled up on my side, while the others in turn sang and prayed and spoke and sat in silence. I was suffering, but I was still aware of what was going on and ready to participate when it was my turn.

"During the fourth hour the blind Indian blessed us with a simple yet sublime prayer: "'Great God, Great Spirit. Thank you for allowing us to send to You our heart's offerings of prayer and song and sincerity. Thank you for the presence of these good people who love You and reverence You, and who care for each other.'

"As he completed each sentence, the group reverently whispered, 'Aho.'

"'Thank you for Mother Earth, for the abundant life She has given birth to: the beautiful butterflies and soaring birds; the fearsome bear and lion; the tall trees waving their breathing, cleansing leaves. Thank you for the honorable people of the world who respect their Mother Earth who brings them life.'

"'Aho.'

"'Forgive us for our ignorance, for our apathy, and for the hurt we do to others and to the earth.'

"'Aho.'

"'Bless the earth with renewal, with strength, and with a forgiving heart. Bless this land, that it may continue to be a place of reverence and worship, that Your presence may continue to abide through the animals and plants and rocks and air which You created, and through the peace and wisdom of nature. Hinder the path of selfish, greedy persons who would strip this land of its purity, its virginity, its beauty. Do not let pride prevail, but let the strength of humility and silence abide.'

"'Aho.'

"Silence pervaded for several minutes while the blind Indian's words lingered in the hot, dark air, and in our minds, while sweat ran from every pore. We listened to the silence, which was not empty, but rather full of energy and vibrancy, full of spirit and heart and soul, full of ripe intention.

"Despite my discomfort, I began to notice within me an increasing comprehension of what was happening in the ceremony, in the turtle lodge. We had entered a place of total darkness and deprivation. To many religious people, this might seem a dismal thing to do. But not to them. These Indians had found a way to leave the earth, to leave their physical, mortal state, by entering a place from which all worldly elements were left outside: light, wind, water, air, food, fancy clothing, pride, luxury. In this place existed only themselves and their Creator, with nothing in between.

"The world's religions, each in their own ways, all provide a means of leaving the earth with its physical worries and mortal cares, sometimes by donning white or ornate clothing and entering sacred buildings full of gold, jewels, sculptures, and other emblems of preciousness, of divinity. Buildings like temples and synagogues, mosques and cathedrals. Entering these buildings symbolizes leaving the earthly world behind and transcending to a higher state of being, or to heaven. In these places, we approach God where He is by leaving where we are and trying to close the gap. We often fast, putting off our bodily needs to seek spiritual strength and insight. That's what the Indians were doing in their sweat ceremony. We had left the world behind and sought to close the gap between heaven and earth, to approach our Creator, to hear His voice through vision and silent inspiration."

As I finished my long narrative, the children watched me quietly, in their own awe, unable to comment or ask questions. I knew that they had not understood everything I had said, but I hoped that they had felt the bigness of my experience, that it was somehow sacred and important to them, as it had been sacred and important to me. They sensed that speaking would break the magic of the silence, would chase away the wonder and mystery of the images filling their minds. They could almost see the people in shorts and jumpers surrounding the rock pit, see the orange rocks placed one by one in the pit, see the canvas flap pulled tight, see the darkness. They could almost feel the unbearable heat, the hot sweat trickling down every wrinkle, dripping off our noses and chins and eyebrows. They did not hear the songs with their ears, but still the songs filled them and moved within them, feeling strange yet wonderful and satisfying.

"Then something really special happened," I gently broke the silence. "The chief invited us to stay awhile longer to join in smoking the peace pipe. Feathers and beads hung from the pipe on leather strips, each object with its own meaning."

The feather was an eagle feather, I explained, which is a symbol of the great God, who lives high in the heavens, as the eagle, the greatest of birds, soars high in the sky.

"The chief filled the pipe with red birch bark, lighted it, and puffed at the pipe. He then softly blew the smoke upward: an offering to God, ascending through the earthly air to the heavens.

"'Don't breathe in the smoke,' the chief cautioned, grinning. 'It will melt your lungs if you're not used to it.'"

"We each took our turn with the pipe, relighting the bark, pulling air through the pipe, and blowing it heavenward. I held the long pipe awkwardly in my hands, sucked hard to draw the air through the smoldering bark, through the small hole. I held the smoke in my mouth for a moment, then blew the smoke gently to heaven, my humble offering to the Creator."

What I had only seen in movies and read about in books had become a reality. I had smoked the peace pipe! I realized that smoking had nothing to do with it. It was all about the offering, an offering taken from the bark of the red birch tree, burning, drawn into me, mixing with my breath, with a part of me, as I sent it heavenward.

"That was special," I told them.

I reclined on the couch, looking at the ceiling. Then I looked at the children with a tired smile, and they knew I was done telling my story.

Erin asked me, "Daddy, what does 'emblem' mean?"

"Oh, I'm sorry," I replied. "'Emblem' is a word that means 'symbol.' Hmm. That doesn't help much either, does it? Well, an emblem or a symbol is a small thing that helps us understand something much bigger. Like the eagle feather, a small thing you can hold in your hand and feel, is an emblem or a symbol of God, a person we cannot fully understand, a being we cannot touch with our hands but can only feel with our hearts. So the scars on the Indians' chests are emblems or symbols of their special sacrifice to know God, and of how he spoke to them and gave them spiritual power and understanding."

Erin brought me another glass of water and some fruit—two oranges and an apple. Lying in bed later, my mind filled with visions of rocks glowing orange in the darkness, of Indian songs, of the smoke from the pipe, and of the Sun Dance. I wondered about my emblems, about my efforts to see beyond what I could see with my eyes, about my attempts to feel more than what I could feel with my hands, about my offerings to the Creator.

HOUSE OF OFFERING

Rocks glow,
like a cluster of orange suns,
shimmering in ferrous shadows
with pulsing heat
in the mid-day darkness
of the stick-framed, skin-clad lodge,
the turtle:
House of sweat,
House of cleansing,
House of song.
Sing of the weathered ancients!
Sing of the laughing children!
Sing of the beasts and the rivers, the woods and the wind!
In this dark other-world:
House of hope,
House of healing,
House of dreams.
Dream of the grizzly bear and bison!
Dream of feathers flying and eyes!
Dream of circles and fire and roads to choose!
Sprinkle now the water,
fill the house with steam,
and breathe,
and sweat,
and renew the chanted song.
Ascend now burning bark.
Fill the house with smoke
pulled from this pipe
and offered up from this
House of prayer,
House of offering, to the
House of God.

Tracks in the Snow

Wherever I am, I find that the road stretches both ahead and behind.

From the airport beacon shine alternating beams of white and green light, ghostly sweeping columns in the crystalline air against the undersides of low-hanging clouds. Here, walking in this desert, I imagine a lighthouse perched on a craggy rock cliff, overlooking ocean waves beating themselves in ferocious crashes against the rock, and ships with trimmed sails rocking, taking on water, close to sinking, with frantic, frightened sailors looking to the light as to a savior, the only thing in the world they can cling to, trust in.

A shallow skiff of snow has fallen in the night on Rabbit Lane and the surrounding fields. It looks as if powdered sugar has been sprinkled heavily on the dark ploughed earth and green wheat shoots. The snow lies a little thicker on the flat surface of the road. Long, parallel tracks from tractors and trucks meander casually down the visible length of the road. Each tire leaves its signature markings, as if its own species traveling through the snow. Narrow, close, twin treads belong to the small front wheels of vintage tractors still used by some farmers. Wide treads with opposing diagonal markings belong to the tractors' huge rear tires. Complex curved and angled markings are those of pick-up trucks.

The tracks of small animals run alongside the tire tracks. Dog. Cat. Skunk. Raccoon. Their tracks meander more broadly, straying from straight lines to collide with and be obliterated by the heavy tire tracks. Does nature always lose against technology? Tiny, articulate mouse tracks cross the road perpendicular to the truck tracks. I cannot tell if the mice have jumped into and over the tire tracks, or if the tires have tread upon the mouse tracks. Forked bird-foot prints appear randomly at places where the birds have dropped to peck for seeds and then fly back to the trees and bushes.

My tracks, the prints of my boots, leave their mark between the perfectly parallel tracks of machines. I purposefully meander within those tracks to join mine to the patterns of nature. But are mine the prints of technology or of nature? Perhaps they are neither, or both, or a symbolic attempt to buffer, to temper, to reconcile, and to harmonize? Whichever, our various tracks frequently converge.

I notice a set of boot tracks that seem to appear out of nowhere, and struggle to understand how that can be possible. These trampled tracks face several directions, connected to a single line of tracks leading to the bank of the irrigation ditch, then to another line of tracks heading back to the trampled area. Quickly I solve the puzzle. Someone has stopped his truck, jumped out, moved around enough to close the door, and walked to the ditch—probably to piss. Then (most likely) he walked back to his truck and drove away.

The snow on Rabbit Lane is also marred by less flattering signs of human presence: hundreds of beer cans, beer bottles, and cigarette butts littering both roadside and irrigation ditch.

Between the various tracks lie areas of undisturbed, crystalline snow. As the sun rises above the mountain peaks to shine directly on the snow, millions upon millions of microscopic prisms reveal themselves in the snow crystals, sparkling in brief and tiny flashes of bright color.

Turning to retrace my steps toward home, I see the footprints I have left in the snow. I look into the distance after them, as if looking into my past. What brought me here, I wonder. Were my steps well placed? The rightness of where I am no longer matters: my steps have brought me here, and I cannot be elsewhere for the wishing. The rightness of where I am going is a more urgent question, answered one purposeful step at a time.

There. There is the house, with its covered porch and green shutters. In the house are Angie, the seven children we brought into the world, the piano, our books, my pen and paper, the dinner table, the crocheted rag rug at the foot of my bed.

Arriving home from my walk, I climbed the stairs to my room and stood in the doorway gazing at baby Hyrum cuddled into his mother, nursing. Hyrum's baby arm suddenly stuck itself up into the air from under the blankets, with his index finger extended. He slowly waved his arm and finger around, pointing at everything and nothing, as if remotely wandering the room, exploring.

I placed on the dresser my hat and gloves, next to a long green-glazed ceramic dish, like a canoe hull, with stubby feet. My father brought it home from a business trip to Brazil when I was a boy growing up in New Jersey. The dish houses my collection of odd little things. Some have been there so long, buried by more recent acquisitions, that I have forgotten them. The collection sits high enough that the children know it is there but cannot see it.

"Can I see what's in it, Dad?" asked John (5), bringing a stool from the bathroom.

He stood on the stool, on tip toes, admiring the collection with his eyes, but being careful not to touch. More recently, I have brought the collection down for the children to see and touch, and also to claim any items that might belong to them.

The collection changes constantly as I find new things and put away the old: a United We Stand pin, in red, white, and blue, from September 11, 2001; a button that came off my slacks two years previous and never was sewn back on; brass buttons from an old blazer that sits in the closet, now too small for me to wear; colored game pieces; three wheat-leaf pennies; a guitar pick with grooves worn in the sides where a child ran it up and down the steel strings; two marbles, one cracked; more assorted buttons, from various shirt collars and cuffs; wood plugs that popped out from covering banister anchor screws; polished rocks that wandered from bags the children brought home from the annual gem and mineral show; seeds from Mimosa and Locust pods; sewing needles and straight pins found on the floor, escaped from the children during their sewing projects; a 1791 tarnished copper Russian coin; Lego pieces; a watch battery, likely dead; small nails and screws; one piece of a 1000-piece puzzle; plastic necklace beads; striped Russian Olive pits from where they fell on Rabbit Lane.

The collection is there partly because I do not enjoy finding little things scattered about the floors of my home. So, I pick them up one at a time and put them in the dish, not always wanting to take the time and the energy right then to find their proper place, but also not wanting to just throw them away. Each item is unique, admirable for its own peculiar qualities. Some are very old (the coin). Some are pretty (the beads and marbles). Some are functional and should be put back to use (the nails and screws). Some form part of a larger whole that is incomplete without them (the puzzle and game pieces). On another level, the collection reflects my fascination for small, beautiful things. Although I am a man, I am also still a boy, a boy that loves his treasure box as much as the little treasures it holds, and a boy that is reluctant to part with the possessions of a child. The green ceramic dish is my childhood pockets that once carried around marbles, pennies, and bits of string. Many children relish the competition of trading treasures with other children. But I relish the little things for the treasures they are.

A short while later, I gathered the children and proposed that I pull them in their plastic toboggans behind the truck in the snow on Rabbit Lane. They practically cheered at the idea. I tied three ropes of different lengths to the bumper, put the truck in four-wheel drive, and started slowly to pull them, gradually picking up speed. The children screamed and hollered with happiness, until the ropes crossed and tangled, the sleds jumped the ruts, and children tumbled out. My biggest worry was that a sled might lurch into the deep irrigation ditch. We refined our ropes and speeds and enjoyed more sledding up and down Rabbit Lane. Except for red-faced and teary-eyed Hyrum (4), who sat in the warm truck recovering from his spill and eating a banana.

I LEFT THE HOUSE

I left the house
to walk a long walk
through the uncertain silhouettes
of morning's pre-dawn dim,
and found that
Heaven had graced Earth,
silently,
magically,
with a covering of snow,
soft on the hard, frozen earth,
pale gray in the lingering starlight.

On the farm road,
tire tracks sliced and sullied the snow,
leaving long, undulating ruts
to follow.
I quickly chose the ease of the rut.
Tracks of other travelers—
mice, rabbits, a raccoon—
meandered, veered, crossed,
as necessary or desirable.
Then I, too, left the pre-established path,
and made my own way through the snow.
Frozen crust crunched and gave way
under the weight of my boots;
each step sent up a small crystalline cloud;
white snow caps clung to my toes;
legs protested with burning fatigue at
the effort of resisting the rut.

The snow turned from gray to white with the fading of night,
tinged with the pink of impending sunrise.
In the undisturbed snow beside the rutted tracks,
Sun's first rays revealed an infinity of microscopic prisms,
sparkling brief flashes of rainbow color.

In the distance behind,
the house waited patiently for my return.

Little Baby

Roger Baker

Witch's Tree

Desire teased spawns a vice.

The noise of my boots on Rabbit Lane's loose gravel reverberates in the air and in my brain and distracts me from the peaceful quiet of my surroundings. I imagine the noise to be similar to that of chewing crisp carrots with tight earphones on. I find myself wandering within the roadway in search of the path of least noise generation. Part of me does not want to startle the wildlife, which in turn startles me with a sudden rustling of wings or splashing of water. I also do not want to interfere with nature's soft voices. A bigger part of me simply does not want to draw attention to myself, not even from the animals. On Rabbit Lane, at least, I can be free of critical eyes and voices. Still, even here, alone, I instinctively avoid the noise that would bring the attention of looks and whispers in other places.

Waking each morning for my walk, I would rise from lying down and sit on the edge of my bed. Each movement on the edge of the bed would elicit a whiny squeak from some unknown location on the bed frame. The squeak often roused my tired wife or lightly-sleeping baby. After so many days and weeks and months of this, I resolved to find and eliminate the source of the squeak once and for all. One Saturday after breakfast, the children watching with interest, I stripped the bed, awkwardly removed the flopping mattress, slid off the box spring, and dismantled the bed frame. I oiled every joint and weld I could find, with newspapers spread out to collect any drips, then wiped the frame clean and reassembled the bed. Tentatively, fearful that I might have to do it all over again, I sat down upon the edge of the bed. No squeak! The children cheered. Then they began to laugh as I repeatedly sat down, stood up, sat down, stood up, sat down, stood up, each time with a new look of triumph. Mother and several babies slept better after that.

I often lie on that bed looking south though the window over the landscape. Erin (5) found me there one evening after dinner.

"Daddy," she asked, "what are you doing?"

I smiled wearily, my reverie having been discovered and interrupted.

"I just needed to stop for a while," I answered. "I'm lying here, relaxing, gazing out my picture window. Come here," I invited, moving to the middle of the bed and pulling her close. Her back to my chest, my arms around her, we gazed out the big window together.

I said softly, "I love to lay here and look out this window. The landscape is so beautiful. So beautiful."

Miles of deep green alfalfa and waving wheat fields stretched south from our house toward the Oquirrh Mountains. An occasional Cottonwood grove or well house sprung up. The church steeple, sharp and white, poked up from the cross-shaped building. Patches of gray and black clouds hung low against the mountains, as if dammed up by the tall peaks. From the setting sun in the west came rays of orange and red, setting the fields and mountains to glowing under the dark cloud cover. *This is beautiful*, I thought. *Does she see it?* The scene was both stunningly beautiful and heavenly soft. Erin squeezed my embracing arm tightly, and I knew.

We laid there a few minutes more when Laura (3) came in and whined hopefully, "Daddy, what are you doing?" obviously wanting to be a part of whatever it was.

"Come on up, little one," I offered, hoping Erin would not mind. "Look out the window with us."

We shifted on the bed, making room for Laura. She nestled her back into Erin, who said quietly, "See how beautiful it is, Laura?"

"Ohh," Laura whispered with awe as we stared at the gloaming scene.

Before long, John toddled in, squealing "Daddy!" at the victory of finding me. John was more interested in us than in the view. He had found us just how he wanted us. He hoisted himself onto the big bed and declared himself king of the family by shouting and smiling as he climbed and crawled over us.

John brought a fun change of mood, but the strong, quiet magic of gazing out the picture window upon the beautiful world beyond remained a powerful image and a sweet memory. Many times after that I laid in bed, soaking in the changing scenery. Hot, dusty brown. Snowy white and bright. Deep green. Cows and horses and the "Er-Er" of a lone cock pheasant. Delicate pinks of sunrise; rich reds of sunset. Gray fog; torrents of rain; lightning and booming thunder. South winds rattling the house and buffeting our young trees. Full moon haloed in mist. Each had its own untouchable mystery. It was as if I were watching through a magic window into a foreign, always-changing world, a world that could be seen only through the picture window.

I heard Hyrum (9 months) squawking, shouting, and screaming happily as he scooted and crawled around the house. He had found his voice. It takes so many of us so long to find a voice. Many people never seem to. Others find it but misuse it, leading people astray, or making noise for the sake of the noise, not for the sake of beauty or for the hearer. What comes out of our mouth cannot be put back in. What our voice utters cannot be silenced. At best we can ask forgiveness, but the pain we cause may linger lifetimes. I have often wondered if my thoughts would ever find expression. I have always hoped that my voice would be a calming, soothing voice, a voice that helps people feel good about themselves and their place in this world, a voice that contributes to making this world just a little better.

Every noise has a cause and an effect. A boy slamming shut the toothbrush drawer rattles the picture frame hanging in the next room. A startled duck's quack from my gravel-grinding boots in turn starts my heart to beating fast. A chorus of goose honks from high overhead reminds me that Autumn's harvests are drawing to a close and that it is time to prepare for Winter's dearth. My baby's cry, urged by hunger or fear or colic, causes me to cradle and coo, to do all I can to comfort.

Carli, a young neighbor girl, told Erin (6) and Laura (4) that the gnarled Willow growing by the irrigation ditch mid-way down Rabbit Lane was named Witch's Tree. A little pond opens up in the ditch to swirl around the trunk of Witch's Tree.

"A witch lives under the tree roots, under the pond," Carli taught. "She rises from the pond to capture stupid children."

For several years, my daughters were afraid to approach the tree unaccompanied, although they disclaimed their fear. On one walk we noticed two rubber boots standing in the mud beneath Witch's Tree, as if the wearer had been quickly spirited out of them. Standing side by side, they pointed toward the road, and toward the children. The two boot leg holes stared darkly upwards as if telling of some awful event.

Erin whispered to Laura, "When that farmer stepped into the mud with his boots on, that wicked witch must have come out from under her tree and killed him, suddenly, so that he didn't fall over or even struggle."

"Yea," Laura agreed, shivering. "That awful witch must have taken the farmer's body away, but left his boots behind. The boots of a dead man. It's a warning: a warning to anyone who might think of stepping near her horrible tree."

Through this conversation the girls had thoroughly spooked themselves. They stood staring, trembling, caught between their desperate desire to escape and their gnawing urge to remain in this spooky and dangerous place.

A few days later, the children noticed that the boots had been moved slightly, the toe of the left boot pointing in a new direction, the right boot moved several feet away and laying on its side. This omen could not mean a happy ending for the farmer, they reasoned.

After another few days, the boots disappeared entirely. Erin and Laura lamented the poor farmer's death. The mystique behind the boots and the missing farmer only increased with passing time. They never asked me who he might be. All the farmers in the area that I knew were alive and well.

Country Quiet

If I say I'll never do something, I never will.

The country was not quiet, not like we all thought it would be. Cows mooed, horses neighed, chickens clucked, dogs barked and howled, cats fought, chasing each other around the house, pea cocks called mournfully, donkeys ee-hawed, and roosters cock-a-doodle-dooed. I had always thought that roosters crowed at sunrise, waking the farmers for their morning chores. But I discovered that the roosters in Erda crow all night long.

About a week after we moved into the country house, another noise began, a horrible grinding, vibrating noise. I liked the cool, aromatic air wafting through my windows at night, but I had to shut them, and use ear plugs, to find enough relief from this new noise that I could sleep.

I complained to Angie about the mysterious noise the next morning. None of us could guess what it was or where it was coming from. We only knew that we hated it, especially me. It sounded like the noise was coming from right outside my bedroom window.

I kept looking out of the window into the darkness, trying to see what was making that dreadful noise. Three days later I announced, "I know what it is," then sat quietly until all the children asked several times, "What? What?"

"It's a pump," I answered. "There's a well over there in the corner of the alfalfa field behind our house, and the farmer runs the gasoline-engine pump so he can water the alfalfa with his line of sprinklers."

"What makes me mad," I continued complaining, "is that he runs it all *night* long instead of all *day* long. Why can't he run it during the day instead of keeping everybody up at night?"

I called a neighbor farmer, Cordale, and asked as politely as I could why the pump ran all night, and couldn't farmers water during the day?

"Thank you, I was just wondering," the children heard me say a few minutes later, and I hung up the phone with my ears burning with embarrassment.

"What did he say, Daddy, what did he say?" the children asked together.

"He called me a city kid," I grumbled. "A city kid that didn't know a thing about farming. A city kid that just moved to the country because he expected it would be all quiet and nice. A city kid that didn't appreciate what hard work farming was."

The mad was all gone out of me.

"At least he said the pump wouldn't run all summer," I sighed, "just a few weeks at a time as they move the sprinklers across the field. Then they'll let the alfalfa grow up and cut it."

For weeks the pump droned on at night until running out of gas in the early mornings. When I thought things could not get any worse, the pump stopped working correctly: the noise would begin to soar upward and then dip down, over and over again for hours until the pump ran out of gas. It sounded like a sick cow mooing forever into a microphone. On and on it ground away, sliding up, sliding down. Oh, how it annoyed me as I jammed in my ear plugs and covered my head with pillows. The rest of the family just got used to it.

The country, it seemed, could be anything but quiet.

Austin

The measure of one's greatness is one's goodness.

Sitting on the porch lacing my boots for a walk on Rabbit Lane, I heard the distant bellowing of a distressed calf. Something in the bray was not quite right, sounded a little off. I had heard lost calves calling for their mothers before. I had heard desperately hungry calves complaining before. I had heard lonely wiener calves bellowing for their removed mothers before. This calf call sounded strange; perhaps, I thought, not even a calf at all. I turned my head to pinpoint the source of the noise. It came from behind Austin's house, where there should be no cows and, in fact, were no cows. An ignorant urgency sent me running through the intervening field to Austin's back door. There lay Austin, helpless, in abject distress, fallen across the threshold of his back door and unable to arise, the screen door pressing upon his legs. He shouted and bellowed with his deep and distressed bass voice. I wrapped my arms around his prodigious barrel chest and heaved as gently yet as forcefully as I could to raise the big man from the ground. Clutching each other, we limped back through the door, up three steps, and into his kitchen, where he sank heavily into a wooden chair with lathed spindles next to a round formica-top table.

"Thank you," he said through heavy breathing. "I don't know. . . what I would . . . have done."

His right elbow and the knuckles of his left hand were abraded and bleeding. I offered to wash and bandage his wounds.

"In the bathroom medicine cabinet . . . the top drawer," he directed.

We chatted a little as I wiped the scrapes clean and applied red Merthiolate to the scrapes and antibiotic ointment to the bandages. Mostly he said nothing and I said nothing as I doctored him.

The round-chested man, a hard-working old farmer, had once been strong enough to hand-sheer sheep and throw cattle, to carry 30-foot sprinkler pipe like toothpicks and toss hay bales like pillows. He had sat 12 hours a day for decades upon the tractor's uncushioned iron seat. He had led congregations and unions and had been esteemed by his peers. Now he could only lie on the ground and shout like a sick calf and sit at the kitchen table while another generation hovered over him.

"I just went to the mailbox to get the mail," he explained.

I did not tell him, as others had, that he should not shuffle to the mailbox, that he should not go to the detached garage to feed the cats, that he should not pick up stray items from the lawn. I did not tell him, as others had, that he should let posterity do his chores. But it did not matter. In his 90s, having now lain helpless and bellowing in the doorway on the hard concrete, he sensed that perhaps his time had passed, that his strength was spent, that instead of ruling the farm and raising the family and controlling life, he might no longer be of any worldly use. He could only be looked after.

A year later the great old man died. At the request of his posterity, I sat in the spindle chair at the formica-top table in the empty old house during Austin's funeral to guard against those who have no respect for the dead, or for the living, or for the property of others. No one skulked by as I sat in the dead man's house, remembering the odd bellowing and his round barrel chest and his dignified silence as he allowed himself to be patched up and then left alone, saying, "I'm fine."

In fact, even during his last year Austin was full of life. In my mid-life, I am full of life. So are you. I am the clicheic "child within." I am still the three-year-old I was, and will always be. I am still the infant newly transitioned from a sea of soft warmth to a world, often harsh, of light and darkness, of truth and lies, of pleasure and pain. I am the 12-year-old, the teenager, the husband, the father, the lover, the old man. Contained within my body and my mind and my spirit are all the prior selves of all the prior years, of each day of those years, of each hour of those days, of each of the infinite moments of my past, into which cascade my futures. We rest only briefly in the present.

Antique Sheep's Wool Sheers

GENERATIONS

I am the center and the circumference,
the present and the past:
the generations are one before me,
the memories of years
a single infinite scene,
shifting and stirring within,
slowly moving to embrace the future
even as it becomes the past.

I am at once a boy and a man,
a son and a father;
my child: my father: myself.
I gaze at my child
and see
my father gazing at me
and feel
a father's agony,
as I look to my father,
and my child looks to me.

Worm Sign

A sincere smile can change the world.

The night's rains have turned the hard-packed dirt surface of Rabbit Lane into a thin slick of mud, with narrow pools in the valleys between washboard peaks. Long earthworms, flushed from their deluged burrows, make their tedious way across the muddy film, seeming to wander without any sense of where they need to go. Slight worm tracks crisscross the slick: shallow smooth ruts, their directions and intersections chaotic, random, crossing over and following each other without discernible pattern. They leave only faint signs of their humble existence. By the time I arrive, the rising sun has begun to warm and dry the clay. Most of the worms have found their way into the softer soil of the farm fields or ditch bank, or have been eaten by ravenous American Robins. In addition to the dangers of birds and desiccation are the perils of ants, cars, bicycles, snakes, and the boots of oblivious humans. One large worm, seven inches long, struggles to cross the stiffening soil, grains of sand sticking to its increasingly gaunt length. The worm's journey seems long and futile. *It need not be*, I muse as I pick up the worm and settle it under a patch of moist grass clippings at the edge of the ploughed field.

Our lives may seem similarly chaotic and random, our direction indiscernible. The slightest storm tends to send us scurrying for safety and shelter. The vicissitudes and dangers of life gobble many of us up or leave us injured or maimed or washed out. We see and touch each other as we ooze about our daily lives. But what is the impact of these connections and intersections upon ourselves and those that we meet? Do we allow these events to possess any meaning, or do we simply move on in the pretense of aloneness to disappear into the grass, down our dark holes?

Certainly we are more than earthworms. Our complex bodies join forces with intelligent minds and sensitive spirits. We are souls. Our life patterns may seem random and chaotic, but each interaction can be meaningful, can teach and edify and even heal.

At American Burger I connected with a man sitting at another table. Our eyes had furtively met several times, and each time we looked back to our burgers and fries, pretending the connection had not occurred. I arose to drop my garbage into the can. Returning to my table for my coat and book, I stopped at his table and said, "For the life of me I can't place where I know you. I'm Roger."

He smiled pleasantly and replied, "I thought I knew you, too. I'm Ray, and this is my wife Betsy. I work at the city sewer plant."

Then I remembered having seen him at company functions, though we had never met.

With a smile of my own, I offered, "Well, Ray and Betsy, it's nice to meet you. Have a great afternoon."

I may never interact with Ray and Betsy again. I gave nothing tangible to them, did nothing visible for them. They likewise gave me nothing. Yet we had connected in some indefinable but real and uplifting way. Our simple, random crossing of paths left me feeling happier.

How many times in a day do we cross another's path? Dozens, if not hundreds. I cross paths with my children each morning as I leave for work. Every day they insist on giving me a hug (or two or three) as I walk out the door. I'm often late and feel anxious to get away. Sometimes I protest, "Just let me go, guys" or "You already hugged me once." Sometimes I stop and put my briefcase on the floor to give them a genuine embrace and a smile and a kind word, perhaps "I love you" or "Have a great day". If I really pay attention to these moments of connection, I notice a subtle but distinct feeling of goodness and happiness, a sense that something has changed for the better. On those occasions when I exit hastily and with irritation, I notice a hint of sadness in myself and in them. I am making a greater effort to be mindful in these moments, to do or say something that makes the connection a happy one, an edifying one.

I can do this in the store, in line at the post office, at work, even in the dentist chair. Connections will happen regardless of how I accept them, for none of us lives in isolation. It seems to be the nature of life to bring us together, to give us these opportunities to interact. Life gives us never-ending chances to cross paths with others and to leave them better and happier than we found them. I often receive these opportunities weakly, being full of worry or sadness or grief or fear. But I can make a greater effort to choose another way. I think we will find, somewhat ironically, that choosing to uplift others will uplift mostly ourselves.

Of Goats and a Pot-Bellied Pig

Our garden is going to grow because of this beautiful rain!
(Caleb-3)

Caleb (2) loved to feed the goats. We kept a bucket under the sink into which we scraped all the table scraps and vegetable peelings. Each time Caleb saw the bucket, he cheered, "Goatie, Goatie!" I carried the bucket in one arm and the boy in the other to the goat yard, dumping the bucket's contents into the lopsided plywood manger I had made. At 14, one of Caleb's daily chores was to empty the scrap bucket into the pig pen, and it was no longer an occasion he looked forward to.

One Fall day I took the children to Pioneer Days at the historic Benson Grist Mill. Men and women in traditional 19th-century dress demonstrated various pioneer crafts, including blacksmithing, preserve making, and grain milling. My attention was drawn to one woman weaving a rectangular rug from strips of wool cloth pulled between strings on a rectangular wooden loom. *That*, I thought, *I might be able to do.* To make such a rug I did not need a forge or a mill or knitting needles, just a framed loom with nails and string, and strips of old cloth. During the following weeks I made a frame from two-by-two lumber and hammered finishing nails, angled outward, at one-inch intervals on the two shorter sides to secure the string. At the local Deseret Industries thrift store, I bought several wool-blend skirts and slacks of various colors and patterns, and cut them into inch-wide strips. (Don't bother with blazers: it takes too much effort to harvest too little cloth.)

The children watched me curiously as I made the loom, cut the strips, and tried my awkward hand at weaving. Soon they began asking for their own looms so that they could weave with me. My loom was about three by two feet; theirs I made one by one. For weeks in the evenings we enjoyed pulling strips of cloth between the strings, watching the rugs slowly take form. Erin (8) and I stayed up too late several evenings, frustrating her mother, who was trying to get the children to bed. We eventually sighed and put our looms away for the night. But we enjoyed many quiet moments together, sitting by the hot wood-burning stove, twisting strips of brown tweed or red plaid from one side of the loom to the other, then back again, talking to each other on occasion, but not needing to talk, merely feeling happy at making art side by side.

One of my rugs sits on the carpet at the foot of the wood stove. On more than one occasion it has rescued the carpet from errant embers popping out through the open stove door as we loaded fresh logs. Another rug covers the tile at the bottom of the stairs, where it has softened the landing for more than one tumbling child. I gave my loom to our neighbor Judy, who wanted to try her hand at pioneer rug-making.

Unbeknownst to me, Caleb (12) had admired my rugs for years. He announced to me one evening that he wanted to make his own loom and rug. We shopped for fabric at the thrift store. I instructed him how to make the loom and how to cut, weave, and join the strips of cloth. In just a few days he proudly showed me his small rug, which he keeps in his room by his bed.

The children and I have not weaved a rug for years now. But I have a feeling that it might be time to weave together again, soon, sitting as father and children near the wood stove, talking quietly but not needing to talk, creating art together. And as we weave our cloth, we will entwine our memories, our feelings for one another, enlarging the patterns, colors, and textures of our connected lives.

Another legacy of Pioneer Days is Piggie, our pet black pot-bellied pig. As we admired the cute black piglets on display at the fair, the owner told us he had one too many piglets.

"You can have 'im if you want 'im," he offered, showing us the runt. "Take 'im home with you. See how cute he is?"

He even offered to throw in the small chain-link pen. I looked back and forth from child to child, each face smiling approval, and could not think of a reason to say no. So we came home with a pet pig that we never named except for Piggie, or just Pig. I did not think Pig would mind. It's not like we named him Horse.

We thought it would be fun to take Piggie for walk, so I bought a body harness such as one would use for a small dog or goat, where the legs and head fit through loops of the harness. Well, a pig, especially a pot-bellied pig, is constructed differently than a dog or a goat. It has an enormous neck and almost no legs. And Piggie did not appreciate me trying to direct his snout and limbs into the harness. Soon he began to panic and squeal and kick with tremendous strength. I leaned into the task and suddenly found myself sprawled spread-eagle on top of the terrified, screaming pig. Hysterical, Piggie wiggled out from under me despite my weight and effort. And he was not the only one squealing. The spectating children laughed and squealed themselves at the sight of their dad wrestling with a screaming pig.

From inside the kitchen, Angie was surprised to see the pig run wildly by, still squealing, followed by her anxious husband, followed by five delighted children. A moment later, Pig ran by the window in the other direction, again followed by me and my entourage. We finally coaxed the exhausted, trembling pig into its pen. We never again tried to walk Piggie. I suspected that I would not ever succeed in harnessing the pig, but I also could not bear to terrify the animal again. It took months before Piggie would let me touch his rough, course-hair hide. But Piggie would eat from my hand when he was really hungry, which seemed to be all the time. Whenever I walk by, he snorts and grunts to let me know he's hungry. He slurps his water and smacks loudly at his slops, eating, well, like a pig.

Harvey brought us our first goat: a skinny, floppy-eared kid. I asked Harvey about the piece of iron baling wire twisted tightly around the kid's testicles.

"Don't worry," Harvey reassured. "They'll shrivel up and fall off in a couple of weeks. No problem."

I smarted at the thought, but trusted that Harvey knew what he was talking about, and tried not to think too personally about the rudimentary procedure. The kid did not complain, anyway, and Harvey's prediction proved accurate.

Sometime later we bought Captain, a white pygmy kid—a male. Remembering Harvey's successful procedure, I thought to replicate it. For the lack of handy wire, however, I used a plastic zip tie, sure that it would work just as well, if not better. I cinched it as tight as I could around the kid's testicles and waited for them to shrivel up and fall off. Instead, over the next two weeks the scrotum swelled and reddened, and Captain retired frequently, panting, to a corner of his pen. When the maggots took up residence, I knew it was time to take Captain to see the veterinarian. The vet had me lead the goat to a concrete pad with a low spot and a drain, where he examined the goat without saying a word. I told the vet about our first successful experience, and that I could not imagine what had gone wrong this time.

"You can't get a zip tie as tight as twisted wire," he shot at me.

He did not say the words *you idiot*, but I heard them plenty loudly, as well as echoes of Cordale's "city kid."

"Hold his back legs!"

Before I knew what was happening, the vet snipped off the inflamed testicles, scrotum and all, and jammed a hot cauterizing iron onto the squirting arteries, holding it there for what seemed like a very long time. Captain bleated and screamed, kicking against my tight grip. The smell of burning flesh turned my stomach.

"Hold him!" the vet shouted as he removed the iron to check for bleeding. A small artery still squirted, and several oozed, so he pushed the hot iron back into Captain's groin.

"There," said the vet, releasing. "He'll be fine. Watch for bleeding or swelling." Blood flowed over the concrete and dripped slowly into the drain.

My mind was still catching up to the sudden stream of events with thoughts like, *Wait, don't you put him on a table and anesthetize him or something?* Before my mind caught up fully, guilt stomped heavily in for having been so stupid with the zip tie and for having caused the poor goat so much suffering. *He'll be fine,* the vet had said. I hope goats do not have memories. If there is a next time, I will take the kid to the other veterinarian to be neutered. No more baling wire for me.

I had just moved another baby goat to a fenced 40 by 40 area of the garden so that during Winter the goat could chew on the detritus of the previous year's garden: crispy corn stalks, hardy Swiss chard, withered pumpkin vines, the tasseled tops of carrots never picked. Some of it was still green despite freezing temperatures. Early snows had insulated the chard from the coldest weather. The carrots and beets had sweetened for months in the cold soil.

The fence was necessary to protect the goat from wandering off and falling prey to speeding cars or marauding dogs and foxes, and also to protect the fruit trees and shrubs. I have learned that goats like nothing better than to eat long strips of tender bark peeled from young fruit trees. Acquiring this knowledge has come with several trips to the nursery to purchase replacement trees.

Out of either laziness or business, I had not yet dragged the goat house over to the new pen. The goat house was a simple four-sided rectangle, the wide front wall taller than the back wall to allow a sloped roof, with an open panel in the front wall for a door. With asphalt shingles on the roof, the shelter was heavy. It could be dragged across the grass yard with difficulty, but across the mud not at all, even with ropes pulled by me and all the children. And I had left it 60 feet from the goat pen for two days.

Early on the morning of the third day, a north wind began to howl, driving before it rain and sleet that quickly covered the muddy garden ground with an icy slush. This was one morning I was definitely *not* going to venture out to walk on Rabbit Lane. Comfortable in my warm, dry bed, I thought vaguely of the little goat, how cold it might be in the icy rain. But it was an animal, livestock at that, and would surely be alright. After all, I rationalized, livestock were hardy and had braved the elements for millennia.

Unable to sleep comfortably for the nagging worries about the goat, I finally arose, dressed, and descended the stairs to look out the living room window. Even from inside the house, I could see the little goat shivering in the unprotected pen, dripping with half-frozen slush. Its Nubian ears hung even slacker than usual with the weight of water soaking its short fur.

Suddenly alarmed, I threw on a coat and ran from the house toward the goat house. Although I knew it would not move, I was desperate to bring the shelter to the goat, and pulled mightily while grunting and cursing in the icy rain. After several minutes, it occurred to me that I could roll the goat house end over end toward the fenced enclosure, then open the fence and roll the shelter into the pen. I heaved up from under the rear end of the goat house, toppling it over onto its front wall, then lifted again, accomplishing a 90-degree roll

with each heave. But this was taking way too long, and despite my heroic efforts, the little goat remained shivering in its pen, the risks of irreversible hypothermia increasing with each passing moment.

Finally, the thought occurred to me to leave the goat house and go directly to the goat. It was the goat that needed me, not the goat house. I heaved once more so that the shelter stood upright, the door available, then ran to the goat. Hopping the short fence, I wrapped my arms around the four little legs and easily lifted the shivering animal off the ground, holding it against my chest. Its head hung, its eyes were nearly closed, it felt cold, and it shivered violently. Stepping over the fence, I trudged through the mud toward the shelter. I dropped to my knees, ducked my head, and shuffled myself and the baby goat into the shelter. By now I, too, was soaked with rain and sleet, and I shivered with the cold. But I gave no mind to my own discomfort and focused on the goat. It lay on my cross-legged lap, trembling and listless, wheezing slowly. I knew that if I did not work quickly we would lose the goat. It would die in my arms. The children would be devastated. And so would I, knowing that its death, and my children's sadness, would be my fault due to my own inaction. I began to rub the goat's hide, rubbing hard and fast, over the withers, over the shoulders, on its back and belly. I felt the heat in my hands as I rubbed, and I hoped that the rubbing would warm the little goat's body.

Unbeknownst to me, the children had followed me down the stairs and had been watching anxiously from the living room windows. Seeing me disappear into the goat house, Brian (10) decided to brave the wet winds to see what he could do to help. I sent him back to the house for towels. Hugging the warm, dry towels, Brian pushed in past the goat and me to get out of the driving sleet. With the towels we rubbed the goat's body completely dry. Brian joined his little hands with mine, and we continued to rub and rub, increasing the goat's circulation and warmth. Slowly, the goat began to open its eyes wider, then to lift its head to look up at me, then to struggle feebly against our aggressive rubbing. The act of warming the goat had also warmed us. Our shivering had stopped.

I sent Brian to have his mother mix up some warm lamb formula and to bring it in a calf bottle. Holding the half-gallon bottle, I squeezed the nipple to exude a drop of warm milk, then coaxed the nipple into the goat's mouth. The kid resisted at first. Then, tasting the warm milk, the kid began chewing at and then sucking on the nipple, drawing in streams of nourishment that warmed it from the inside. After several minutes, the goat released the nipple and laid its head back down on my lap, resting contentedly, breathing easily without a wheeze.

There the three of us remained for a long time, steam rising from our wet but warming bodies. When the freezing rain stopped, we crawled, sore and stiff, from the goat house. While Brian stood with the little goat, I opened the fence and rolled the goat house into the pen. We carried some old oat straw from the chicken coop to put inside the goat house, covering the cold mud. The revivified goat trotted happily into the shelter, its low ears swinging, and laid itself down on the straw, where it went peacefully to sleep.

Never again did we think of that little goat as livestock, not even when he was fully grown and butting heads with his companions. I had almost let him die. Then we had worked together to revive him from his suffering. He had become a beloved pet, almost a member of the family, and we loved him. His fur was colored mostly white, with splotches of black. We named him Oreo.

A season later, Laura (5) was determined to walk Oreo in the mid-July Erda Days parade. I loaded Oreo and the children into the bed of the Chevy truck.

"Hold on tight to his leash, so he doesn't jump out," I told her as I hooked the loop of Oreo's leash onto the truck bed and drove slowly off.

Oreo was much bigger and stronger than Laura, however, and he jumped out of the truck bed despite her efforts to restrain him. I heard Laura's scream and saw a blur in my rearview mirror. I jumped out of the truck and rushed to pick Oreo up so he would not hang himself on the leash. *Stupid goat,* I whispered to myself. Of course, it was I who should have anticipated this moment. I asked Angie to drive the rest of the way, and I sat in the back with the frightened goat, which had never before gone for a ride in the bed of a pick-up truck.

The parade line was forming on Liddell Lane, near Rabbit Lane. Some of my children had woven brightly colored crepe paper between the spokes of their bicycle wheels. They joined other children to ride happily up and down the parade line. Laura stood proudly and patiently with Oreo, who munched contentedly on the sweet clover growing randomly in the borrow pit next to the church-owned alfalfa field.

The parade began to move. Parents pulled wagonloads of children behind four-wheelers. Dozens of children rode their bicycles. Many children and their parents rode horses. Some neighbors drove their restored vintage cars. A few teenagers rode motorcycles. Laura began to walk with her Oreo, a bright yellow bandanna tied around the goat's neck. Along the parade route, neighbors sat in their lawn chairs and camp chairs next to their parked cars, cheering and throwing tootsie rolls and salt water taffy. Laura and Oreo both stopped to pick up candy, but Oreo ate it wrapper and all.

I walked behind Laura to keep the goat in check. It's not easy to keep a goat walking in a straight line down an asphalt road when fields of ripe, fragrant alfalfa clover are burgeoning ten feet away. The crowd of neighbors cheered praises for Laura and Oreo. Some neighbors even stopped Laura and Oreo to take pictures of them with the neighbors' grandchildren. The parade ended at the church, where we tied Oreo up underneath a tree on the thick green lawn. Oreo showed his delight by tugging intently at the grass. The children chewed happily on frozen otter pops.

"Hi Laura," I said over the phone. "I have an exciting surprise waiting for you when you get home—*very* exciting."

I had just brought home from Ken's menagerie a small black pygmy kid for Laura (7) to have as her very own pet. The other kids had grown into full-sized goats that had been much too large and aggressive for a small girl. Not to mention the fact that I could not keep them contained: them jumped handily over my five-foot-tall split rail fence. They had been sent to other homes, leaving the goat pen empty and a little girl wanting a pet.

The little black kid was adorable: cute and precocious. I put her in the fenced enclosure to await Laura's arrival. I had lined the white split-rail fence with cow panels to keep the goats from slipping out between the rails. The 12-foot-long panels were made of welded steel squares about eight inches on a side. Surely these panels formed a sufficient enclosure for the new kid, I reasoned.

Returning from a short errand, I felt sudden panic at not seeing the baby goat in the fenced enclosure. I jumped the fence and searched in the tall grasses, calling, "hey goatie, here little goat," but saw no sign of the kid. The new baby goat must have pushed through the panel squares. Dusk was turning to dark. Laura would be home soon, expecting her surprise. I set out to find a small black goat in the dark.

I walked and then drove on Church Road, Rabbit Lane, Bates Canyon Road, Tom's Lane, and Warr Lane, calling all the while. I asked every neighbor I saw if they had seen a little black goat. None of them had. Chelsea jumped in her car to help in the search. All to no avail. Thousands of acres of pasture and farm fields opened up on all sides, and I did not know where to look. The chance of a small black goat being hit by a car on a dark night on a road with no street lights grew from a mere possibility into a probability. My anxiety rose to desperation. My prayers for assistance had become mendicant pleas. By the time Laura arrived home, I felt depressed and empty, and could only inform her that the baby goat I had brought home for her had run away. She cried herself to sleep, and I laid awake all night, sick with worry for Laura and for the baby goat.

The phone rang early the next morning.

"Did you lose a little black goat?" asked Cloyd.

"Yes. Yes! YES! I did!" I could barely answer.

"Well, I have her in my pasture," Cloyd explained. "She's hanging out with all the little black calves. I guess she got lonely and came over for a visit. I'll go catch her and bring her right over."

All the worry of the night before melted away with the sunshine of the new day as Cloyd returned the little black goat. Laura held her close and petted her and fed her Dandelion flowers.

"She didn't run away from me, huh, Dad?" Laura asked hopefully. "She was just lonely. She won't be lonely anymore."

"No, she won't be lonely anymore," I affirmed, so totally relieved and grateful. "What are you going to call her?"

Laura released the little goat, which immediately ran and jumped and twisted in the air in obvious delight.

Laura laughed and exclaimed, "I'm going to name her Merrylegs!"

CUPCAKE AND OLIVE

Olive is a pygmy goat,
white with black splotches,
or black with white,
two months old, almost.
You brought her, two days old,
home, with little cousin Cupcake,
and bottle fed her
four times a day.
She doesn't bleat like Cupcake
(oh, my goodness),
even when hungry,
but cocks her head to one side,
just so, as if to say,
And where, Mama, have you been?
Olive will only suck
from a bottle held by you,
having jumped and flopped
onto your mother's lap.
You stroke her neck
with a free hand.

No Trespassing

A butterfly graces equally the idyllic mountain meadow
and the urban flower box.

On a cedar fencepost near Rabbit Lane an old sign announces "No Trespassing." The letters were burned or carved into the worn and weathered plank. The sign has been cracked by the black head of a rusting iron nail driven into the cedar post, and hangs upside down. Long ago the sign lost any intimidating aspect, and it now resembles the endearing smile of a gap-toothed old man.

On Church Road, long rows of abandoned pens are all that remains of the Russell mink farm. The corrugated metal roofing flaps like flimsy paper in the wind, anchored by a few remaining nails. The sheet metal crumpling and twisting in the wind groans and booms like distant thunder claps.

Old, white enamel bathtubs spot the pastures along Rabbit Lane. Once enjoyed by luxuriating humans, they are now used as watering troughs for cows. Clean water arrives through an assortment of pipes and hoses and valves and clamps. One tub still sports its antique clawed feet.

    Fields of grain stretch out before me as I walk. The grassy stalks rise high and green, with the tassel tips just beginning to turn yellow. The crop seems to be a feathery soft sea, the supple stalks swaying in unison in the breeze, undulating gently with the slopes of the submerged soil. I desire suddenly to leave my feet and swim, snorkeling, through the swells in search of hidden treasures of sea life. The breeze falls suddenly, and the sea turns in to a still life, looking for all the world like an ocean stroked with Van Gogh's colorful textures.

A humble stream trickles and winds through the irrigation ditch, choked with Willow bushes and Watercress, coursing inexorably on through heat and drought, through intense cold dipping at times below zero. In the night, a Raccoon left its tracks in the mud as it searched for Crayfish and munched on Watercress. Its prints look like the hands of a small, long-fingered child.

In the dim light of early morning, I see a young Raccoon curled up asleep at the base of a tree growing out of the ditch bank. The iconic masked face does not stir despite the loud scuffing of my boots on the gravel. It sleeps on despite my soft calling, followed by my less timid "good morning" salutation. On my return trip, the awakened Raccoon looks sleepily up at me, uncaring, unperturbed. Having expected it to scamper anxiously off, I wonder if it is sick.

A powder-blue butterfly the size of my fingernail, a Blue, lands on a patch of ditch-bank mud. Crouching for a closer look, being careful not to block its sun, I can distinguish its pretty markings and tiny tails, two on each underwing. The delicate arrangement of shapes and colors on the wings astonishes me. I have looked at such wings under a microscope, and have seen vague beauty transformed before my new eyes into exquisite tapestries of color and design, texture and pattern, more beautiful than anything the artist can paint. Even most photographs do not capture the vibrancy of the life, let alone the beauty, possessed by tiny creatures like this Blue.

Water trickling through the ditch slowly erodes the soft soil shoring up the Weyland grain field. Each Spring a few inches, sometimes more than a foot, sloughs off and tumbles down the steep bank into the water. Enough of the bank has worn away that several of the old cedar posts have toppled into the ditch, wrapped in their rusted barbed wire. The whole fence line will eventually fall over.

By the month of June, shiny young stalks, green laced with purple, have pushed up through the hard dirt at the edges of the road. Leaves have begun to unfold. At the top of the stalks sit clusters of little balls, hints of buds, that in a month will burst open to form generous heads of small, pink starlets. The Milkweed bloom is a convex, spherical arrangement of petite, pointy, pearly-pink flowers emitting a rich, sweet fragrance. Milkweed perfume is compelling and attractive, rich and sweet, with just a touch of tart. I bend over to breathe deeply of the exotic fragrance, and am overcome in a moment of aromatic ecstasy. Stop and smell the roses? I say, stop and smell the Milkweed.

In September, milkweed seeds sit white in their pods, packed tight, each pod holding a baseball-sized poof of cotton. Winter's big winds will spread and scatter the seeds across the fields, each seed floating on a white, downy sail. Walking with Hannah (6) in October, she observed a single milkweed seed caught in the tall, dead weeds. She rescued it with clawed fingers. Holding up her open palm, she blew the seed high into the air, setting it free to float slowly to the soil to sprout in Spring.

A flutter of orange and black—a Monarch butterfly—descends upon young Milkweed plants to deposit her eggs. The larvae will eat only Milkweed, filling their plump, tiger-striped bodies with the plant's bitter juices that birds dislike. The eggs on the plants set farther back from the road's edge will survive. Other eggs, like the plants to which they are glued, will fall prey to the county mower. The Monarch does not know any better. She has done her job and trusts the other players—water, sun, and soil—to do theirs. The natural instinct inside her has no way to account for man's machines.

Several years after planting seeds in the tulip beds in front of the house, Milkweed plants finally sprouted. They proliferated ten-fold the following Spring. The plants are tall and gangly and drab, out of place juxtaposed with tulips, daffodils, and low groundcover. They wave fragrant clusters of pink star flowers in the breeze. I asked Angie to tolerate the plants until the blooms faded, promising to cut the plants down before the seed pods grew. This would not hinder the perennials from rising again. Approaching the house one evening after work, I startled a Monarch feeding on the flower clusters. I froze and stood completely still, hoping the Monarch would return. She soon did. I watched her land on a leaf, cling to its edge, and curve her abdomen to press it against the underside of the leaf. With a thrill I realized that I had just witnessed a Monarch mother deposit an egg. I hurried to retrieve my jeweler's loop (which I had bought years ago for rock hounding that I never did much of), put on my reading glasses, and examined the tiny, delicate, striped, cream-white egg up close.

Over several weeks the egg color turned to charcoal with silvery stripes.

Clusters of small Sunflowers grow on the rough berms piled on the east side of Rabbit Lane, between the road and the irrigation ditch. The new gravel-and-clay berms are not bare for long, the weeds and grasses growing eagerly within mere weeks. Sunflowers and Milkweeds follow the next year. In the dark of my early morning walks, the sleeping Sunflowers still bow to the west, acknowledging the faded warmth and light of yesterday's setting sun. An hour later, the yellow heads have turned to the east, welcoming the sun's new rise.

As I walked with Brian (12) and Erin (9), Brian explained with superiority to Erin, "They turn their heads toward the sun."

"Nu-uh," retorted Erin testily, mostly to avoid conceding to his apparent knowledge. Still, her admiration for the bright flower overcame her pride, and she whispered a fascinated "wow."

To the Sunflowers, the sun means more than mere light attracting the attention of curious petals. The light of the sun is to the Sunflower the source of simple but life-sustaining truth. With an instinctual faith, the Sunflower relies on the sun as the plant sinks its roots into the soil in search of stability and moisture, as it sprouts new leaves and pushes its stalk to greater heights, as it soaks in water and breathes in air and manufactures energy through the miracle of photosynthesis. Sunflowers love light and life. The sun invites them to grow, to extend, to become more today than they were yesterday. Each day they begin again the truthful task of looking to light, of recognizing truth and power. They are not ashamed to yearn upward and to seek light.

A black Llama browses amongst the sheep. Sitting obscured in the tall grass, chewing its grassy cud, the Llama's head resembles in shape and movement a submarine periscope rising to see the undulating ocean of new green grass. Wanting another bite, the periscope submerges through the grass to the unseen craft below. The Llamas are unconcerned at my approach on the crunching gravel of Rabbit Lane. They sit monk-like in the grass amidst the flock of sheep. They do not twitch their heads nervously to see who I am, if I'm a threat. Unlike the sheep, they do not tense their muscles from a pre-decision urge to bound away. They hold their ground, unintimidated. They turn their heads slowly toward me . . . if and when it suits them. Masticating their course grass cud, the Llamas lower one ear, then the other, then both, as if the ears are each consulting with the brain, and then both ears lift sharply up again.

"Llamas keep away the coyotes," Craig told me.

Craig's llama-guard sits demurely in the field. Its body obscured by the tall grass, its head and neck poke up out of the grass, looking like a mammalified duck, its snout the magnified bill.

Of Foxes and Hens

You are my best friend and my big buddy.
(John-3 to Dad)

The day-old chicks arrived at the store in a box delivered by U.S. mail. While I had ordered only half-a-dozen specialty breed pullets, they came boxed with two dozen unsexed White Leghorns for cushioning and warmth. I had hung a heat lamp—a warm if impersonal surrogate for their mothers' downy breasts—in a makeshift pen because the chicks were too tiny and frail to generate enough of their own body heat against the chilly Spring nights. The hanging lamp radiated light and heat downward to make a spot of warmth in the straw where the chicks gathered close to rest. I do not think they ever fully slept, for the light. But they were warm and safe and comfortable.

The children were thrilled with the new chicks. Each child cupped a fluffy golden chick in their hands, bringing it up close, looking into infant chick eyes, rubbing the fuzzy little creatures softly against their cheeks. Holding a chick was like holding life itself: sweet and simple, full of love and innocence. A chick was like the earth, the sky, and the trees, like the aromatic Spring breeze, and like the rain that turns the alfalfa a deep green.

The chicks were three weeks old and slightly larger and fluffier when the lamp bulb cracked and the element burned itself out on a rainy night in May. Bringing water the next morning, I found the pen dark and the chicks huddled in a corner of their pen. With instinctual faith, they had waited out the dark and the chill, not knowing that the sun always rises. Despite the cold, they were just old enough to have slept soundly, wrapped in their collective warmth. That evening, I screwed a new bulb into their artificial sun, just to be safe.

The chicks were growing bigger, and I was worrying more and more about them in their temporary pen in my garage. I knew nothing about building chicken coops. Driving home from work I noticed a "Free Firewood" sign at a snowmobile and ATV store, and wondered at the seeming incongruity. Pulling my truck in to explore, I learned that the free firewood consisted of snowmobile and ATV pallets, some as long as ten feet, and all made of hardwood. I suddenly had the idea to build a chicken coop, at almost no cost, out of the free pallets. Several pick-up loads brought home enough pallets. I scooped out a level spot by the garden, then dragged over the pallets and started banging them together to make walls. The pallet wood was so hard, often oak or poplar, that the iron nails bent prematurely more often than they fully penetrated.

Before long I had turned three pallets into the front wall: twelve feet long by ten feet tall. I steadied it with two-by-four props, warning the children to stay away, then put a side wall together and attached it to the front wall. The side wall tapered from ten feet tall in the front to six feet tall at the back, and was eight feet deep. Harvey came over to help me finish the walls and frame the door, which swung on some old barn door hinges. For the roof we slapped on an assortment of old planks (two-by-sixes, -eights, -tens, and -twelves). Plywood scraps covered the walls and roof. Two thrift store windows allowed in light and warmth even in winter. The children excitedly set the chicks free in the completed coop. The chicks peeped gleefully and pecked around as if they thought they were real grown up chickens. I admit to stepping back as the sun began to set and standing melodramatically with my hands on my hips, smiling with pride at my meager accomplishment. In truth, the coop looked like a jigsaw puzzle with pieces from several old puzzles forced awkwardly together. But it worked. The walls stood up; the roof stayed on; the door opened and closed. The chicks seemed happy with their new home. What more should a coop be?[1]

Building onto the coop a few years later, Caleb (4), who wanted to be a part of the project, squatted on the low, descending, back part of the roof, six feet above the ground, near where I was working.

"Be careful," I had warned him. "You don't want to fall off."

A moment later I watched him, as if in slow motion, as he somersaulted off the roof, turning a perfect front flip and landing unharmed in the soft earth to squat on his feet and bottom. How grateful I was that he landed unharmed. Thereafter, he watched me from the ground.

Brian (9) had the job of feeding and watering the chicks, which grew quickly into hens. Now I had a new problem: I had not built any nesting boxes, and we did not want the chickens to lay their eggs on the ground where they would sit in the dirt and manure and get stepped on. So we assembled a bank of eight nesting boxes out of scrap plywood, this time following instructions in a book: the nesting boxes looked like they were meant to be nesting boxes. Attaching the row of boxes to the back wall of the coop, we filled each box with dry weeds because we did not yet have any straw. The chickens cautiously jumped up to the top of the boxes, but did not go inside. It took months for them to start laying, but the children checked every day anyway because each of them wanted to be the first to discover the first eggs.

Erin (6) stared one day at a hen sitting in one of the nesting boxes. The hen was moving around and clucking in a funny way. Erin saw an egg squeeze out and plop onto the weed bedding, and screamed to the world, "A chicken laid an egg! A chicken laid an egg!" She ran

---

[1] For more on chickens and coops, see *Round Shells Resting* in the Appendix.

into the coop to grab the egg as Brian, Laura (4), and John (2) came running to see.

"Let me see! Let me see! Don't push!" they whined at each other, both jealous and excited.

Erin carried her prize delicately across the back lawn to the kitchen and held it out for her mother to see. Mom's jaw dropped in open-mouthed surprise at the soft, pastel green of the egg. Erin placed the egg on a saucer on the counter, where it waited until I came home from work. Every day after that, Erin was the first one to the chicken coop, and found more eggs. I encouraged her to let the others have a chance, especially little Laura, who desperately wanted to find an egg. Erin wanted to share the fun, but it was hard for her to put aside her eager excitement and watch while someone else found the treasure she knew was there. To her, reaching under the soft, warm hen to find the smooth egg was like finding buried gold. But we had several hens, which soon all started laying, and so there was plenty of gold to go around.

The next year I decided I wanted to try pheasants, ducks, and different kinds of chickens.

"Not turkeys or geese," I said. "Too temperamental."

Along with the specialty breed chicks, I had brought home a dozen White Leghorn chicks that the hatchery had put in the box to keep the others warm. The store owner had given them to me free when I picked up my chick order.

"I don't know if they're hens or roosters," he had told me, "but if you want them you can have them."

As the Leghorns grew bigger, so did the red combs on the tops of their heads. They all turned out to be roosters.

At breakfast one Saturday morning I said to no one in particular, "What do you do with a dozen roosters when all you wanted was a few fresh eggs?"

When I came home from work a few days later, Angie informed me that Teancum (or "Tank"), our huge yellow Labrador, had escaped from his dog run and killed several of the young white roosters. Without a word, I dropped my briefcase, took off my jacket and tie, and headed for the dog and dead chickens. I picked up the dead chickens by their feet, grabbed "Tank" by his collar, and (to the horror of the children) began beating the dog with the dead chickens. Tank yelped and whined as I struck him repeatedly across the face with the carcasses. After about ten lashes, one of the chickens ripped open and made a mess on Teancum's face. The sight and sound and feel of the tearing chicken turned my stomach; I stopped the beating and locked the dog in his run. The children hid quietly behind their mother as I stormed into the house muttering, "Damned stupid dog" and stomped up the stairs to clean up.

At the dinner table, my nerves had settled enough to see that I had upset the children's nerves. Feelings of guilt began to replace feelings of frustration.

"I'm sorry that I blew up like that, children," I offered. "I just felt so angry at the dog for killing my little chickens, even if they don't lay eggs. And I've heard that if you hit a dog with the chickens he has killed, he will be afraid of them and won't kill any more. I'm not so sure. We'll see. But I'm sorry if I scared you."

My friend Don slaughtered his own chickens every year to stock his freezer. With an abundance of non-egg-laying roosters, I called him and asked if I could help him slaughter his chickens, with the idea of learning how to slaughter my own.

"Sure," Don said. "Come on over."

When I returned home an hour later, the children found me looking a little pale and a little tired.

"Well," I told them, without any pride, "I've slaughtered my first chickens. I can't say it was fun, but I can say I know how to do it. We'll be eating home-grown chicken soon."

The children did not exactly rejoice at the thought. The chickens I was going to kill had become their friends.

"They're not chickens, their roosters," I protested. "And I don't want a dozen roosters. There is nothing to do with them but to kill them and eat them."

My logic meant nothing to the children. They liked the white roosters. But I stuck to my guns and told them I had to do "the job" before the roosters got too old and tough. They were already starting to crow, which meant they were full-grown.

"How will you do it," Erin asked sadly.

"Well," I said stupidly, "you just hang them by their legs with wire, slit their jugulars, and then skin them. That way you avoid all the mess of dipping and plucking and gutting."

Mom took the children to the Tooele public library the next Saturday, and I stayed home to slaughter the roosters. When they came home I had a bucket full of ice and chicken meat, and a black garbage bag full of feathers and guts. The cats slinked around greedily, smelling the blood and meat. My hands and arms were a bloody mess, and it was obvious to everyone that I was not happy. I had only slaughtered a few of the roosters because of how hard the job had been. I learned later that Don's hens were bread specifically for skinning in this manner, whereas my roosters were not. My roosters were not bread for anything. It had been very difficult to cut through the feathers and thick skins, to find the jugulars, and to pull the skins off of the meat.

We baked the chicken for Sunday dinner the next day. The children picked at their drumsticks, knowing that the day before the legs had been attached to living chickens running around our garden catching bugs and crowing. They just could not eat their chicken. Neither could I, I confess. We ate a little, then gave our Sunday meal to the cats.

"I'll never slaughter another chicken," I declared after dinner. "I'll buy it at the grocery store. All I ever wanted was a few fresh eggs, anyway."

With an incessant guttural groan, the pump pushes water through the neighbor's sprinkler pipes. Water squirts rhythmically from the sprinkler heads and sprays wildly through leaks in the pipe joints. Still, I can hear the crickets singing to each other in the grass.

In the day's last light, after an evening rain shower, Barn Swallows flit and swoop in the cool air. Inside the coop, a mother Swallow broods over her chicks in her mud-and-horse-hair nest pasted to the side of a chicken coop roof truss. A black-eyed mouse nibbles at crumbs of helpfully ground grain, sweetened with molasses, ignoring the poisoned bait hidden behind wire in a corner of the coop.

The heat lamp sends a warm, yellow glow seeping out through the cracks in the scrap-lumber walls, beaming weakly from the windows cut in each pen, where the glass has been broken out by errant children playing soldier fort in the coop rafters, covered now by wire against the raccoons, the skunks, and the Red Fox that hides in the corrugated culvert down the street.

Looking out over a grain field, I watch a kit Fox standing high on its haunches to see over the ripening oats. Mother Fox, a soft, rusty red, hops high through the ripe oats as if on springs, her bushy tail, as long and thick as her sleek body, rising high with each descent of her head and torso. They are such wild, beautiful creatures, even if they do kill my hens. It is my fault for leaving the hens out at night. The Foxes do not kill for sport, but for survival, leaving only the clawed chicken feet and a few feathers in the place of consumption. I do not worry for the farmers' new lambs: the Llamas stand guard.

Around the Fire Pit

I'll help you learn to walk.
(Erin-10 to Hyrum)

One Monday evening after dinner, the whole family walked on Rabbit Lane. The sun was setting large and red, and the chilly Spring air settled upon us as we returned home. We gathered around our new fire pit to tell stories, sing songs, and roast apples and marshmallows, sitting on camp chairs and logs. I felt especially proud of the pit. It was more than just a shallow hole in the ground. I had lined it with large smooth sandstone boulders harvested from the commercial lot of a friend who had excavated for the foundation of his new building. He was happy to have me take as many rocks from the dirt piles (more rock than dirt) as I wanted. Each stone I took was one less stone he had to pay to haul off.

The day of the rock haul, I laid protecting plywood in the bed of the truck and drove the children to the lot. The only limitation to the size of the rocks we harvested was our strength to pick them up. I gathered the largest ones, while the children tossed smaller ones into the truck bed. Too late, I instructed the excited children not to throw their rocks into the truck, but to gently drop or set them in. The truck body still shows the several dents made in those few minutes. At least no windows were broken. Back at home, we rolled the rocks out of the truck and over to the spot chosen for the fire pit. We laid the largest rocks in a ring, then filled in and around with the smaller rocks.

Home from our walk, we crumpled newspaper and piled kindling.

"Can I light the fire?!" the children each clamored, as usual, for the privilege of lighting the fire.

I resolved the conflict by giving each child a match and letting each light a different section of the tinder pile. Soon the fire was roaring, the sudden heat taking away the evening chill. We sang a few silly campfire songs, like *Do Your Ears Hang Low*, and some family favorites including *White Wings* and *Swing Low, Sweet Chariot*, songs my father sang with the family when I was a boy. They were songs his father had sung with him when he was a boy. The children frantically blew on their lighted marshmallow torches and carefully tasted their roasted apples. Slowly, as we interacted, the burning sticks and logs made a heaped bed of shimmering orange embers. The warmth reached out and enveloped us all, together.

After a while, everyone grew quiet, staring into the fire. Angie and I began to tell the children stories of others who had walked little dirt roads like Rabbit Lane, in other times and under other circumstances. I told them of their fifth-great-grandmother, Susanna Ann, whose nursemaid smuggled her as a baby out of France during the French Revolution, walking obscure dirt roads, filled with the fear of being discovered and imprisoned and executed. No one knows the real names of either the smuggling nursemaid or the contraband child. But the grownup baby's daughter, Jean Rio, herself grown up, had joined herself to the new Mormon religion in England. Leaving the cobbled streets of London, she sailed with her young family across the

Atlantic Ocean and up the Mississippi River. Little Josiah, only four, sickened and died aboard ship. The vast Atlantic was his grave. From Illinois, Jean Rio and her children walked and rode in ox-drawn wagons over 1,000 miles of dirt trails to arrive expectantly in Salt Lake City, the center of the Mormon faith. Jean Rio, a woman of some means, brought with her Utah's first piano. Angie told the children of how one of her ancestors, Sarah, a pioneer midwife, had frequently left home in the middle of the night to walk the dirt roads of the Salt Lake valley to help her sister-women deliver their babies. She delivered over 300 babies, and never lost a single baby, or a mother either. We told them how many others walked hot and dusty roads, stubbing their toes and turning their ankles, wiping the dust and sweat from their faces, jumping away from coiled, rattling snakes, but always looking forward and upward toward their destinations, toward places of hope and promise.

MONDAY NIGHT

Monday night,
and we gather again,
a family:
sitting on cinderblocks
around the fire pit;
holding long applewood sticks,
like fishing rods,
with points in the flames,
connecting
with the warmth, the glow,
the power and mystery of fire.
A family:
singing songs about
head, shoulders, knees, and toes,
and the beauty of God's creations;
reading poems about kittens and calves,
and forks in the forest path;
telling stories of inspiration and faith;
munching popcorn and brownies;
keeping the cats away from our cups of milk.
The children
toss sticks into the flames,
poke smoking sticks into the ground,
carve their special sticks
with knives that are somehow always dull.
The sun sets behind towering pink and orange
cumulous that dwarf the snow-capped mountains.
The fire settles into a ringed bed of shimmering coals.
The children quiet themselves
and stare into the ebbing heat and color.
Mom and Dad look to each other
and share an unspoken gratitude that,
for this moment,
life is good.

Foreshadowing

The Milkweed *will* push through to grow tall, fragrant, and beautiful,
to call the Monarch.

The disc cushioning my lumbar 4 and 5 vertebrae has been bulging capriciously and desiccating prematurely since I was 12 years old. It was then that I experienced my first unexpected spine-twisting spasms that paralyzed me sitting in my church pew. A flattened, bulging disc means a frequently aching back, with locked joints and tense muscles. The pain is always different depending on which way the disc is bulging and, more importantly, which area of the spinal nerves the disc is irritating. While it becomes difficult and painful to bend, I somehow always manage to dry my feet after a shower, to shimmy on my socks, to tie my shoes, and to drive to work, even if I do have to lie occasionally on the floor during the mayor's staff meeting.

One morning, every forward step with my right foot triggered stabbing back and leg pain, and my bowels and back burned intensely with each deep breath. Slowly, as I walked, the tightness began to ease and I could walk and breathe more comfortably. Despite the pain, I was still able to enjoy the early morning peace of my surroundings on Rabbit Lane.

Limping slightly, I noticed a car turn onto the dirt road, its headlights glaring in the dawn. As the car approached, I began to emphasize my limp, just in case the driver was, coincidentally . . . and it was. Though I had never seen him on Rabbit Lane before, now I saw my chiropractor, Glenn, driving slowly by, taking his son to high school. Recognizing me, he grinned his hello and waved. I made sure my face showed the pain I was in as I grimaced and waved back.

I had just seen Glenn the day before, in some desperation, and was seeing him again the following day. I did not want him to think that I was moaning on his table one day and doing triathlons the next. Not that I was doing a triathlon, or could have done a triathlon. My back did hurt, I rationalized, and part of the limp was genuine.

Of course, Glenn was not worried about what I was worried about. He was only worried about me feeling better. I, on the other hand, was worried about what he was thinking about me. But I needn't have worried about his perceptions. Why did I worry in the first place? Should it matter what he thought about me? Of course not. What counted was what I thought about myself. I was happy to be walking at all, happy that I managed to roll out of bed early enough to walk, happy that I could tie my shoes. I was doing my best to take care of myself, and that was enough.

At about three-quarters of a mile long, Rabbit Lane can be driven in just 90 seconds, at an undisclosed speed. At this speed, however, the driver risks flattened tires, broken axles, wheel disalignments, and cracked teeth, not to mention missing every virtue revealed only at much slower speeds. I have found a slow walk to be the best speed for traveling Rabbit Lane.

The grains of sand in my shoe irritate me terribly as I walk on Rabbit Lane. I feel annoyed at having to stop, sit down on the dirt, take off my boot and sock, clean each thoroughly, then put them back on to resume walking. Sometimes I decide to resist my normal compulsion to remove all discomfort, all distraction, and to learn to go on in spite of the pebble. Rarely, I begin not to notice the irritation, or am able to diminish its importance, to keep the tiny grain in perspective. After all, it is not crippling me, or even paining me, just annoying me.

It may seem too obvious to point out, but life is full of events and notions that distract me from who I really am or want to be, from where I really want to go and what I really want to do. Many of these are merely annoying; some are quite painful. So, it is up to me to decide what kind of pearl my life will make of me. Will I be flaky, fractured, lumpy, or stained? Or will I be whole, having learned to live with my annoyances and disappointments and pains? It is comforting to me that we can all become pearls, and more so that God is no respecter of pearls, valuing each alike.

At the edges of Rabbit Lane, budding, volcano-like peaks pock the hard-packed clay and gravel. Emerging from the peaks are tiny slivers of green from seedling weeds that push persistently up to reach the light. Though the sprouts are tender and soft, still they possess the power to slowly displace the infinitely harder compacted earthen road.

One summer day I awoke to the noise of a heavy diesel engine belching over its labors near Rabbit Lane. Driving past the lane on my way to work, I saw a giant, rusty grader scraping away stands of flowering Milkweed and Sunflower, white-topped Parsnip, and Willows that thrive along the edge of the road above the irrigation ditch. They have formed a green and living border at the edge of the water as it trickles through the Watercress. On my way home from work later that day I saw that new dirt and gravel had been brought in and steamrolled to fill the ruts and potholes. Tons of gravel have been shaped to form a bermed bank above the ditch, replacing the vegetation.

As much as the potholes were a nuisance to drivers, my children have loved riding their bicycles into the holes and popping wheelies on the other side. As a walker, I had come to enjoy the puddles, thinking of them as eyes in the earth looking toward the heavens, reflecting the blue skies of day and the starry skies of night.

To me the road has seemed somehow alive, with pulse and personality. Now the road is blind, filled in and covered over. After maturing for many years, it has again become a mere thing to be used, trodden upon, driven over, instead of part of the history and landscape, instead of a companion to the farms and fields, to the flowing water and waving trees, to the Milkweed blossoms and Sunflowers. Perhaps I am selfish in wanting the road to remain as it was for my pedestrian purposes in the face of the need for a more utilitarian street for cars and trucks. But whether I walk on the road or not, its nature has changed, its character covered over, its memory dimmed.

I knew, then more than ever, that someday Rabbit Lane would be paved over with a steaming strip of burning black asphalt. I knew that I would lament that day and would see the glistening blackness as a shroud upon the once living road. It is only a matter of time. The ditch will be dredged and piped, the long line of trees removed, and a full road paved and striped. The Muskrats will expire in their collapsed burrows. The Owls will fly away and not return. The Mallards will find wilder wetlands. The haunting echo of the Snipe's winged acrobatics will no longer float over the ground-creeping fog at twilight. The farms and fields will be carved into five-acre mega slices

of the American dream that brokers market cleverly as ranchettes.
Mostly they will be five-acre weed patches.

Mary

Bend, bend, but do not break.

I had rescued Austin from his fall just two years before. Now the barrel-chested man was gone. Mary, his widow, a diminutive black-haired woman in her nineties, lived alone. We tried to visit her one afternoon. We knocked and knocked, but no one answered the door. Later we learned that she sleeps during the day and lives her waking life at night. I now understood the dim yellow light that glowed late at night from her living room window.

With a plate of cookies and five children in tow, we tried again to visit, this time at about 9:00 p.m. We knocked and waited for a long time, with Mary's numerous cats brushing against our legs and purring. A hand finally turned the dead bolt, and Mary opened the door. She invited us in with a pleasant but tired smile, seeming very small in the door frame. We sat and stood around her kitchen table, talking agreeably but with the natural awkwardness of new acquaintances. She chatted with the children, often asking them to repeat their shy responses due to her deafness. She quietly thanked us for the cookies we had brought, and said she would enjoy them. Then we left.

Mary's world had shrunk to the size of her little brick house. I wondered about her being so isolated and enclosed. She existed within a small world of familiar floral wallpaper, dusty drapes, cracked and glued nick-knacks, and worn easy chairs. Misty memories hung heavy in the stale air. She no longer ventured into the light of day, staying indoors in the light of her dull lamp. Would anyone notice if she died?

I felt different after leaving her house. Something had changed in me. We had connected with a noble, ancient matriarch. I sensed the humble grandeur of her life and spirit. I knew that she had lived powerfully but quietly. She had made the type of maternal contribution to the world and its people that changes civilizations yet goes largely unnoticed. She had not needed notoriety or accolade, but was sustained instead by meeker motivations. She had improved others through calculated sacrifice. She had persevered through human adversities. She did not care that no one remembered. She knew, and that was enough. She had made a mark on the world, invisible to all but a few, that left the world better than she found it.

Mary died later that year. I learned about it when one of the family asked me to sit in the house during the funeral to protect it, as I had when Austin died, from heartless burglars who read obituaries and preyed on the deceased's belongings even while the family prayed over the deceased's grave. I sat in the worn arm chair surrounded by the faded olive wallpaper, the dusty drapes, and the china cups on saucers lining a shelf. Austin's austere sepia portrait hung on the wall, next to Mary's. The weight of their lives at once pressed me into the chair and inspired me to rise above my own fear and mediocrity.

Others have moved into Mary's little brick house. I see the house as I walk back from Rabbit Lane, and I remember Austin and Mary. I wonder if the newcomers know.

Porn

The Sego Lily is the most delicate and elegant of chalices,
a veritable grail.

The state highway traverses the valley three-quarters of a mile away, perpendicular to Church Road as I approach Rabbit Lane. In the dark morning, a long line of white headlights travels north toward the Great Salt Lake, becoming red taillights as I pan from south to north.

Where do they all go? To work? To the airport? To breakfast at the all-you-can-eat truck stop buffet? On vacation? It occurred to me rather absurdly that if everyone that was going switched places with everyone that was coming, no one would have to go anywhere. They could stay home, play with their children, make love to their partner, read a classic book, work in the garden—enjoy life. Instead, they rush off in one direction only to rush back in the other, with little of substance, perhaps, filling the void. I do the same.

Water moves slowly through the wider parts of the ditch, reflecting the bluing early morning sky in its glassy surface. It trickles through the green Watercress to smooth again downstream. As the sun prepares to crest the Oquirrh mountain peaks, the sky explodes with pink and orange hues, reflecting gloriously in the water's calm.

Ron and Mary often heat their home and cook their meals with coal in the wood stove and wood in the cook stove. The smoky smells of burning coal and wood, mixed with the sweet aromas of frying bacon and baking bread, together with the crisp morning air of Fall, transport me momentarily to a place of transcendent bliss, into the happy ending of my own fairy tale, where I wish I could stay.

Ron farms the 18 acres on the corner of Rabbit Lane and Church Road, with alfalfa hay or silage corn during the growing season, and grazes cattle in Winter. The corn he cuts down, chops up, and dumps, stalk and all, into a ten-foot-deep silage pit, which he covers with tarps. Beneath the tarps, the corn slowly ferments in the cool Fall temperatures. During Winter, Ron pulls the tarps back several feet each week and scoops the silage out of the pit with his 1950s Case tractor bucket to feed to the hungry, black Angus heifers.

Cheap newsprint porn floats open on the water near Witch's Tree. I pause a moment, then turn away and move on past dozens of crushed beer cans thoughtlessly tossed. Further along, I walk atop a low ridge of soft earth and gravel pushed up against the ditch bank by the county grader that has smoothed out the washboard ruts so annoying to strollers and cars. From this short height, I can see deeper into the ditch, and find hundreds upon hundreds of beer cans lining the banks and floating in the water. I even found an old vending machine sunk deep in the mud. Weeks later, the children and I brought rakes, bags, and a wheelbarrow, which filled up quickly. The cleanest cans were recycled. Cans full of mud went to the county landfill with the crayfish still inside. I walked slightly ahead to keep an eye out for stray porn.

Another day, I invited my two older daughters Erin (15) and Laura (13) to join me for a walk on Rabbit Lane. After a few minutes, the peacefulness of the summer afternoon settled in, and I pulled together the courage to broach with them the sensitive subject of sexuality. I did not talk about anatomy; their mother had expressed her opinion that the topic of sexual anatomy should be discussed with daughters by their mother, not their father. I did not object.

I began by explaining that a woman's body has the power to excite certain sensations and emotions in a man. This is why modest dress is so important for young women, not to restrict them from the popular styles of their peers, not to hide their natural beauty, but to help them both to avoid drawing unwanted sexual attention to themselves and to avoid creating sexual tensions within young men. While feelings of sexual excitement are normal and healthy in young people, I expressed my conservative opinion that these feelings should not be intentionally magnified by wearing revealing clothing. I do not apologize for this opinion. I believe that modesty in attire and speech will allow a young person's nascent sexuality to be kept in balance with his/her greater needs for real friendship, acceptance, understanding, and love, without premature sexual entanglement.

I moved from the topic of modesty to the subject of pornography. I explained how the pornography industry makes billions of dollars annually by using women's bodies to excite men's fantasies. While my opinion about modesty comes from sincerely held beliefs, my aversion to pornography comes less from a sense of traditionalism or conservatism than from a pragmatic understanding of the very real and very dangerous effects of pornography on the human mind.

From a place of reason and experience more than religion, I cautioned my daughters about marrying men that had spent any significant time with pornography. For these men, pornography will have defined their sense of what a woman should look like, of what a woman should act like, of what a woman is for, of what intimacy and sexuality are all about, of what feminine beauty is, and of what marriage is. I believe that a man trained by pornography will never be content with the woman he marries. Her breasts or buttocks or thighs or waist or face or hair will never be right, and he will always be wishing and yearning for someone else. As exciting as pornographic images may be in the moment, they will taint every true image that follows. A woman married to a man filled with the propaganda of pornography will not be appreciated for who she is as a woman, but only for how she looks and how she performs sexually. In his mind, she will never measure up to the idyllic woman sold by clever and calculating pornographers.

Rabbit Lane was not long enough for this discussion. My beautiful daughters and I had turned the corner onto Bates Canyon Road, walked its length, and were now retracing our steps toward Rabbit Lane. What I was telling them seemed to make sense to them. It was rational and understandable. Without their own experience, they nevertheless knew intuitively that what I was saying was true. Still, I reinforced the message by pointing to the failed marriages of several beautiful women they know, and the behavior of the men in those marriages.

What I did not reveal to my daughters at that time is that my opinions about pornography derived in part from personal experience. I did not tell them the story of when, as a 12-year-old boy riding my bicycle to church, I found a *Playboy* magazine in the parking lot. I did not tell them of my unfortunate decision to pick up the magazine—to keep it, to take it in, to learn from it, to taste and feel the power and excitement of its images—instead of to ignore it or to reject it. I was a young boy, barely into puberty, and, contrary to my indoctrination, had invited this magazine to shape my beliefs about womanhood,

manhood, sexuality, pleasure, beauty, happiness, contentment, relationships, and marriage. Since that first day, I have expended enormous energy and effort, not always successfully, to maintain internal integrity toward womanhood, manhood, and marriage. I did not explain to my daughters the anguish that the lies of pornography will bring in the pursuit of real manhood, of a true relationship with real womanhood, and of real, lasting, and happy marriage.

Was I a coward not to confess to them the mistakes of my youth? Was I afraid to show them their father's imperfections? Was I afraid to disappoint them, to have them feel ashamed of me, to relive my own shame? I'm not sure. I think I decided that it was not necessary for them to know. I love them and they trust me; that is enough. I do know that I feel keenly, to this day, a sense of my own shame for allowing myself to fall prey to pornography, for allowing the pornographers to teach me about womanhood and love. But I have sought truer teachers since, and have worked to transform that shame into wisdom and truth.

My daughters were kind to me. They did not reject or challenge or blush or avoid. They simply took in what I had to say. To my relief and joy, they began a conversation about what they hoped for in a husband. They each hoped to marry a man that would be their friend, that would talk with them and listen to them, that would laugh with them and cry with them. They each hoped to find a man that would love them. It is really that simple: they want to be loved. My prayer is that they will each find a man that will have eyes only for them, and not eyes that wander, yearning, to other women's bodies, or to the pages of a magazine, or to a computer screen—that is when love will leave.

I have repeated iterations of this talk with my sons, sometimes on Rabbit Lane, sometimes on a drive to the movies, sometimes in the privacy of their rooms.

I hope for my daughters. I fear for my daughters. I hope and fear for my sons. I see pornography as a great threat to the happiness and durability of any marriage, of any intimate adult relationship. I pray to God that my daughters will find men worthy of them, men who will love them for who they are and not for what a pornographic magazine or website says they should look like, should be. I pray that my sons will learn about womanhood not from a magazine or a website but from the wonderful women in their lives—their mother, their grandmothers, their aunts, their teachers, and their future wives. This is my prayer for all daughters and sons. As mothers and fathers, as aunts, uncles, and grandparents, we can help God answer this prayer.

The road in front of Ron's and Mary's house is edged by a tall, tangled hedge of Wild Roses. The bushes rise in long thorny tendrils that at about six feet long finally arc under their own weight and return to ground. In mid-May, little green buds suddenly burst into hundreds of thousands of soft-yellow and scarlet-orange flowers. They lay themselves open, more like daisies than commercial roses. But the rich perfume is unmistakably and completely rose, with a hint of citrus. Wild Roses in bloom are like bursts of exotic orange and yellow fireworks frozen at the moment of explosion. After one or two weeks, the dazzle fades and the bushes thicken into a deep green mass. Like the once ubiquitous Hollyhock flower, these wild rose bushes are the vanishing vestiges of pioneer landscaping. Few remain, like most things pioneer, being replaced by exotic hybrids possessing their own merits.

FALL

Fall has become
in my advancing years
a sweet season
sending forth
a settling sense
of things slowing down
preparing to rest
under white blankets
that warm and moisten
against year's end.
Nights are cool
and days are sunny and cool.
Rows of dry corn
sheaves rasp each other
in the evening air.
Geese wave
a noisy farewell
overhead on their way away.
Greens melt
to candy yellows and reds
smelling earthy sweet
drifting down to become
the richness in the soil
where sleeping segos and tapertips
wait for Spring.

WINTER

Winter has lain
long and heavy
on the landscape,
pressing pliable grass blades,
weighing down supple apple boughs.
Too long
has the sky hung
gray overhead.

Of Cows and a Stray Bull

Cows have such large, glossy, gentle eyes.

    Ben was attempting to herd his cows from one field to another as I walked in his direction on Church Road. The process first involved opening the gate at the receiving field, then opening the gate at the sending field. In theory, Ben would then shoo the cows out of the sending field down the road and into the receiving field. At the open sending field gate, Ben's wife and children lined themselves up across the street, arms outstretched, forming a barrier the cows were supposed to respect. The kine, however, had ideas of their own, and strolled indolently between Ben's kin. The human line instantly disintegrated into a chaotic chasing mob, which I enthusiastically joined. Determined to be a helpful neighbor, I chased a particularly errant cow. But when I cut left, she ran right, and when I cut right, she ran left. She simply refused to be caught. (It had not occurred to my brain what I would do if I "caught" the one-ton cow, or what "catching" her might mean for me.) On one run I headed the cow so effectively that she veered ninety degrees and careened full speed into four strands of barbed wire. The wire held, and the cow backed out, seemingly unfazed and unharmed. As I continued to wave my arms and holler, however, the cow turned to face me, lowering her head while fixing me with furious eyes. This time it was I who ran to the right and to the left, terrified as the enormous cow trotted after me, albeit with not much interest. At that moment, I decided that if I were going to be a cowboy, I would need a horse, or an ATV, or a truck. Actually, I decided that I was not meant to be a cowboy. I also decided that I was of no use to Ben, and left him to his own devices. Somehow, he managed to corral the cattle later that night, probably with the help of a real Erda cowboy.

I stood near the kitchen sink one morning, in my suit and tie, preparing my breakfast and sack lunch. Glancing through the west window, past its white grids, I started at the sight of an enormous black bull standing in my back yard contentedly cropping the thick Kentucky blue-rye blend grass. I stepped onto the back porch and down the few wooden steps to the grass, feeling foolishly safe so close to my house and the open porch door. The bull munched on, paying no mind to my waving arms and shooing voice. I ventured ten feet closer to the bull (and ten feet farther from the house) and raised my voice to catch his attention. More quickly that you would think 2,500 pounds of animal could move, the bull squared off, facing me directly, and lowered his head, ready to charge. I did not wait to find out if it were a bluff, but ran instead through the open doorway and slammed and bolted the door, moving more quickly myself than one might expect for a 200-pound lawyer. I felt relieved that none of my family had witnessed the showdown in which their father had run for his life. The bull's intimidation objective accomplished, he returned to eating my grass. I called the sheriff's office to request an animal control officer, but no one came, and the bull eventually wandered off. Had I known the bull was Charley's, I would have called him and informed him calmly and politely that his bull was in my back yard. Charley later told me that I had had no reason to worry: "That bull is as gentle as a lamb." I said nothing, but silently begged to differ.

On another morning, thankfully a morning without bulls in the backyard, Hyrum (2) announced that he was going to run circles around the house. I followed from inside, watching through the several windows of the various rooms. Barefoot, he rounded one corner, crossed the front lawn, disappeared behind the garage, then crossed the back yard. He sang joyfully as he ran, with a full-arm swing and a bouncy, quick step.

Even more frightening than my encounter with the bull was the morning I left the house early, in the dark, walking across the front lawn toward Rabbit Lane. The stray black cows and I did not see each other until we were only five feet apart. When I finally detected the hulking black shapes, I jumped with such a start that it seemed as if I might land on a cow's back like a spaghetti western cowboy jumping over his horse's rump to land in the saddle. Instead, I ran one way, the cows ran a few feet the other, then we both realized that neither was a threat to the other.

Charley, Cloyd, Craig, and Ron all raise black Angus beef. The cattle roam the pastures lazily, constantly chewing their hay and grass cud in rounded, grinding motions. In Spring their calves run and dance playfully, chasing each other and jumping clumsily in the air.

On Rabbit Lane I see cows from just a few feet away, only a few strands of barbed wire between us. They look at me curiously but cautiously out of large, soft, brown eyes set in gentle, jowly faces. A sudden movement from me in their direction spooks their bulk into a surprisingly quick retreat. Though monstrous in size, the cows appear such gentle creatures. They nuzzle and lick their calves between bites of grass. The calves suckle and run off to frolic. In a few months, millions of people, including myself, will be eating these animals, in delicious ignorance of the peaceful lives they have lead in country pastures.

Confined to small barred pens, several cows on Church Road stand in puddles and piles of their own urine and manure, gazing at the grass that grows thick and abundant outside their enclosures. For these cows, the grass is truly greener on the other side. In fact, the only green thing inside their pens is manure. The welded pipe manger lies on its side in the muck. Any hay it held has long since been eaten or trampled into the mud-manure mixture, as if by slaves mixing mud for bricks. Dark muck oozes through the cows' cloven hoofs and covers their legs up to their knee joints. As I walk by, the acrid odor tries to knock me over, but succeeds only in pushing me to the other side of the street, where I hold my breath.

On Rabbit Lane, a young wiener calf reaches to scratch some teasing itch with its incredibly long tongue. I wonder why it does not simply raise a hind hoof to scratch its haunch. Seeing that it is standing in wet, green, steaming shit, I think that I might avoid using my hoof if I were in its place. I feel grateful for two hands that can do my scratching even though I might be standing with my feet in fresh dung. I would do well in life to keep my knuckles from dragging in the shit of life, instead raising my hands at least to my empty pockets, or preferably raising them high in finger-stretching ebullience. My tongue, after all, is entirely too short.

THE CALF

The calf
lay beneath the rusted barbed wire fence
by the side of Rabbit Lane:
a lonely, black puddle in Winter's whiteness,
salted with slowly settling snowflakes.
Death's sadness reached into me,
a dull ache in my empty stomach.
It drew me to the calf.
I came near and reached out to touch the black fur.
At my touch,
the small, black head lifted weakly,
turning big, moist eyes
to meet mine.
Those glossy eyes spoke to me,
a simple, sad story:
of bewilderment, exhaustion, loneliness, and despair,
of wandering from its mamma,
of slipping between the loose, rusty strands,
of learning it was lost,
of growing cold and weary,
of slumping down to die.
I strained to heave the baby animal from the snow,
and trudged with my burden to
the dilapidated farmhouse.
I knocked shyly, a stranger,
whispered at the back door,
transferred my quivering bundle
to the thankful farmer,
to the warmth of a coal fire and a tender expression,
to a promise:
to find a mother,
to restore the proper order of things.

Cricket Chorus

Hyrum, you're my little bug.

Under low, heavy clouds and a light, misty rain, the lighthouse beam shines in a shaft for miles as it slowly sweeps the sky.

European Starlings gather by the thousand in the neighborhood Cottonwoods, with grease-black feathers and cheddar cheese beaks. Their wild chatter resembles radio static blaring in a range of high pitches. The Starlings do not enjoy seeds so do not compete with the House Finches and House Sparrows that crowd the feeders. Instead, the Starlings flock to the Mulberry tree above the porch, waiting for safe moments to descend upon the unguarded cat food bowl. Within minutes they fly away, leaving a near-empty bowl and a redwood porch painted with splotches of white-and-brown guano like a dubious modern art masterpiece. What the starlings leave in the bowl the skunks will eat before morning. Considered by many a ubiquitous pest, at least the Starlings do not worry about how they are perceived. They go about casually and confidently doing their business, unheeding of the judgments of others. In that sense they are as genuine as I could ever hope to be.

A gray cloud of swarming Starlings moves chaotically yet algorithmically through the sky, expanding, shrinking, changing shape, diving, ascending, with never a bird out of synchrony. The avian cloud drops suddenly upon a broad, dead Cottonwood, which instantly comes to life with cacophonic chatter, as if one-thousand concomitant voices are announcing life to the world. What the birds' squawking lacks in song it makes up for in eager ebullience, in happy, boisterous communication to their family and community, celebrating their togetherness, absolutely free of concern for any listener. Without apparent signal from any leader, the birds suddenly lift off the tree, leaving it again a silent giant, and the noisy cloud hurries amorphously away over the ploughed fields.

Jeanette called me one Saturday afternoon. I sat in the living room as we spoke, looking out at the birds clamoring over and around the bird feeders. With excitement in her voice, she told me that she had just seen a beautiful black bird with a yellow head, and asked me if I knew what it was. I had seen hundreds of these striking birds clinging to tall reed grasses near the Great Salt Lake.

"Sure," I told her, doing my best to sound intelligent. "They are Yellow-Headed Blackbirds."

"Oh," she responded, and I could tell she felt dumb.

Outside my window, a pair of Red-winged Blackbirds was doing its best to chase a hundred House Sparrows away from the best feeder perches. Jeanette ventured another bird question.

"What about those black birds with red bands on their wings? What are they called?"

"Well," I responded, pausing as if searching my memory, "those are Red-winged Blackbirds."

"Oh," she said again. "Okay. Thanks."

"That's alright," I tried to reassure her. "I just happen to know their names, and their names just happen to be exactly what you see."

She did not ask me any more bird questions. But today she knows as much or more than me about birds.

Some creature rustles the tall grass, shrouded by drooping Russian Olive trees. It's big, I can tell, by the volume of sound. Stooping to glimpse under the tree branches, a Mule Deer starts up from its bedding place to bound away over the grass and through the alfalfa. Deer do not belong here. Their territory is in the mountains and foothills. But this lush lowland, covered with sweet alfalfa and willow bushes, food and shelter, together with seeping springs, provides excellent year-round habitat. They escape the starvation and predation common to the mountains, and are free from the pressures of the hunt, unless the farmer tires of their presence. This deer, a small doe, is followed by another I had not seen in the thick grasses that reach taller than her withers, the doe's chestnut blending with the lighter brown grass. Farther away, a two-point buck stares at me intently, its haunches taught, its large ears pointed forward and twitching. Caleb (2) once pointed after such a deer and called out "moose-doggies!" Discovering little piles of deer droppings, John (4) told Caleb it was "moose-doggie poop."

The sound of bowing and pizzicatoing crickets and katydids hovers over the pasture lands in the approaching twilight. As I enter a copse of Russian Olives flanking Rabbit Lane, the sound becomes more than a merely pleasant ensemble ambiance. Walking past the first trunks, underneath their boughs, I find myself suddenly inside the sound. It surges rhythmically around me and through me. It is as if I have stepped into a powerful magnetic field that excites and repolarizes all my trillion cells. My body seems to pulse amidst the air and trees in which the invisible insects sing to one another. I slow my pace to prolong the music. Passing through the small tree cluster, I seem to step out of a symphony hall, where the sound was big and beautiful, and into the corridor with the music muted by insulating doors, a still audible and pleasant sound, but no longer compelling, no longer strumming my soul strings. The orchestral cloud calls me back, and I succumb willingly, to linger even as the song dwindles in the evening's waning warmth and light.

SUMMER SONG

Ground-line sprinklers in the green alfalfa hay
make such pretty music,
like the field song of crickets and katydids
on a hot, summer evening.

Cows' tails swishing in the tall, dry grass,
and the breeze fluttering stiff poplar leaves,
add apropos percussion
to the sublimity and song.

Summer Night

Roger Baker

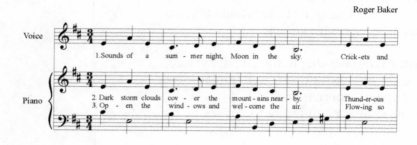

Reza

Good men and good women make a great difference in the world.

My Persian friend, Reza, joins my family on occasion for Sunday dinner. Over several Sunday visits, he told us parts of his life story, including how he left his homeland of Iran. Reza had been a wealthy industrialist in Iran: young, educated, and ambitious, with millions of dollars invested in an industrial complex fabricating modular housing units. Then the Ayatollahs overthrew the Shah and began their reign. The new regime did not at first seem to pose a threat to Reza or his industrial operations. Soon, however, they began to appropriate the proceeds of his operations while at the same time demanding that he continue to incur all his operating costs.

"They made me continue to operate my facility, to purchase materials, to manufacture my products, and to pay all my laborers their wages," said Reza.

In this way, the regime reaped the benefits of Reza's industry with no political or monetary cost, while impoverishing him. Without cash flow, it was only a short time before Reza's costs depleted his once vast reserves. A friendly tip alerted Reza that the regime, having taken what they wanted from him, no longer needed him. His freedom, if not his life, was in danger.

"I had no other option," Reza explained. "I took only a small case, drove toward the mountains, parked my car a safe distance from the border, and walked out of Iran. I crossed the Pyrenees on foot and stepped into Turkey."

He left everything behind—his wife and two sons, his kin, his inheritance, his career, and his properties—knowing that he might never be allowed to return.

"Turkish authorities immediately arrested me," Reza recounted. "They thought I was an Armenian terrorist."

During his weeks behind bars, his captors beat and tortured him. They connected parts of his body to a car battery to torture him with severe electric shocks. His pleas and protests availed him nothing, for the prison authorities did not speak Persian, English, or French, and he did not speak Turkish (or Armenian). Finally, he found someone in the jail that spoke enough French to communicate with the Turkish authorities. Reza convinced the officials that he was not a terrorist, but an asylum seeker, a victim of the new Iranian regime, and posed no threat to Turkey. They finally released him, and he made his way to Spain, then to Los Angeles, where he became a United States citizen, and finally to rural Utah.

After one Sunday dinner, I invited Reza to join us for a stroll down Rabbit Lane. As we walked, the sun slowly lowered toward the Stansbury mountain tops, and the sky's soft blue transformed to a delicate orange and peach. We talked of his challenges as a developer and home builder, and mine as a father and public servant. Developers and city officials are not always on the best of terms, but I have always experienced Reza as an honest man who keeps in view the public good even as he pursues his private gain.

Although I set a leisurely pace, Reza labored to breathe.

"Are you feeling well?" I inquired.

He responded that he had been experiencing unusual fatigue and shortness of breath, without apparent explanation. I encouraged him to see his doctor, and he assured me he would. A month later, Angie and I visited him in the intensive care unit of LDS hospital, where he had undergone a heart valve replacement and five bypasses. I learned that when Reza first awoke after surgery, he had begun to pull out all the tubes and catheters in a delirious frenzy; he thought the hospital staff were prison officials trying to torture and kill him. The physicians induced a coma to reduce the mental and physical stresses to Reza's barely living body. Seeing him in a coma, connected to IVs and with tubes in his nose and mouth, he appeared more dead than alive. I sensed a foreboding feeling, and knew that he was close to death. When I came a few days later, his condition appeared unchanged. I wondered if the strength I knew he had would be enough to pull him through.

We had brought a vase of delicate Bluebells from our flower garden to leave by his bedside. We wanted him to see something beautiful and natural and living when he awoke, if he awoke.

"Um, you can't take flowers into cardio ICU," a nurse instructed us.

She seemed happy to have the vase on the bare counter above her work area. If we were not permitted to brighten Reza's day with flowers—he was still unconscious, after all—then we were happy to brighten hers. Reza not only survived, but made a remarkable, if slow, recovery. After nearly three weeks in a coma in ICU, he was moved to a recovery room, then to a rehabilitation center, and finally to his home.

This was not the first time I had been in a hospital with Reza. Years earlier, he had told me that his granddaughter, less than one year old, was dying in Tehran of liver disease. He had arranged for her and her parents to come to Utah, where expert organ transplant surgeons at the University of Utah medical school hospital would remove a lobe from her father's compatible liver and transplant it into her body. I went to visit Reza and his family in the hospital the night before the operation.

Little nine-month-old Diba lay peacefully in a hospital crib. Her abdomen was terribly distended, and her skin was a drab green-brown because her sick and swollen liver had ceased to filter the toxins in her blood. As poisoned and distressed as her tiny body was, Diba smiled shyly at me as I looked into her large, soft brown eyes and said hello. I knew instantly that we were friends. I reached in and held her little hand for a moment.

The adults and I spoke quietly together for a few minutes. Then we gathered around Diba to pray, asking God to guide the hands and enlighten the minds of the surgical team, to bring recovery and healing to Diba and to her donor father, and to comfort her mother and grandfather. In the silence that followed we felt a peaceful reassurance that all would be well. The transplant succeeded, and both Diba and her father recovered fully.

Not everyone likes Reza. But he is appreciated by those who have glimpsed his true nature. He quietly goes about doing kind deeds. Funding scholarships for local youth to attend college. Cooking Thanksgiving and Christmas meals for families who otherwise would go without. Keeping employees on payroll during hard economic times when a sterile business model would have them laid off. It has been my privilege to share Rabbit Lane with Reza and others like him. And I am relieved that his breathing is no longer labored, but deep and calm.

The Day's Song

The music is everything. Can you hear it?

Erda and Rabbit Lane lie in the low lands of the Tooele valley. Still, we are high enough to see the silvery ribbon of the Great Salt Lake lining the horizon. Northerly breezes often bring with them the smell of salt in the air as it brushes over the enormous lake, transporting me through the darkness to days of my youth spent beach combing and sailing near New Jersey's Sandy Hook, looking across the bay to the iconic twin towers that exist now only in memory and in mourning, and in old photographs.

Each day brings its own song. Yesterday's song has faded into memory. It can be recalled but vaguely. Attempts to retrieve it are vain. So, let the old song go. Find today's song and rejoice in its tune, whether it be happy or sad, ebullient or contemplative.

We are influenced by what we see and hear, smell and taste and feel, by what is going on around us. Honking taxis. Smelly steam from manholes above the subway. Trains rattling on overhead tracks.

Rain-wet concrete under foot. A hot pretzel around the corner. Deep green alfalfa with small, purple blooms. Freshly cut hay drying in long lines down the length of the field, waiting to be baled. Cows bellowing as the farmer forks out their evening meal. A vase of summer sunflowers. A glass of fresh-squeezed orange juice. Children laughing at the playground. The words *I love you*. The music is everything. Can we hear it?

Russian Olive trees, despised by farmers and ranchers, grow wild and tangled along portions of Rabbit Lane's ditch, invading the pasture and sucking at the water. Their hard thorns can grow to a length of two inches and snag the shirt or hair of any careless passerby. One would never think of climbing a Russian Olive. From a short distance, they resemble the true olive trees of the Mediterranean. Their leaves grow narrow and long, in color a powdery blue-green-gray. Late Spring produces strands of tiny yellow flowers that fill the air with a sweet pungency, pleasant but at times overpowering. In late Fall, millions of dwarf olive berries fall from the trees and litter the roads. The pits, tiny striped footballs, can be drilled and strung for necklaces.

Fields of wheat, barley, and alfalfa hay sprawl adjacent to Rabbit Lane. Farmers irrigate these fields with great wheel lines. A wheel line consists of six-foot-tall metal wheels with flat rims and spindly spokes connected to 42-foot lengths of four-inch-diameter aluminum pipe. The resulting line can be half-a-mile long. Sprinkler heads rise periodically from the pipes, connected by brass fittings. Drug addicts at times break the sprinkler risers off the pipes to harvest the brass fittings, scrapping them for cash. The thieves are usually caught and prosecuted, spending years in prison while the farmer has suffered tens of thousands of dollars in damage to his sprinklers, while being unable to irrigate his fields.

Each pipe segment is centered at the wheel, with 21-foot lengths of pipe welded to each side of the wheel, forming an axle. Double wheels at the center of the line house a two-cycle engine that slowly drives the center wheels. When a line of crop is sufficiently irrigated, the farmer shuts off the water, allows the water to drain from the line of pipes, and fires up the motor. The motor slowly turns the center wheels with a chain and sprockets. The resulting torque gently muscles the entire wheel line slowly across the saturated fields, using the pipes themselves as the great wheel line axle, moving the machine to the next irrigation position, whereupon the farmer kills the motor. The torque is sometimes too great, or the speed too fast, or the ground too uneven, and a pipe twists and tears off from the line, irreparably damaged. Some fields are littered with torn sections of pipe angling up from their single wheels.

Underground water mains cross the fields unseen and sprout risers at predetermined intervals, connected to the end of the wheel line by a securely clamped flexible four-inch hose. The artesian pressure from some farm wells remains sufficient to run the wheel line sprinklers without the aid of a pump. Not-so-lucky farmers supplement with electric or petroleum pumps. Increased development has dropped the water table and the historic, natural artesian pressure.

Ron flood irrigates his 18 acres, pumping water to perforated pipes, a square, one-inch hole at the head of each ploughed furrow. Water flows down each furrow, soaking into the ground, hopefully making it to the end. Slight imperfections in furrow slope result in low spots that pool water and high spots that do not receive enough water, leaving a spotty crop. The State Engineer estimates that about one-half of this water is consumed by the plant crop or by evaporation, with the other one-half returning to the groundwater system, and requires that farmers own water rights to four acre-feet of water for each irrigated acre of farmland. In the old days the whole valley was flood irrigated from spring-fed ponds that dotted the farmland.

Ground line sprinklers are a less expensive but more labor intensive method of irrigation, each length of pipe lying on the ground and needing to be lifted and relocated by hand. Ground lines are four-inch-diameter aluminum pipes with periodic two-foot-tall risers from which sprinkler heads churn out water. This method is ideal for small or uneven patches of alfalfa, but less so for larger fields or taller crops.

The most modern irrigation method is the pivot. A pivot consists of an elevated pipe suspended on a metal superstructure mounted on rubber wheels. The sprinklers hang down from the pipes, spraying mist directly onto the crops. A motor at the pivot point slowly swings the pivot around in an arcing circle, irrigating 60 or more acres without any human intervention beyond turning the water on and off. The corners of the fields still need to be sprinkled manually.

On cold Spring mornings, when the air is frigid but the ground still thawed, the sprinkler spray freezes to the aluminum wheels and spokes, forming great white mounds of ice and thousands of icicles, each flashing brilliantly in the morning sun, while the surrounding ground is the rich, dark earth of a newly-ploughed field or the lush green of a new crop.

The *whump whump* of an old baler pulses in the still-hot air of the fields long after dark, reaching with its mechanical arm and rake fingers to pull the dusty hay tightly into itself, wrapping it with taught orange nylon twine. Even for this old baler, baling wire is a thing of the past. The baler measures not only the length of each bale but also the passing hours and days of the farmer's field, the moving moments of his life.

Whump! Whump!
Whump! Whump!

The sound ceases only when the low-mounded rows have changed into oblong cubes of compressed hay, still green, ready for stacking and storing for Winter's bovine hunger.

Before moving to Erda, I thought that straw and hay were two words used to describe the same substance. Perhaps hay was the green living stuff, while straw was the cut, dried, baled, and stacked stuff. Just different forms of the same commodity, like cow and beef. I soon learned how wrong I had been. Straw is, in fact, the harvested stalks of grain plants, commonly oats. Straw is used for animal bedding, not animal food. Huge harvesters separate the grains from the reedy stalks, which stalks are cut and fed into a baler and bound tightly into bales. Enormous clouds of dust follow the harvesters as they glean out the grain and chop down the stalks, also called chaff.

Oat straw is soft and smooth, making great bedding for animals. I stuff straw into the hens' nesting boxes to make comfortable beds for egg laying. I also spread straw around the chicken coop floor. The hens peck and scratch through it all year until it is pulverized and mixed with droppings, making an ideal garden fertilizer. Hay, on the other hand, is rough and prickly when dried. Sleeping in a bed of straw would be quite comfortable, if dusty, while sleeping in a pile of dried alfalfa hay would be oxymoronic. Climbing over or throwing hay bales without long pants, long sleeves, and gloves will leave you punctured, scraped, and sore, not to mention itchy.

While straw is not another word for hay, hay is another word for alfalfa. Hay is to alfalfa what hamburger is to beef. Hay is the end product: cut, dried, baled, and fed to livestock in winter. Alfalfa, a type of clover, is the living plant. The alfalfa plant does not grow kernels of grain atop tall waving stalks, like wheat or barley, rye or oats. Rather, alfalfa grows close to the ground in tangled green bushes with small clover leaves. The plants produce abundant clover blossoms of white, purple, or yellow, depending on the variety.

The farmer harvests the plant when it is a deep green, just before blossoming. The swather tractor has huge rolling blades on the front, like a giant, old-fashioned, non-motorized push mower, which cuts the plants off close to the ground. Stiff, spinning wires behind the tractor rake the cuttings into long, narrow windrows.

The same rakes are used to turn the cuttings over to thoroughly dry in the summer sun. The cuttings must be fully dried before baling, or mold will grow inside the tight bales, making the hay unfit for feeding to horses. When the plant has fully dried, another tractor pulls a baler, which gathers up the tangled stems and leaves and binds them tightly with nylon twine, yellow, orange, or red, into rectangular bales about three feet long and one-foot tall and deep. Thirty bales make a ton.

The last machine to come along is the bale wagon, which scoops up the bales one by one and stacks them high behind the driver.

A farmer that does not have a bale wagon pulls a flat-bed trailer onto which the hired hands, amidst clouds of hay dust, grab the bale twine with gloved hands and heave the bales. Some farmers use balers that make huge half-ton rectangular bales that have to be lifted and moved with a forklift.

Others use machines to roll the hay into six-foot-tall rolls. The neighborhood cats follow expectantly behind the helpers, hunting for

gophers and mice disturbed by the machines and exposed by the bare fields.

Erda farmers pray anxiously for rain, except during the three or four alfalfa harvests of the year, when they pray for blue skies. A poorly timed rain (or rather, a poorly timed harvest), can ruin the drying hay. The water quickly leaches out the nutrients and leaves the windrows of hay a mildewing mess. Once the hay is baled and stacked, rain can do them little harm, though covering the tall stacks with tarps provides further protection.

Behind Lucille's small clapboard shack sits a twisted, rusted dump rake. A bare iron seat, without springs, rises from the horse-drawn implement, where the pre-tractor farmer sat holding the reins with his hands and controlling levers with his feet. The rake, a dozen feet wide, scratched at the fresh-cut hay with curved iron tines two feet long. When the tines gathered hay to capacity, the farmer pressed a pedaled lever that lifted all the tines at once and dumped the hay in a neat row just behind the spoked iron wheels. Continuing on, the farmer let fall the tines and began another hay row, and another, until the field was bare but for the raked hay rows. Leaving the rake, the farmer folded each row onto itself in thirds, forming hillocks of hay, or haycocks. He loaded the heaped hay with sharp-tined forks onto wheeled slip carts. The open-bed carts, fully loaded, were rolled to where a cross beam hung on two upright poles at the same height as the cart bed. Pushing the cart under the cross beam caused the hay to slip off the cart, still in a neat haycock. Moving the beam to an adjacent location, the cart slipped stack after stack of hay in the stacking yard, forming what looked from a distance like a line of fresh bread loaves. With the advent of balers and bales, dump rakes became rusting relics in suburban rock gardens.

A favorite sight walking on Rabbit Lane, along with breathtaking sunsets and soaring Red-tailed Hawks, is the sight of a ripe alfalfa field. A field of ripe alfalfa is a deep, vibrant green, homogenous but highly textured. A ripe alfalfa field looks as if a green leafy mass had boiled excitedly up from the earth and suddenly frozen in a photograph, or like the soil has sprouted a curly, green, foot-thick carpet. My favorite of all aromas, even above lasagna or fresh wheat bread or watermelon or lemongrass tea, is the sweet and cleansing smell of a newly cut hayfield steaming in the afternoon sun after a light summer shower, though my olfactory pleasure is not as pleasant to the worried farmer.

Bringing home our first ton of alfalfa hay was an adventure that fulfilled in me a longing to connect with the romantic notions of both the cowboy and the farmer. We had acquired two young goats from an entrepreneur trying his hand at making goat cheese. They quickly cropped down the native grasses that can grow six feet tall. Some yellow and purple clover alfalfa sprouted up here and there in the borrow pits where the wind had blown random seed. The plants were tough, but I could yank the stems in just the right way to make them snap off at the base of the plant. I did this every morning I walked on Rabbit Lane. The goats devoured the rich alfalfa like hungry children munching candy at Halloween. But there were not enough plants to give them more than a snack, and winter was on its way.

I called Evan, who was still growing alfalfa and throwing hay bales in his seventies, about buying some hay. To neighbors he sold at the discounted price of $100 a ton.

"Drive your pick-up over and I'll help you load up," he offered.

The children all wanted to come, so I let them hop into the bed of the truck. I drove them slowly over to Evan's house. He opened the gate that kept the sheep away from the tall stacks of hay bales, and let us through.

One ton of hay turned out to be 30 bales. I was sure he could never fit 30 three-foot-long bales into my six-foot-long short bed, but he assured me that he could. Instructing the children to stand back, he climbed onto some nearby bales, reached a rake to the top of the stack, and brought several bales tumbling down. The ensuing cloud of green alfalfa dust pushed its way up my nose and into my eyes. I sneezed repeatedly. Somewhat recovered, and wanting to be helpful, I grabbed a bale by the yellow nylon twine and pulled it up to my waist, trying to muscle it into the bed of the truck. I learned quickly that I could not throw the heavy bale, and instead rather awkwardly rolled it onto the tailgate, then maneuvered it toward the cab. The twine cut into my fingers, and rough, dry hay particles scratched my arms and flew into my face and hair and down my shirt.

Evan, 40 years my senior, with leather gloves and long sleeves, adeptly hoisted a bale and raised a knee to at once lift and push and throw the bale onto the truck. He patiently instructed me on how to arrange the bales so that I could fit them all, effectively removing me from bale-throwing duty. I discovered that bales of hay do not slide against one another at all. Instead of sliding past one another, they bite into each other like two sharks biting into each other's flanks. Veritable velcro. It took repeated jostling and muscling and lifting to align the bales side by side.

After the first layer was neatly blocked in, I began to lay the second tier, hoisted the third layer, and somehow managed to heave on the fourth. My hands shook with fatigue and exertion as I wrote the $100 check. With a sincere thank you, I carefully maneuvered the heavily-laden half-ton truck down the dirt lane past his house, then down Liddell Lane to Church Road. The huge one-ton stack of green hay bales rocked above and dwarfed the white truck. The children all begged to ride atop our new haystack, but I did not dare let them. The danger of them falling 15 feet onto the hard road was all too obvious. And I remembered the story of my grandpa Wallace breaking his neck when as a boy he fell off the top of a tall hay stack loaded in the horse-drawn hay wagon. He miraculously survived to live an exemplary life, dying in his sixties of cancer. But I was not going to take any chances with my children.

At home, the children rolled the bales off the truck while I stacked them neatly next to the chicken coop, where they would provide some insulation from the winter winds. As the sun dipped toward the Stansbury mountaintops, we climbed the bales to sit proudly on top of our hay stack and watch the sunset. The hay was not soft at all, but instead painfully prickly to any skin that pressured the hay. Mom brought out a pan of hot chocolate. As we sipped, the sun sank below the mountain peak horizon, and the sky rewarded us with a brilliant crimson panorama.

Remembering the Day

What I like best is being with you.

The hour was 10 p.m., long after the children's bed times. I had come home late from city council meeting, and had settled into the sofa with cookies and cold milk, grandma Lucille's crocheted afghan over my lap, and a book of Sherlock Holmes mysteries in my hand. Finally, it was time for a little quiet enjoyment.

The phone rang in the other room, injecting me with adrenaline, and I swore under my breath at the jarring ringing so late in the evening. Mom was helping the baby fall asleep, or stay asleep, each of equal virtue. By the time I reached the phone, it had stopped ringing. Not recognizing the number on the caller ID, I did not call back, but returned to the couch.

I wrapped myself in the afghan and settled in again, with the handset nearby and its ringer volume turned down. Laura (5) suddenly stepped sleepy-eyed into the living room.

"I can't sleep," she complained. "The pillow is too scratchy."

She had used a pillow with a cotton flannel pillowcase, not being able to find her own favorite pillow with the silky, pink pillowcase.

"I don't know where it is, and you'll just have to make do," I told her.

She slinked bank to bed, dejected.

A paragraph into Dr. Watson's first story, Erin (7) walked in with a smile and dobs of tri-colored toothpaste all over her face. Next came Brian (10) to show me the new socks his mother had bought him earlier that day, along with his latest Lego creation. I nodded and smiled stiffly to Brian, told Erin to wipe the toothpaste off her face, and ordered them gently off to bed.

In the middle of page three, John (3) cried out from his room. He had woken up hot and sweating. I ran up to his room, folded back the quilt, and rubbed his back to help him back to sleep.

In the second paragraph of page eight, Brian and Erin descended the stairs again for their ritual drinks of water. They really were not thirsty; they just wanted to prolong their day and avoid going to bed. As they came to me for their third good-night hug, I resisted a roar and instructed them to go to bed and not come down again.

At the end of page 11, Angie came down, released from her servitude to the fitful one-year-old Caleb. She leaned softly into me and began to talk about her day. Trying hard to listen to my wife, I still held the open book as a silent statement of my longing for quiet time alone and my intention to obtain it. I listened dutifully, allowing myself to be drawn into her narrative. She soon went off to bed.

Close to midnight, I finished the first Holmes story. Enough for one night. At least church did not start till 11:00 the next morning. Lying in bed, I remembered each child as they came to me and interrupted my time. I could see their innocent, loving faces and, despite my momentary annoyance, was glad that they had each come to me. I chuckled at the toothpaste polka-dots on Erin's face; I sympathized with Laura for her scratchy pillowcase and with John for waking up hot and sweating; I admired Brian's creation. How precious each child was to me.

The detective story I had read did not inspire me, and did not stay with me. But memory's reflections of my children's faces did stay with me. For some reason, having their lives rub up against mine can be irritating. I sometimes chafe at their questions, their stories of the day, their little hurts that no longer hurt or never really hurt in the first place. I misconstrue their approaches as demands for my time and energy, when in truth the children are coming to me to give, not to take.

In the weeks that followed, these reflections came back to me as I walked on Rabbit Lane. Words and music began to fall spontaneously into place and soon became the song, *Remembering the Day*:

What was your favorite part of the day?
I loved our picnic by the bay.
And what about the thunderstorm?
I'm glad you kept me safe and warm.
What I liked best was being with you.
Thanks for the day. I love you, too.

Caleb (10) had a habit of coming to find me wherever I was to tell me about every little hurt and owie he had acquired through his work and play. Sometimes he called me at the office to tell me he had bonked his head or scraped his toe. He always sounded so sad as he told me his story. I confess to having been often insensitive and impatient with these accounts of his little hurts. I could see that nothing was bleeding or broken. So I would grunt or nod distractedly or with annoyance, and he would walk away. But on the occasions when I listened to him and acknowledged his pain, he always brightened up, said "Thanks Dad," and walked away cheerfully, no longer troubled. As I am with so many things, I was slow to discover that all Caleb wanted was for someone to care, not by fixing his hurt but by listening to his heart. He wanted me to reassure him that I love him and that he matters to me. I am his father, after all. What more important service can a father offer to his son than to listen, to express sympathy, to show love—in short, to help the healing of inside hurts while the outside hurts heal themselves? Sure, I could tell him to be tough, to be a man, to stop crying; I could characterize his hurts as insignificant. But he would have plenty of time and occasion to toughen up. Life would do that to him on its own without any help from me. What Caleb needed from me was to buoy him up in his moment of need, so that when life did get tougher later, he would be sure enough of himself to ride the tide.

OPEN EYES

when
we open our eyes
the places we walk
will show us
wonderful things
but also hard
heart-wrenching things
beauty and sorrow
sometimes each alone
often all together

Remembering the Day

Roger Baker

Rabbit Lane

Shining Shoes

Knock, knock.
Who's there?
Shampoo.
Shampoo who?
Made you look! Made you look! Made you eat your underwear!
(Caleb-3 to Dad)

As a four-year-old, Caleb loved cowboy boots, though he did not have any of his own. Somewhere he found some hand-me-down boots, one brown and one black, different sizes, both for the left foot. He wore them everywhere, without socks, running in shorts and a t-shirt around the yard, whooping and hollering, digging in the garden, shooting his stick rifle, tromping in the pig pen.

My dress shoes hold their shine quite well for several months. But eventually the time comes when I need to polish them. Shining my shoes quickly becomes a family affair. It seems that the moment I open the can of polish, the strong smell runs throughout the house, as if summoning the children, and they in turn come running, each with at least one pair of their own shoes. They watch me patiently for a minute or two.

"Can I help you shine your shoes, Dad?" they each ask. Next, "will you help me shine my shoes?" Then, "Can I shine my shoes too?"

When I was a small boy, my father made himself a wooden shoeshine box. He made one for me at the same time, with my initials carved artistically in one end: *REB*. The ends of the shoeshine box are shaped like broad spades; the sides slant inward and down to form a narrow bottom. The wide lid is hinged, and a cross bar connects the tops of the two spade-handled ends. The box is stained a rich walnut. Inside the box sit various cans of polish: dark brown, light brown, tan, cordovan, ox blood, white, and two cans of black. The black polish gets used up the quickest, because I use it on every shoe to dress up the sole and heel edges. Mixed in with the cans are various old gym socks and toothbrushes. My favorite item is the wood-handled horse-hair brush made in Israel. Over more than 30 years of polishing shoes, the horse hairs have shortened to about half their original length. But the hairs remain just soft enough and just course enough to give a perfect shine to the polish.

I formerly used the old gym socks, wrapped around my fingers, to apply the polish. But I grew tired of dark stains on my fingertips where the polish seeped through the fabric. Now I use old toothbrushes to wipe the thick polish out of the can and work it into the leather. When I'm done, the toothbrushes go into the socks to keep the box clean. The polish dries and flakes inside the toothbrush bristles, so I vigorously work the bristles back and forth against the inside of the sock, both when putting the brushes away and when retrieving them for the next job, to avoid scattering specks of dried polish that stain my clothing and the carpet the next time I pull them out to polish.

I usually have enough patience to polish three pairs of shoes. The number reduces to two if the children are clamoring to help. Allowing a child to participate in shining shoes complicates the process significantly. I place the can carefully on a rag so that the helping child does not smear polish on the carpet or furniture. I make sure he does not scrape too much polish onto the brush to prevent globs from falling onto the carpet. I see that she does not fill the crevices and holes in the leather with polish, like so much putty. I double check that every bit of leather has a film of fresh polish. I let the children help with the polish for a little while. What works best is for me to apply the polish and to let them shine the shoes with the horse-hair brush. Nothing can go wrong with shining. Shining works best by placing one hand inside the shoe and passing the brush over the shoe with even, swinging strokes with the brush hand. The in-shoe hand turns and angles the shoe to allow the brush to shine every part of the shoe. I show the children how, then hand them the shoe and the brush. Their little hands do not fill the shoe like mine, making it harder to hold the shoe steady in the face of the swinging brush. But when their hands grow, they will know how to hold the shoe steady for the best polish. Their feet will grow, too, and their hearts and their minds, and will fill larger shoes than mine.

Many times after church and our mid-day meal we have taken a family walk on Rabbit Lane. I sometimes forget (or am too lazy) to change out of my newly-polished shoes. Back from our walk, I see that fine dust from the dirt road has settled upon my shoes, covering the polish. A few strokes with the horse-hair brush usually restore the shine.

I find myself shining my shoes less and less over time. As my shoes age, I feel less motivated to keep them looking nice. I wear them scuffed, unpolished, and old. Some lawyers I work with never seem to shine their shoes. If the polish gets significantly scuffed, they simply buy new shoes. I wear my shoes until they are worn out, polishing them (or not) for years. Even an old shoe assumes new respectability with a fresh coat of polish.

I like the pungent odor of shoe polish: it reminds me of my childhood home and the aroma of my father's regular shoe polishing.

He kept his wooden shoe shine box in his walk-in closet, with his initials carved in the side: *ONB*. But not everyone enjoys the strong odor. I fret that if I polish my shoes in my closet, it will smell up Angie's clothing. Maybe I should polish my shoes on the porch, or in the tool shed, or in the chicken coop, where the smell will not bother anyone.

To preserve the tradition, I have made spade-sided shoeshine boxes for each of my sons. Each box boasts a different color stain and unique hinges, and each is filled with polish and old socks and old toothbrushes and a horse-hair brush. My boys are now men in their own right, shining their own dress shoes. Soon they will be hearing the call, "Can I help, Daddy?"

Of Dogs and Cursing

Kind words counter the world's cruelties.

Quiet is a rare luxury at our house. If not the cows or dogs or pumps, I can usually count on my children to fill my quiet moments. But not all noise is unpleasant.

One day Hyrum (2) said sternly to his big brother Brian (14), "Brian, don't *keel* anyone. OK? Because it's dangerous."

He was dead serious, as if in grown-up conversation. It was apparent that the word *kill* had only a vague meaning to him. It did not equate to the loss of life, but related more closely to roughhousing or child's play, as in "Bang! Bang! You're dead!" A short time later I heard a brief but violent interaction between Hyrum and Caleb (5):

Hyrum: "I *keeled* you!"
Caleb: "No you didn't. I killed *you*."

Hyrum: "No! I keeled you *first!*"

I chimed in at that point: "It seems that you are *both* dead, so be quiet!"

Home life is hectic for a mother at home with a house full of children that she feeds, bathes, clothes, plays with, reads to, listens to, cries with, nurtures, educates, and puts to work. At times when I call from work, Mom steps into the pantry or coat closet to find a moment to speak freely and without interruption. I have found her writing while sitting on the floor in her closet, or reading a book while sitting on a lowered toilet seat lid, to find some personal quiet space. I wonder if, when the children are grown and gone, the house will seem too quiet. But this is what our house has often sounded like at night:

"Can't you read to us a little longer, Daddy?"

"No. It's time for each of you to wash your dinner dishes and get ready for bed."

"But it's *her* dish night!"

"Just wash them! I was washing *your* dishes until midnight last night."

"But I'm still hungry!"

"And your clothes don't belong in a heap at the bottom of the stairs—put them away."

"But tomorrow's cleaning day—can't I put them away then?"

"No. Put them away now. And if you don't do your homework you can't go to the church dance!"

"Dad! He called me a jerk!"

"When can we go to the movies?"

"Dad! She won't let me in the bathroom!"

"I need new shoes."

"I know you can brush your teeth yourself, but when you're done, I'm going to brush them again anyway!"

"There's no more bandaids, and my blister hurts."

"It's 10:30—no more talking! And I mean it!"

"You heard Dad: BE QUIET!"

"Turn your lamp off, stupid! Dad, make him turn off his lamp!"

"Dad! He called me stupid!"

"Shut up!"

"*You* shut up!"

"*Both of you shut up!*" . . .

. . . "Sing me a song, please, Daddy."

Somehow, each day ends with hugs and I-love-yous, but I am left feeling fatigued and empty. Visiting with my father on a Sunday afternoon, he smiled and observed with wry satisfaction, "Isn't life wonderful!"

Angie and I occasionally find the space to walk together. I invited her one evening to join me on a Rabbit Lane walk.

"Caleb," I ventured to the three-year-old, "Mommy and Daddy are going out for a little while. Do you mind?"

He responded matter-of-factly, "I don't mind. I don't have a mind. It disappeared."

As I leave the house and turn down Church Road, I pass Teancum's expansive pen and turn my back to him, rounding the corner onto Church Road. He begins to bark and howl as he perceives that I am not taking him with me on my Rabbit Lane adventure. Teancum, the enormous yellow Labrador, begins a forlorn howling lamentation, as if being left behind is his life's great disappointment. He is no less disappointed for his third-of-an-acre dog run. The whole town must hear him and grumble or chuckle at the sound.

"Not today, Tank!" I shout over my shoulder.

I am determined to not be dragged through this morning's walk. But I begin to feel sorry for him as he howls mournfully, even though he lacks nothing but loving attention, and I go back to clip on his leash to take him with me down Rabbit Lane. Lacey is no less desperate in her supplications, and I relent. No sooner do we embark than the two dogs begin to pull and tug at me in conflicting directions. I find myself exerting all my strength to keep my direction, even at times to stay on my feet, tripping over twisted leashes. Teancum pulls like an angry ox while Lacey stops determinedly to sniff at a marked power pole. All hope I have of a peaceful walk has quickly vanished, sacrificed to the dogs.

I have often taken Teancum walking with me on Rabbit Lane. His huge paws, fully the size of my hands, dig in and pull his bulk against the leash with such force that I, at over 200 pounds, can barely hold on. He gasps inside his collar, not appearing to apprehend that he is strangling himself. All of my effort during my walks with him is focused on not falling over. Tiring of the walk, he pulls harder as we near home. A walk with Teancum is simply not enjoyable.

The situation strikes me as a comical microcosm of life. How often we are pulled in opposing directions, delayed, dragged along, distracted, twisted up in life's leashes, only to finish the day utterly exhausted for our efforts. Most days! I have not learned to find peace amidst life's pullings and tuggings. But I have learned that peace can be purposefully pursued, and that we will not always find peace despite our best intentions and efforts. I have learned that we should probably not expect our life's comings and goings to be serene and restful. And I have learned that we sometimes need to leave the dogs at home.

A particular neighbor dog, a German Shepherd, displays a twisted pavlovian response to my daily appearance, like some dogs do with uniformed mail carriers. The brute barks and growls menacingly at me, like a hungry wolf, lifting its lips to bare yellow, saliva-dripping teeth and splotchy pink gums. It harasses me mercilessly from behind the cow panel fence. Thank the Lord for that fence. Attempting to soothe it, I speak to it calmly, although inside I am cursing its very existence. I know better than to throw rocks or make aggressive moves. As I approached its yard with dread one day, it looked at me with a kindly tilt of the head and trotted along beside me for the length of the fence with nary a bark. That dog never barked at me again. The dog's epiphany, however, did not change my opinion of dogs that delight in molesting walkers, joggers, and cyclists.

I came home from my walk one evening to see Caleb (18 months) pretending to be a puppy playing fetch, crawling around the kitchen floor with a stick in his mouth. As I came through the door, he looked up at me hopefully, then brought me the wet stick and laid it at my feet.

Parents and religious instructors taught me well not to swear or curse or use profane language, especially language that degrades women. I remember the first time I uttered a frustrated *"DAMN!"* at the age of 12, while struggling with some outside chore. I craned my neck toward the heavens, eyes squinting at the sun, expecting a bolt of hot lightning to flash down and extinguish my sorry life. Of course, no lightning came; neither was I consumed by an earthquake, or by fire, or by a whirlwind. In fact, I received no rebuke of any kind, earthly or divine. The Universe had allowed me to live another day.

Through successive experimentation, I found that a good swear word seemed to fit many situations like no other word could. It even felt good to swear at the stupidities and annoyances of life. I also learned, upon close observation of my emotional states, that angry cursing and swearing always brings immediate and subtle, but noticeable, negative feelings.

I believe that, while swearing can give the appearance of providing momentary release, it brings no long-term relief to the underlying emotions that give way to the swearing in the first place. Instead, cursing tends toward an addictive cycle of tension building and emotional explosions rather than healthy tension management and the difficult but possible process of learning to be stronger than our impulses.

Still, while I believe this principal to be true, a good "oh hell!" once in a while just seems to hit the spot.

The wood burning stove inset into our faux river-rock wall is the one upgrade we allowed ourselves in the new house. I grew up with fires in the open fireplace of my home on Schindler Court, and wanted the flickering light, comforting warmth, and crackle of wood fires in the home in which I raised my family. Winter fires, however, require Summer wood cutting and splitting. The more wood I cut in Summer, the longer we would have fires during cold Winter evenings.

At times splitting wood tries my patience, especially when, try as I might, the work-a-day stresses build up inside. While I have always left my work at the office, I have never learned to leave my work stress at the office. With some taps of the blunt end of the maul, I set the wedge into a particularly knotty piece of elm. Taking aim and swinging with all my strength, I brought the steel maul down to meet the steel wedge. But I did not hear the ring of metal on metal. Instead, I extended my reach too far and missed. The wood handle crashed down onto the iron wedge, and the steel head snapped off, struck my booted foot, and bounced away. My hands stung painfully at the jarring vibrations that shot up the broken handle.

"You stupid goddam piece of shit!" I shouted, enraged, unable to contain my internal tensions any longer.

I put the finishing touches on my fit by kicking over the log and throwing the broken handle across the garden into the neighbor's grassy field.

What I did not know was that my children, admiring their lumberjack father, had been watching from the porch. Turning toward the house, my eyes met theirs, and I saw looks of shock on their faces. Seeing their stupefied innocence, I slumped my shoulders and bowed my head in shame at my mistakes, at my lack of self-control, at my anger.

"I'm sorry kids," I offered repentantly. "I'm not a very good example."

After a stunned moment, the children rushed toward me and all embraced me at once. I knew then that they loved me anyway, and that they felt sorrow for my frustrations, for my penitent self-loathing, and for my bruised foot.

"Did you hurt your foot, Dad?" Brian (12) asked.

In pain, I stared silently toward the mountains, then began to chuckle with the ridiculousness of it all.

"Hurts like he. . .ck!" I said, laughing.

The children all began to laugh and hugged me again, this time with relief.

Picking up the decapitated maul head, I commented, "Looks to me like it's time for a break!"

We all laughed harder. Limping, I led them into the house to stir up some cooling lemonade.

The family is fortunate that Mother generally possesses more equanimity than Father. One day two children were screaming at each other while pulling at a gallon-size box of fish crackers. The box ripped open suddenly, and little golden fish flew everywhere. The two fighting children fell away from their positions, mashing the crackers into cheddar-cheesy crumbs. Suddenly frightened, they looked toward their mother and saw the brewing storm. But Mom found the strength within herself not to be angry or to break down in tears, but to laugh, to help the children change from anger and fear to laughter, and then to cheerfully enlist their help to clean up the mess.

Fifteen years later, the old, dying cottonwoods were coming down to make way for development. I asked if I could harvest the wood, inasmuch as the trees otherwise would be hauled to the dump. With a borrowed 20-inch chainsaw, freshly sharpened and oiled, I cut into the 24-inch diameter trunk, first with upward-angled cuts, which I met with slightly higher straight cuts from the opposite side of the trunk. These several cuts were calculated to make the tree fall *away* from our neighbor's house. That is what the saw owner's manual said would happen. But the tree was so big, and my cuts were so numerous and so imprecise, that when I barely managed to pull out the binding blade, the tree merely sat down on its trunk, under its own enormous weight. While I had cut the trunk clean through, the final shape of my many cuts resembled more of a bowl than a slanting wedge, and in its bowl the tree sat. Fortunately, the typical Erda winds were silent. Suddenly terrified that the slightest breeze might topple the tree in the wrong direction, the direction of our neighbor's half-a-million-dollar house, I ordered the children away, grabbed two iron wedges and a sledge hammer, and began banging the wedge blades into my chainsaw cuts with strikes of the sledge. After several desperate minutes attempting to insert the wedges into the cuts, I felt greatly relieved and rewarded to hear a faint creek of the tree as it began to lean in the correct direction. With several more swings of the hammer, the giant tree finally fell with a loud groan and then a huge shattering crash upon the ground. The tree from which a Bald Eagle had once stared down at me was now flat and dead, and would now warm my house for several winters. From its clay-encrusted roots, my sons harvested beautiful burled wood, which, when cleaned, stained, and varnished, made gorgeous living room lamps, similar to the lamp my father made from the five-foot twisted pine root he carried off a mountain in 1959 and that now sits in my living room.

Like an electron in chaotic orbit around its nucleus, a single fly had followed me the entire length of my walk on Rabbit Lane—both directions. It landed on the tips of my ears and nose and in the stubble of my thinning hair. No amount of swatting or frantic arm waving would convince it to leave me be.

"Dumb ass fly!" I finally hissed, responding to the rising temperature of my temper.

The fly did not leave. My cursing had no effect upon the fly. None. I chided myself in rebound to my curse: *I am cursing at a fly! The fly is not stupid. Nor is its rear end. If I had the persistence of that fly . . .*

Sparring Skunks

I heard the sun and waked up!
(Caleb-3)

The Stansbury mountain range is a succession of high peaks, some above 10,000 feet, each a lighter hue of gray proportionate to its distance. In the moments before sunrise, the clouds and sky form a sea of swirling scarlet, orange, red, and pink. The western face of the Oquirrh range once boasted thick pine forests. But over-harvesting, together with decades of settling particulate pollution from the now-defunct Anaconda smelter, denuded the mountain slopes of their forests. They now show mostly fault-fractured bedrock, studded with a few hardy junipers. With the smelter gone, the pine trees and aspens are slowly returning, starting from deep within the canyons and creeping back onto the slopes.

A mat of thick clouds hangs low and gray above Erda and Rabbit Lane, with soft, curving undulations, resembling piles of crumpled flannel sheets on an endless up-side-down bed. I imagined myself lying upon it comfortably, floating, swaying in the pre-dawn breeze.

Near midnight the night before, munching on cold cereal, I heard a strange sound from the living room: a spooky, vocalized hissing. My heart pounding with sudden adrenaline, I poked my head around a corner wall. The porch light dimly illuminated the room. Through a living room window, I detected movement on the porch, in the vicinity of the cat food bowl. Tip-toeing closer, I saw a furry black tail raised stiffly in the air, with white stripes. A skunk, raiding the cat food. The tail twitched, and the whining intensified as another bushy tail appeared. Since the window was closed, I felt safe to step closer. One skunk munched eagerly at the cat food, monopolizing the bowl. Another hungry skunk tried to push its nose into the bowl. The first skunk hissed and whined, and the second skunk hissed and whined and nipped, but backed down for a moment before trying again. Their bushy black tails, pointing straight up, were as large as their bodies. The second skunk made another attempt at the bowl, and the hissing and nipping began again. The sparring never became violent or vicious, but did serve to establish dominance over the bowl. Having apparently eaten its fill, the dominant skunk waddled off, tail erect, allowing the second skunk to move in.

I occasionally catch the whiff of skunk on Rabbit Lane. The smell is sickeningly pungent no matter how old or faded. The slightest whiff fills me with instant tension, and I am on my guard for any movement of black-and-white fur. Close to the site of a recent spray, the smell is more than an unpleasant aroma, but a tangible breathing in of revolting vapors.

Several weeks after finding the dead Red-tailed Hawk on Rabbit Lane, I observed a dead skunk lying on the dirt in the middle of the road. Sure this time that it was a skunk, I stopped and watched for signs of movement. Seeing none, I threw a rock at the carcass just to be sure. I crept closer, holding my nose against the unique and awful stench. Despite the stomach-turning smell, I noticed the animal's beautiful fur: jet black with shapely white stripes joining at the head.

For a moment I wondered if Rabbit Lane was a road of death, but quickly pushed that thought out of my brain. Though the occasional death crossed the lane, even those creatures were regal in their own way. Rabbit Lane is a road full of life. I have heard and seen its abundance: owls, snipes, muskrats, hawks, ducks, Canada geese, herons, sparrows, foxes, raccoons, insects, and even the domesticated cows, horses, sheep, llamas, and chickens of adjacent farms. Add to this the purple and yellow blossoms of the Bitter Nightshade, the pink crystalline flowers of the Milkweed, the dripping sweet aroma of the Russian Olive, the Evening Primrose's yellow four-petalled evening blooms, and the Virginia Creeper vine, brilliant scarlet in Fall.

Barbed-wire fences line the pastures and fields bordering Rabbit Lane. Four or five strands of often loose, rusting barbed wire span from post to post. The posts are the trunks of Juniper trees, often referred to as cedars.

Orange spray paint on the post tops warns: *no hunting.* Juniper is the preferred wood for fence posts because it is resistant to rot. The old-timers must have cut whole juniper forests for fence posts. Angie's father, Darwin, tells of the days in the 1950s when his father would drive him in the old pickup truck out to the western Utah deserts to cut Junipers. It was sweaty, scratchy work to fell the trees and cut off their evergreen limbs. He earned a dime for each juniper post: in his words, "good American money (when it had value)."

Severe winter winds from the south roust up the tumbleweeds and send them rolling and bouncing northward. Tumbleweed, that nostalgic icon of the romantic western film (*"rollin' rollin' rollin'"*), is what we call the skeleton of a short bush whose stiff branches grow in a spherical shape. Strong winds snap the dead bushes off at the stem and send them rolling as far as the open land will allow. Arrested by miles of east-west fences, the tumbleweeds stack deep and high against strands of barbed wire strung between old cedar posts that long ago shed their scraggly bark. Occasionally, a particularly spirited tumbleweed will bounce against the pile and vault itself over the tumbleweed wall to continue its journey. In Spring, Cloyd squirts the tumbleweeds against his Church Road fence with lighter fluid and burns them away with a hot, quick flame that blackens but does not burn the cedar posts.

Cattle often stare at me over or through the barbed wire fences with huge glossy black eyes and twitching ears, some stopped in mid-chew with grass protruding from between their thick lips, some looking at me over their backs, some boring into me head on. I take one step toward them and the calves trundle away in the distress of uncertainty. A cow turns to face me squarely, and I am glad for the barbed wire.

Every afternoon, Ron's slow approach on his grumbling tractor sets the cows to singing. With the bucket raised high, holding bales of hay, the cows, usually quiet, become a cacophonic chorus, trotting and mooing in bellowing harmonies toward the tractor. A few cows sing above the rest in a descant that blends surprisingly well for a chorus of cows with only a lumbering tractor for a director.

Outbuildings and sheds dot the homesteads and farms. The older ones are made of railroad ties set between upright posts. Some are sided with rough wood planking. Wood shakes cover the roofs. Newer sheds are clad and topped with corrugated aluminum or steel that often works loose and flaps loudly in the desert winds.

FENCES

Grain-field fences march
away in a disciplined line,
cedar post after cedar post,
rough-barked,
each tugging its barbs
taut as burning guns
at soldiers' cheeks, marching
straight and away at an acute angle
to the way I would go,
hemming me in with wicked wire
points, urging me down, at the risk
of gash and scar, the direct
and dusty disciplined road,
while a tiger swallowtail
lazily wafts its easy way across
the fence to flutter above
the ripe wheat tops,
and a western kingbird
darts here and there,
erratic, up and down,
above all artificial lines, chasing
invisible insects overhead.

Away with Murder

People who destroy are people who have not created.

Rabbit Lane is a peaceful place. The water trickling through Watercress in the deep ditch, the exotic purple and yellow blossoms of the Bitter Nightshade vines, the gently waving and rustling fields of ripe oats, the deep green of the ripe alfalfa. The solitude. After a few minutes on Rabbit Lane, all of this works together to settle my turbulent mind. Usually.

On occasion, though, troubling memories from a piquant past press themselves upon the serenity of the present. Images of a mother and her three children sometimes appear, without apparent cause, from many years earlier. I have tried to forget these images, but cannot. I also cannot forget how a guilty man got away with murder.

I was a new lawyer working for the Salt Lake County District Attorney's Office when I learned about the Kastanis murders. Kastanis had murdered (allegedly) his wife and three children. Morgan, the prosecutor, was determined to put him behind bars for the rest of his life. Morgan invited me to help him with the prosecution. He became my mentor and friend. I was thrilled to work on a case worthy of any 30-year career, and my career was only days old. My blood surged with the excitement of the opportunity.

I learned quickly that the word *spatter* is defined as "to spurt forth in scattered drops." In the field of crime scene investigation, blood spatter analysis is the art and science of reconstructing a brutal series of events by reading the patterns of blood spattered onto walls and doors, ceilings and carpets. Blood spatter paints a picture of violent trauma. From the number and size of spatters, an astute and experienced investigator can determine the severity and location of a wound. From the shape of the spattered droplets, the trained detective can determine whether a victim was stationary when stabbed, or running for her life. Multiple areas of spatter can actually be read, as if they formed words and phrases from a dying victim, silently telling the story of an occasion that had been anything but silent.

To cipher the blood spatter code in the Kastanis house, the County had brought in an expert from California, a retired veteran homicide detective who had acquired a wealth of knowledge on the subject of blood spatter. The expert's conclusions were to be portrayed graphically in a computer-generated video. If admitted into evidence, it would be the first time in Utah's history that a computer-generated video would be used to portray the prosecution's interpretation of the crime.

Morgan had instructed me, "I want you to work with the computer graphics team. I want you to work with the detectives. I want that video to be accurate. The right number of strikes with the hammer. Every stab with the knife. The right depth, the right angle. It's got to be right or it's not worth shit."

Morgan had the detectives give me boxes full of photographs. Like most movie-hungry Americans, I had seen my share of action movies. I had stayed away from the horror shows, but had seen the occasional *Rambo* or *Commando*, people flying about riddled with machine gun blasts. But nothing had prepared me for what I saw in those photographs. There were hundreds of them, separated into two groups. Group one: crime scene. Group two: medical examiner's lab.

The video's computer graphics were quite rudimentary. These were pre-*Toy Story* days of the early 1990s. Partly to keep from sickening and offending the jury, and partly because the computer graphics experts just were not that expert, the computer representations of the murdered mother, daughters, and son were green, boxy, stiff-moving forms that resembled humans but could have equally been any upright hominids on the homo sapiens ancestral family tree, or even humanoid aliens. The bodies had a basic human form, but were sexless and had no sensory organs (eyes, ears, nose, mouth). The green forms moved slowly and robotically through the halls and rooms of the house, with the larger form of the father following.

Sitting with the computer graphics team, I watched as the father, in slow motion, followed each of his four victims, stabbing them as he went, to their final destinations in a bathroom and two bedrooms, where he alternately bludgeoned their heads with a hammer and cut their throats with a hunting knife.

Having been introduced to the video, I now watched it again, and again, charting in detail the number, location, depth, and angle of each strike. Carefully cataloguing them, I now turned to the photographs and autopsy reports to verify that the video was accurate. The blood spatter expert had determined the location of each person when the various wounds were inflicted. But it was my job to check the details. The crime scene photographs of the bodies where they were found were shocking and gruesome, but they were not particularly helpful to my task, other than to make sure the video showed each body as it was found, e.g., curled around a toilet fixture, prone on a bed, crumpled on the carpet.

What I really needed to do the job was the autopsy photographs, correlated with the autopsy reports. One by one, I studied hundreds of photographs showing the washed, naked bodies of each of the four victims: a mother and her three children. I noted on my chart each knife and hammer wound, to make sure they corresponded with the wounds depicted on the video. The hammer wounds, of course, could be seen best from inside the skulls, for the hammer had crushed the skulls and pushed them inwards, bruising the brains. Thus I discovered the Y-cut, in which the medical examiner makes an incision from the base of the neck, with two widening incisions across the skull, enabling him to pull back the skull to examine it, and the brain, from the inside.

I tried to be businesslike as I dutifully performed my work. I tried to put my emotions aside. It was important to me that I do my job, and do it not just well, but perfectly. A man's life was on the line, for a conviction could bring the death penalty. I must not believe that the father had murdered his wife and children based on my feelings about the brutal manner in which they were killed. Doing that, I would fall prey to the very trap the courts seek to avoid by not allowing overly gruesome photos to be shown to the jury. So, I had become a sort of gatekeeper. All the gory photos had to pass through me, and to stop with me, to present a version of the evidence that would spare the jury the horror of what I was seeing. But I got the video right. The judge made legal history by admitting the video into evidence.

More than twenty years later, I can still see their clean, white faces, their chests and arms and stomachs, their legs and feet, and their brains.

In the end, the video did not matter. The jury acquitted Kastanis of the murders of his wife and three children. He won. Kastanis escaped earthly accountability. But I know the truth as no one else does: I got the video right.

Gardens

Knock, knock.
Who's there?
I got up.
I got up who?
(Hyrum-4 with Dad)

Despite the bright blue sky and the sun's brilliance dazzling from millions of ice crystals in the fresh skiff of snow, I felt crushed by life's burdens as I trudged alone along Rabbit Lane. The burdens of being a husband and provider and father to seven children. The burdens of being legal counsel to a busy, growing city. The burdens of maintaining a home, of participating in my church, and of being scoutmaster to a local boy scout troop. The burdens of being human. While the sky above me opened wide to space, these responsibilities bore down heavily upon my heart. They seemed to darken my very sky.

As I was wishing it to be otherwise, a subtle impression came to my mind. It suggested that I had the power to reposition these burdens in a way so as to relieve myself of their weight. Not knowing what I was doing, I reached out with my mind and gently pulled my burdens down from over me, as if clearing cobwebs. I pulled them down to where they surrounded me, loosely, even comfortably. Some even moved under me in a supporting cloud. They danced slowly around and beneath me, holding me weightless and unburdened.

While my responsibilities had not changed, somehow their power over me had quickly and unexpectedly transformed into a subservience to my mastery over them. Rather than being a source of stress and worry, they had become a means to my success in being the best man that I can be and making the best contribution to my community and my world that I can make. The existence of my life challenges had not changed. My burdens had not disappeared. Rather, my perspective of them had somehow changed, and so dramatically as to alter their appearance and modify their nature.

Walking toward home, I knew that I would still struggle to fulfill my duties, and still grow tired with the effort. But I could begin to see a way that I might find joy in the effort, instead of suffering as if with the doomed labor of bucket-bailing a sinking ship.

The world is an awfully big place, with expanses of forest and prairie and desert, vivified by pulsing flows from glacial peaks to vast saline seas, by the breath of the sun on the water, clouds in the sky, and tearful, rejuvenating rain. The world is an awfully full place, hosting seven billion humans who each need water to drink, food to eat, energy to sustain, love to warm, and who each desire a spot to call their own.

I have decided that the two hardest things in life are, first, to discover who you are, and, second, to actually be the person you discover. Very often, our notion of self-identity is formed by outside influences that do not necessarily have our interest in mind. Even the strongest of us will struggle our whole lives to know who we are, to be true to who we are, and to resist the seducing and demanding voices that whisper and clamor for us to be who they want us to be.

"I am discouraged because. . . ." How often have I begun a sentence that way? My friend asks me how I am. Another wonders how was my day. "I'm discouraged. . . ." I have said and thought this sentence so often.

There will always be a personal weakness to worry about, a problem to bemoan, a fault to fret about, something broken to fix, a debt to pay. If I strive to conquer myself but only examine what remains to be conquered, I will always feel discouraged. We need to find a way to put aside our whips of self-inflicting pain and remind ourselves of our personal victories, or our inherent human worth.

In the quiet of Rabbit Lane, I often ponder the purpose of life. Has it occurred to me that the purpose of life may be simply to live? Not just to breath and have a pulse, of course, but to live the best life we can every day, slogging through the sorrow and the suffering in exchange for hope and a greater measure of joy and contentment, seeking to attain our full potential, to find the best that is within us.

And a vital part of living is learning. What are we to learn if we are to live? Here is my idea. Learn to shun betrayal and embrace fidelity. Learn to defer shallow, selfish pleasures in exchange for paving a path toward a depth of happiness unknown to mere pleasure seekers. Learn to create rather than to be entertained. Learn to forgive and to not boil in bitter begrudging. Learn that learning is an endeavor that requires patient effort. Learn that we learn from all experience, the good and the bad, the joyful and the grievous, the sweet and the bitter. Learn that what we learn is what we choose to learn.

Without the regular addition of organic material (manure or compost), the garden turns to hard clay and grows only weeds whose roots are impossible to extract. Angie and I had an intense desire to grow a vegetable garden. This translated quite naturally into an intense need to bring in truckloads of manure. Mother, father, and six children loaded into the white pickup truck and drove to Richards Dairy farm for the family's first adventure in cow manure. I can honestly say that we were excited.

With each tractor bucket load, the pickup sank lower on its springs, until I wondered if we would make it home. But the truck maneuvered reasonably well on the state highway at 60 mph.

"Mom, the manure is blowing out of the truck!" One of the children shouted suddenly.

I looked in my rearview mirror and saw, to my horror, that dry manure dust was blowing out of the truck bed, it seemed by the ton, to settle on the cars behind us. I slowed the truck to 50 mph, although this only brought the following cars closer. I discovered that manure dust flies just as well at 50 mph as it does at 60 mph. I was careful not to look at the cars as they passed us. I'm sure a few drivers waved hello.

Finally, we turned onto Bates Canyon Road, then took Rabbit Lane, nice and slow, with no cars behind, and with no one caring if manure dust blew out.

Arriving at home, Mom announced happily, "Well, that was so easy, we'll have to get more, lots more."

"Children," I responded, straight-faced, "I want you to know that one of the reasons I married your mother was that I knew, someday, she would have me bring home truckloads of manure for the garden."

And I have. Except that on every other occasion I strapped a tarp over the manure pile to avoid spraying highway travelers with manure dust.

Bringing the manure home was only half the adventure, though. Next, I parked the truck at one end of the garden, gave each child a shovel or a rake, and instructed them to start digging. Some children would stand atop the manure pile pushing and digging the manure out. Inevitably, shovels would clash like swords, manure would be thrown on some poor child standing outside the truck, and harsh words would fly. Moving the truck slowly across the garden, we managed in an hour to empty the truck and spread the manure fairly evenly over the garden. Once I moved the truck too fast, and Caleb (3), sitting on the manure facing forward, somersaulted backwards right out of the truck bed onto the garden soil. Happily, again on this somersault, he was unhurt.

Dry manure is not so unpleasant to work with, despite the manure dust in the nose and teeth. Wet manure is a different proposition altogether. It is so much heavier, clumpier, stickier, and smellier. After two hours, an exhausted and ornery father chased all the children away to finish the job by himself, with manure adhering to his boots and the bed of the truck being coated with a black, slimy film that resisted washing.

Each Spring I till the garden with my red, five-horsepower, rear-tine tiller. It is a loud job, but a job that I enjoy. It takes two hours and three passes over the garden before the earth is well turned and soft. Laura (5) ventured into the garden one Spring and stepped toward me as I tilled. She reached out to me and I clasped her small hand in mine, steadying the bouncing tiller as best I could with one hand. After a minute I slipped her fingers into my back pocket and grasped the tiller with both hands. She walked with me for a few minutes, holding onto my pocket, digging her bare toes into the cool, soft soil with each step.

Holding baby Caleb in my left arm, I muscled the tiller with my right, guiding it in ever smaller circles. Caleb never seemed to tire of this, although I did. Each child has enjoyed working the tiller with me, either holding a corner of the handle and walking by my side, or walking in front of me holding the short cross bar, my legs awkwardly straddling theirs. John came to the point where he could work the tiller by himself. I instructed him about never putting his feet or hands near the turning tines. With a stout pull on the cord I started the motor, put my hand on his to engage the tines, positioned his hands on the bar handle, and let him go. After watching closely for a few minutes, I felt satisfied that he would be fine. He smiled proudly back at me as he followed the tiller around the garden.

Charley has come with his tractor several years to till in the new manure and the previous season's weeds and garden plants, vastly simplifying the tilling task. When I use my tiller, the garden soil remains rough and clumpy, with plant stems poking everywhere, no matter how many passes I make. When Charley tills with his tractor tiller, the garden soil transforms to soft powder a foot deep, much to the delight of running and dancing children. My tiller keeps the weeds down thereafter.

Working the soil together brings a mysteriously sweet satisfaction, somehow connecting us in ways that words and movies do not. As wonderful as it is to bite into the sweet corn freshly pulled from the stalk, sinking our fingers and toes into the soft, cool, living soil brings moments of unexplainable joy. Between the happy days of the Spring until and the Autumn harvest, seemingly endless hours of weeding can cause us to forget that joy. But the soil is always there, ready to receive our bare fingers and toes.

In late May, the tilling accomplished, we scratch out the garden rows, dozens of them, with a hoe point or shovel tip. Then we plant the seeds, seeds of many varieties—and then we wait. While planting may be my favorite part of gardening (even more so than the harvest for my hopeful expectations), waiting for germination and sprouting is my least favorite. It can be hard for me to believe, despite what I know factually, that the seeds lying in the ground will actually sprout and grow. Days pass, adding to weeks, without visible signs of plant life, except new weeds. My doubts tell me that the seeds will never grow. They will just die. All my efforts were for naught. The whole garden will remain barren dirt.

But one day new green plants shoot up from the soil, each with its own stylish blade or leaf. Despite this miracle of life, proven to my eyes, my doubts persist and whisper at me that these sprigs of green, so small and fragile, could never become corn and squash and heads of lettuce and cantaloupes. But the stalks and vines grow irrespective of my doubts; they blossom unaware of my fears. Each seed, with its own shape, size, color, and texture, has somehow become a mature plant bearing its unique fruit, each with its own shape, size, color, and texture.

Each year the process tries my faith in the processes of nature. I cannot quite bring myself to believe that nature works, despite the fact that every year nature, in fact, works. Perhaps it is because I do not understand well enough the natural processes at work— germination, transpiration, photosynthesis—or because I cannot see what is happening in the warm, moist darkness of the soil. I do know that I cannot force the process. I cannot make the seeds germinate faster, the plants grow quicker. I cannot make a carrot seed produce a tomato, or a squash vine grow an ear of corn. The best I can do is to help each plant be what it is, what the seed has determined it to be. The most I can do is to nurture: with water, fertilizer, cultivation, weeding, staking, pruning, squashing the squash bugs, keeping the hens away from the ripening fruit.

I have found it to be the same with my children. Despite mother's swelling abdomen, it was hard for me to really believe that it would produce a baby. Then each baby was born: tiny, helpless creatures. When they were infants, I could not imagine them as toddlers. When they were toddlers, I could not imagine them as adolescent youth. When they were teenagers, I could not imagine them as parents of their own infants (or myself as a grandparent). Yet none of my shallow doubting affected the natural processes of growth and maturation. All I could do was to add to Nature my own nurturing: smiling and laughing, playing games, talking, singing, reading books, assigning consequences, taking walks, sharing tidbits of wisdom from my own trial-and-error life, working to overcome my personality weaknesses, and praying. These humble efforts will hopefully make the blossoms brighter, the stalks taller, the vines stronger, and the fruits more robust and sweet. I need not allow the strain of my daily labors to create doubt about the end result. My children will become who they were ordained to be. The laws of nature demand it.

SUMMER CORN

Lay with me between the rows of summer corn.
Don't speak, yet.
Listen
 to the raspy hum of bees gathering pollen from pregnant, golden
  tassels,
 to the hoarse soft rubbing of coarse green leaves in the
  imperceptible breeze,
 to the plinking rain of locust droppings upon the soft soil.
Listen
 to the neighbor's angus wieners bemoaning their separation,
 to the pretty chukars heckling from the chicken coop,
 to the blood pulsing in your ears, coursing through your brain.
Don't speak, now.
Reach to touch my hand.
Listen to the world
from within the rows of summer corn.

Look Out the Window

Roger Baker

2. Crawl through the garden, what do I find?
   String beans, tomatoes, squash of all kinds.
   Dirt on my fingers, toes, and behind.
   Mamma gets angry. Dad doesn't mind.

3. Sit in the flowers, who comes to me?
   Lady Bug, Beetle, Bumblebee.
   Butterfly flutters silently.
   All show their colors beautifully.

4. Down goes the sun all orange and red.
   Dad puts the tools away in the shed.
   "Where are you hiding, sleepy head?"
   "Here I am already in bed!"

Good-Bye, Harv

To change the world, we must first change ourselves.

Harvey had to leave. He lost everything he owned. He moved out to the West Desert to live with a mountain man friend who lived in a teepee. He said he would do fine, but worried about staying warm enough and getting enough to eat in the freezing winters. I worried for him, too. I did what I could to help Harvey, examining legal documents, but it was too late.

The children were so sad to have to say good-bye to Harvey and his animals, especially Lucy and Charlie. All his animals are gone except for a couple of peacocks. They call out at night with a lonely, despairing cry that fills me with sadness. Harvey gave me two jungle fowl, a rooster and a hen. They look like small chickens, but Harvey says they are very smart birds from the jungles of Mexico. The rooster is beautiful, with florescent blue, red, and brown feathers. The hen is dainty and pretty. The two of them stay close to each other, and the rooster protects the little hen from the other chickens, never leaving her side. We hoped they would not die or fly away.

The petite jungle fowl turned out to be the mildest of hens. But the hatching of her chicks turned her into the fiercest of protecting mothers. As I approached to apprehend a stray chick, she attacked me through the wire wall, throwing herself at me claws first, like a hawk about to clasp its helpless prey with black talons. Frustrated by the wire, she strutted like an angry rooster, her wings lowered to the ground in an indignant expression and signaling her readiness to fight. I eased the chick through a crack in the door, then backed away to spare the hen needless stress while she ran to shoo her chick to safety.

When Harvey moved, part of the magic of the country left with him, and part of me felt dark and sad. Erin (8) was particularly disappointed. She adored Harvey, and thought of him as a beautiful man, despite his tangled appearance.

"This isn't right," she declared. "I am going to change the world so that bad things like this don't happen to good people."

She moved quickly, braiding for Harvey a bouquet of dandelion flowers. He knelt down and smiled with his small blue eyes into hers, tears forming in the corners.

"Thank you," he whispered, and then walked out the door.

I started showing Erin magazine articles about people who worked hard to make the world a better place. I read to her about one woman who lived for two years in the top of an ancient 300-foot tall Redwood tree to save it from being cut down by loggers.

"Two years!" she exclaimed. "I wonder how she went to the bathroom?"

The logging company announced that it would save that tree and lots of others.

"She did it!" Erin exclaimed again.

I told her about other people who worked to save coral reefs, silver back gorillas, fresh water fish, the ozone layer, and endangered species. I read to her about scientists who marched through tropical forests collecting seeds from trees so that if the trees became extinct the seeds could be planted and bring the species back into existence.

I told her about Rachel Carson's *Silent Spring*, chronicling the excesses of the 1950 chemical industry, about DDT and soft bird egg shells and defoliating entire fields and poisoning lakes and fish to kill mosquitoes.

Angie told Erin one night, "The best way to save the world is to be kind. If you're kind to one person, you will brighten their day, and then that person will want to be kind to someone else, and it goes on like that. You cannot change the world all at once, but you can change it one small step at a time."

She encouraged Erin that if she saw someone that needed help, and she helped, she will have changed the world a little bit. If she resisted the temptation to scream at Laura, and showed love instead, she will have made the world a better place.

"As you get older," Mom went on, "you will learn how to make bigger differences for more people. Try not to worry about where to go or what to do to change the world. The opportunities will come to you. The world will come to you. And you will be there, ready. Just keep your heart in the right place."

The next morning, while her mother applied her makeup in the master bathroom, Erin stole into our room and made the bed. She pulled the covers up and tugged the corners tight. She fluffed the pillows and arranged the stuffed panda I had bought for Angie on a business trip.

"Who made my bed so nice?" Mom called out a few minutes later.

Erin smiled and knew that she had made a difference.

Erin and Laura decided they wanted to help the poor. They set up a street-corner stand to earn money for that purpose. Their wares included lemonade from real lemons, summer squash from the garden, homemade butter, and fresh eggs of several colors and varieties: white (Leghorn), tan (Orpington), brown (Rhode Island Red), and olive-green (Araucana). They sat for hours trying to sell their goods. Mostly they watched cowboys in pick-up trucks speed by, and mostly I watched to see if any of the trucks slowed down or stopped. A few kindly neighbors stopped and purchased produce with coins and smiles. The day ended with disappointing sales and disappointing proceeds for the poor. But the girls gave everything they earned to charity. And they learned a few good lessons, like how to keep a tidy shop, how to display merchandise so prospective customers will want to stop and buy, how to be patient with the ignorance of others about the value of your products and the worth of your cause, and how hard it can be to make a dollar.

I believe that beautiful music changes people and changes the world. When John was nearly two years old, he awoke several times at night, crying for his mommy. I tried to help him go back to sleep, but he became infuriated and screamed louder because he wanted his mommy to nurse him back to sleep, and he knew that I could not do it. One night John finally gave in, lying on my chest while I sang little songs to him.

"Do you like my songs?" I asked him. "I'll make one up for you if you want."

John nodded sleepily. "About bee-bee zee-ba," he surprised me with his particularity.

"OK," I said. "Baby zebra. Hmm."

Within a few minutes I had composed a little song about a baby zebra, and John was sound asleep. John still wanted his mamma when he woke up in the night, but he quickly succumbed to my question, "Do you want me to sing Baby Zebra?" to which he sighed a long "Yeaahhh."

"Okay," I said.

Here are the lyrics:

Baby zebra: running on the plain.
Baby zebra: dancing in the rain.
Baby zebra: happy all the day.
Baby zebra, come and play.

I was amused one night to hear John demand, "Uh-uh bee-bee zee-ba; bee-bee hor-hie."

"Baby horsey?" I asked.

"Yeah," confirmed John.

So I substituted *horsey* for *zebra*. John quickly found that most any animal could be substituted for his zebra. For example:

Baby birdie, flying in the sky.
Baby birdie, flying way up high.

John, grown to four years old, often broke out in spontaneous song. He loved to sing about Jesus, with lyrics like, *Oh I love Jesus. Oh I love God. Oh I love you, Jesus and God.* His songs about Jesus made baby Caleb happy, and he in turn would sing, *Song, Jesus God.* In John's prayers, he would say, "Please bless Jesus and God."

A year later, I laid myself down by Caleb (2) to help him fall asleep. He looked out the window at the moon and asked me if I would "make" a song just for him, about the moon. Now, I am not a trained composer, but I do love music. These moments with my young children were so magical that simple tunes and lyrics seemed to come easily. Within minutes of vocal tinkering, I was singing to him this song, which became his song, and which he still loves to hear even as a 6-foot 4-inch tall teenager:

Moonlight shines bright.
Stars add their light.
The heavens, they watch
Moonlight shining bright.

Now sleep, my child,
In moonlight mild.
May God delight
In thy pure light.

Moonlight, shine bright.
Stars, add your light.
The gods, they watch.
Moonlight, shine bright.

Baby Zebra

Roger Baker

Ba - by ze - bra run-ning on the plane. Ba - by ze - bra

danc-ing in the rain. Ba - by ze - bra hap-py all the day. Ba - by ze - bra

come and play.

(Repeat as many times as the child wants, using other animals.)

Moonlight

Roger Baker

2. Now sleep my child in moonlight mild.
   May God delight in thy pure light.

3. Moonlight shine bright. Stars add your light.
   The gods, they watch. Moonlight shine bright.

Hurry Up and Play

I'm rich!
(Caleb-3, upon finding two pennies.)

Though running late for work one morning, I felt a determination to take my walk on Rabbit Lane. Quickening my pace on the crunching gravel, I found myself thinking: *If I hurry, maybe I can finish my 30-minute walk in 20 minutes.* The absurdity of this thought struck me instantly. I chuckled to myself, but could see that my thinking deserved further study. I might as well have said, *If I hurry, maybe I can short-change myself.* Thirty minutes of exercise can only be had in 30 minutes. Thirty minutes of meditation cannot be experienced in anything less than 30 minutes. Thirty minutes of quality time with my children cannot be condensed into less than 30 minutes. I lack the power to compress or expand time. I cannot run it backwards, chop it up and rearrange it, hurry it along, alter its linear nature, or stretch or squeeze it. I can, instead, choose to use my time well, to make all 30 minutes of exercise exercise, play play, meditation meditation, work work.

Several weeks later I took my children to my favorite park, the county's Legion Park in Settlement Canyon. The park sits on a narrow, flat, grassy area between two ridges covered with Mountain Maple and Gambel Oak. The children waded in the creek that trickled over rounded cobbles at the park's edge, searching for Rock Rollers. We enjoyed a picnic lunch under a huge Willow, listening to the Red-shafted Northern Flicker chicks clamor as their parents swooped up to the nest hole high in the tree with food. The children then moved to the playground, in the shade of more giant willows. A young mother joined us at the playground with her toddler. After a short while, the mother called testily to the little girl, "Hurry up and finish playing!" My initial reaction to the mother's demand was silent but harsh judgment. How absurd to tell the child to hurry her play. Hurried play isn't play at all. It isn't spontaneous. It isn't fun. But my heart softened as I remembered my own recent ridiculous inclination to hurry what cannot be hurried. I, too, have frequently thought that maybe I could play more if I crammed it in, instead ending up with no play at all. I, too, have often worked to accomplish more by rushing impatiently through, leaving all enjoyment behind. My mist of thoughts cleared into a sincere hope that someday this mother could learn, just as I was struggling to learn, that you cannot hurry play.

Next to the park is an area with concrete pads for recreational vehicles. Every pad was full, forming a neat line of RVs parked very close together. These people had escaped their suburban subdivision homes to "camp" for the weekend in yet another subdivision.

Each day is a lifetime to be lived. Each waking is a birth with infinite opportunities to go here or go there, to do this or do that, to think sundry thoughts, to feel rainbow feelings, to peruse the scenery of choices and destinations, to study the horizon of consequences. Each night brings a new sunset, a new reflection upon the day and how we lived it. It is sometimes brilliant, sometimes sublime; sometimes dull and hazy, sometimes unspeakably beautiful; sometimes unspeakably sad, sometimes holding a glimmer of hope. Each sleeping is a passage to newness. Each waking begins a voyage. Do we know our desired destination? Wherever it is, at the sun's setting we will have arrived. But is it where we wanted to be? Is it a place where we feel happiness and hope for tomorrow's waking? We will always arrive . . . somewhere.

In my youth I hunted beauty. I hunted butterflies and moths with a net made from a broom handle, a pillowcase, and a steel clothes hangar clamped tightly to the broom handle. I hunted and caught my prey, stilled it in an alcohol killing jar (I did not know how to get ether), and pinned it to a cork board. In high school shop class I built a display case, a full three by five feet, and filled it with 183 different species, each checked off in my Golden Guide book. Thirty years later, I still remember their names: Red-spotted Purple; Pipevine Swallowtail; Tomato Hornworm; Question Mark; Cecropia; Polyphemus; Wood Nymph. The case hung in my bedroom, on the wall, where I admired the beauty of the butterflies and moths each day. It was important to me to capture this beauty, to hold it, to make it my possession, my trophy. Returning from college, I found that tiny worms had worked their way into the display case and had ruined my collection. Only dusty, disintegrating remnants remained. The beauty was entirely gone.

In my middle age, I find that I am loath to capture beauty. I learned long ago that beauty captured quickly fades. Rather, I am content to let beauty fly beneath the blue sky, to land whimsically on this bloom or that, and to be carried away effortlessly on a zephyr. I bring beauty into my home as often as it comes to me: an injured bird; a colorful leaf or berry; a start of wild roses; a bald eagle seen from the porch through binoculars. But I no longer attempt to make it my prisoner. It lives on, alive and vibrant.

Many of life's great intangibles—like love, joy, and beauty—cannot be captured or held on to. We often try to capture them, however, because we do not want to be without them. But the harder we try to grasp hold of these intangibles, to keep them close, to control them, the quicker they escape and are lost to us. Certainly feelings of love and joy follow our specific efforts to create them. Just as surely, our specific efforts to control them chase them away. Discover the principles of thought and behavior that bring happiness, and let it come. Resist the urge to capture. Let it be.

Milbert's Tortoise Shell

Laura (10) and I found a yellow-and-black striped Monarch larva on a Milkweed leaf while walking on Rabbit Lane. With an excited smile, she brought the caterpillar carefully home. We made a safe box with air holes, a door for placing fresh leaves every day, and a clear viewing screen. The larva swelled as it ate. One morning it appeared as a powdery turquoise chrysalis with shining spots of gold, hanging from the box top on a button of sticky silk. After several weeks the pupa darkened to almost black. Then its thin, dry membrane cracked, and out crawled a Monarch body with shriveled, wet orange-and-black wings. The butterfly hung from the shell while trembling, urging blood into the veins of the expanding, drying wings. Laura and I watched this miracle of metamorphosis in awe, appreciating but not understanding, filled with wonder. When the butterfly stopped trembling and its wings were fully extended, Laura coaxed the gentle creature to step onto the tip of her finger, then released it with a puff of breath into the wide world to be drawn to the Milkweed growing along Rabbit Lane.

Five years later, Laura and I went for a walk on Rabbit Lane. She talked with me about the biography of Helen Keller she had just finished reading. Helen "listened" to people either by placing her hand lightly on their lips as they talked, or by having people sign the letters into the palm of her hand. Laura brought up the question of beauty.

"How do you comprehend or appreciate beauty without light, color, or sound, when you can't see or hear?" she asked.

Yet, somehow, Helen found beauty, in her own way. Our notion of beauty may in fact be superficial. We see and hear beauty, but do we really experience it, appreciate it, comprehend it? Does the beauty become part of us, or remain distant, separate? Laura's thesis for a short essay she wrote was that the essence of beauty is simplicity, not complexity. The most beautiful things, perhaps, are the most simple in color and design: a daisy; the sun; snow on the mountains; a lullaby.

LIFE ETHIC

"I caught it! I caught it!" cried the boy
over the weed-whacker whir
after waving his pole-clamped pillowcase
across the sky.
Two wide eyes and a victory smile
raced to the porch where
       two trembling hands
       coaxed the delicate creature
       through the screened bug-box door.
A bundle of awe,
the boy sat still and stared
at this astonishing bringing-together
of color and form,
at this life.
Father watched from the garden rows,
remembering his own youth's hunt
for small, helpless prey,
whose fate was to rot
with a pin through the thorax,
and a tag with a name and a date.
But the magical fluttering rainbows had faded
fast behind their showcase.
"Nice catch, son," father admired
with a pat and a ruffle.
"What are you going to do with him?"
"Well, I think I'll watch him for a while, and
then I'll let him go."
Good boy, father sighed, as
a boy released his heart's hold and
a captive rainbow again
graced the sky.

Sun Has Gone

Roger Baker

Sun has gone and moon has come. Time for bed my lit - tle one.

An - gels watch from heav'n a - bove. Go to sleep my ba - by.

Snow Angel

Sweetness: that which induces a slow rolling of the tongue, a gentle closing of the eyes, and an escape from the lips of a sensuous, sighing, "ahh."

Two young girls rode their bicycles down Church Road coming from the direction of Rabbit Lane. Working in the yard, I looked up just as one bicycle, ridden by the younger girl, slid on a gravelly patch, and she fell face forward onto the asphalt. I ran toward the crying girl, about six years old, with my concerned children following close behind. Blood oozed from abrasions on the girl's knee and elbow and cheek, and a tooth was broken.

I spoke to her gently, scooped her up, and carried her to the house. She continued to sob as I set her down in the bathroom to clean her wounds.

"We weren't supposed to be this far from home, but she insisted, and I couldn't let her go alone," her older sister offered an unsolicited rationalization.

The little girl began to cry louder. I tried to soothe her as I dabbed at the painful scrapes with a clean wet cloth.

"My daddy's . . . gonna . . . kill me," her choked words escaped through sobs. "I wasn't supposed . . . to be riding here."

Renewed sobs. I smoothed anti-bacterial cream and applied bandages.

"It's okay. Don't worry," I tried to reassure her. "I'll talk to your dad."

Her crying slowed.

With the girl calmed and her injuries mended to the best of my meager ability, I carried her to my truck and set her in the passenger seat. The bicycles we put in the truck bed. Her sister and Brian (11) hopped into the back seat. I drove the girls to their home, a drab little cinderblock box rented from a Salt Lake lawyer-turned-landlord. Holding the little girl's hand, we walked slowly to the front door. I knocked, and the father opened the door. His face filled with anger immediately upon seeing his daughter, bandaged, by my side.

"She took a nasty fall," I offered, "not far from here. I bandaged her up as best I could."

The girl's crying started up again as her father grabbed her arm and pulled her into the house. Her sister quickly followed, quietly and with eyes focused on the floor.

"She's really worried," I continued in a firmer tone. "She's worried about you being angry with her. I hope you won't be too harsh with her. She was not doing anything wrong. She just fell. She's hurt and she's frightened."

I did not know if what I had said would make the situation worse for the girl, or better. But I knew I had to say something, and said what I thought best, without challenging or accusing him. He glared at me for a long moment, then nodded slightly and shut the door. I hoped I had seen in his eyes a hint of softening as he closed the door of the dismal little house and closed me out of the little girl's life. I hoped he would not be mean or angry. I hoped he would not punish the child for riding her bicycle, or for falling. She deserved better. I hoped.

Seeing that father's anger reminded me accusingly of the many times I have become angry with my own children. How easily I can become angry when they call endlessly for my attention, when they leave my tools on the workbench or spill the nails, when they break the eggs in the chicken coop, when they are slow to go to bed, when they dent the walls, lose the ping-pong balls, pee on the floor next to the toilet bowl, break a dish, or spill their milk. I hope I do not punish my children for being children. They deserve better. I hope I can learn to be more kind and patient, more gentle and loving, more appreciative of the beauty a child brings to the world. I hope.

Laura (5) came limping into the kitchen, complaining that her foot hurt and that she could not walk. I asked her what had happened, and where it hurt. Just then her mother called to her from upstairs. I watched with surprise as she bolted from the kitchen with an enthusiastic "Yes, Mamma?" I heard her bounding up the stairs, and followed curiously. At the entrance to my bedroom at the top of the stairs, Laura suddenly resumed her limp and complained to her mamma, "I hurt my foot. I can't walk. Can you hold me and carry me?"

Years later, Caleb (4) came to me in obvious distress.

"I hurt myself," he whimpered, tears gushing freely.

"Where does it hurt," I sighed, and he pointed to his arm. "Come here and let me see," I offered.

He came to me, and I gently felt and moved his arm. He did not complain of any pain.

"Is it feeling better now?" I asked.

He stopped crying and nodded, venturing a timid smile.

"Yes Daddy. Thanks."

We hugged, and he ran back out to play, his pain forgotten and a smile on his face.

Very slowly it has dawned upon me that children complaining of small hurts may not be hurt at all, not on the outside, at least. But something inside hurts, or is lonely or scared, and wants to be comforted. Very slowly I am learning to not react to the injury, to not judge the injured or the injurer, but just to accept the child's expression of pain. This alone is often sufficient comfort, but how much better when followed with a smile and a hug.

Adults suffer the same hurts. Many of these injuries we have carried, unassuaged, since childhood. Other injuries are new, and remain fresh. We ask for comfort with tears. We ask for reassurance with expressions of disappointment. We lash out in anger, because we hurt, but what we really want is love. We reach out to touch, hoping that we will be touched in return. We ache inside and want healing. I think that most of us do not know where to find comfort, do not know how to find healing. We carry an increasingly heavy burden of hurts inside of us. How fortunate the man or woman, how blessed the child, that has people in their life that know how to give comfort and offer love. Now turn this around. How fortunate and blessed the man or woman that offers comfort and love and healing. Advice is frequently hollow. A listening ear is often best. A smile and a hug are often enough.

A simple smile is unlikely to earn one's fortune or to garnish power. But the virtues of kindness and tenderness, quietly expressed in a smile, will yield hope in the heart, create energy in the mind, and spark passion in the soul, transforming first individuals and families, then communities, institutions, and nations. A sincere smile can turn a hundred frowns and lift the human spirit.

At church one Sunday morning, John (4) balked at going to his primary class. When he got to the door, he turned toward me, puckered up, and burst into tears. His resistance and fears annoyed me, and my reaction showed my irritation.

"I just want to be with my family!" he explained plaintively.

His sweet expression of love instantly softened my heart. I knelt next to him and hugged him, talking softly with him. We decided together that it would be alright for him to go to Laura's (8) class. She held his little hand in hers as they walked into her class together, his heart comforted.

I sat against the wall in the church nursery, where Erin (18 months) was attending for the first time. She was frightened and anxious, and cried at the thought of me leaving. So I stayed. She held on to me for a long time, then ventured off to play timidly with the other toddlers.

I leave the house one morning to find the world covered in fresh powdery snow, six inches deep, brought in during the night by a north wind blowing over the Great Salt Lake; "lake effect," people call it. Only a few cars have braved the unploughed roads. My boots cast up puffs of powder with each step. Though the snow is light and airy, each step requires an additional effort, and my pace begins to lag. Despite my growing fatigue, I stay in the untrodden snow, refusing to follow the ruts established by other travelers. Cows and horses huddle in the poor lee of leafless trees, flanked with white snow and facing away from the cold wind.

Dropping my adult resistance, I yield to a growing urge to plop myself down in the powder to make a snow angel, waving my arms and legs to form the angel's wings and robe. Lying in the middle of the road, I feel my muscles begin to relax, and the tension from my trudging begin to fade. I know no cars will come from either direction for at least the minute or two that I recline in the snow. As I gaze up into the thin gray snow clouds, a partly-obscured passenger jet flies high over me, heading south. Closer to earth, a Downey Woodpecker flaps northward over me and swoops up into a bare Siberian Elm tree growing in the ditch bank. I hope he can find a few life-giving grubs hibernating under layers of sloughing bark.

Turning toward home, I hear what sounds like the anxious ticking of a too-fast clock. In the frozen alfalfa field, the 42-foot-long wheel-line pipes vibrate quickly up and down between six-foot-tall wheels. The air is moving at just the right speed and angle to create resonance, playing the pipes like giant violin strings—not with singing, but with the clicking and creaking of frozen aluminum joints as the pipes bounce in waves. I remember the remarkable film footage of the Tacoma Narrows suspension bridge swinging and bouncing in resonance with the wind that played it until it crumbled and fell into the river flowing far beneath.

Closer to home, I cross the road to walk in the footprints I made on my outward journey. I wonder at the merits of where and how I have walked in my life. Have I walked well? Has my direction been true? It can be hard to know the answers to these questions. I think that we have to trust that if we walk the truest path we know, it will suffice.

My walk ends as I step onto the porch and into the laundry room to fill a bucket with hot water. A half-gallon each for the pig and the chickens, to melt their frozen drinking water. Carrying the bucket toward the chicken coop, a Red-shafted Northern Flicker calls at me from the volunteer Siberian Elm tree, then dives away, showing his rich-orange primaries. I step through the chicken coop door into a swirling vortex of 200 House Finches flying madly and noisily above me in the 8x12 coop. Having taken shelter inside the coop from the cold, where they also pilfer $17-a-bag lay mash, the sparrows form a panicking swarm searching for the way out, but not finding it in their panic. The chicken wire that I have stapled against the eave cracks, to keep out unwanted critters, is just the right size to allow the sparrows to leisurely squeeze their way in. But in their hysteria, they cannot think to squeeze back out. As I stand astonished in the open doorway, a few of the braver birds whiz through the inches between the frame and my head, brushing my hair with their wings. I pour the hot, steaming water onto the block of ice in the rubber basin, in the center of the vortex. One by one, the sparrows begin to push through the cracks and holes through which they entered. I pull away a section of chicken wire to ease their escape, strangely pleased that my coop houses a sizable sparrow flock in addition to my small brood of hens. Throughout, the hens sit calmly on their winter roosts, either oblivious or uncaring. Yesterday's eggs lay frozen solid and cracked in the straw-filled brooding boxes. I put the eggs in the scraps bucket for the pig.

MY CHILD

Small child
clinging to me.
Soft cheek against my roughness,
delicate arms draped over my drooping shoulders.
Sooth your fears.
Let your tears fall and
wet my sleeve.
Let your love flow and
seep into my craggy heart.

Soon healed, your troubles forgotten,
release and turn away to play,
a smile on your small-child face,
a greater love in me.

Shooting Stars

Be kind. Always.

Turning from north to south at the half-way point on my Rabbit Lane walk, I look southeast toward the mountain peaks still sleeping under the early-morning sky. A star rises from behind a peak and continues its slow journey toward zenith.

To the east of where I walk, strings of lights move slowly in the distance, white lights crawling forward, red lights inching away, two parallel lines of progress making their way to and from the offices and factories and stores of wares. They send forth a collective engine-and-tire hum to hover over the fields with the fog. A Union Pacific train's whistle flows out gently over the valley from its tracks on Lake Bonneville's fossil bank. In the west, the lighthouse, itself out of sight, emits soft sweeping beams: white-green-white-green. The beams penetrate Winter's ice-crystal air to trace slow arcs across the gray belly of the sky, a ceiling above me, above Rabbit Lane. The universe of stars—the heavens—are out there, somewhere farther above, hanging mostly hidden by clouds. My fingers, toes, ears, and nose ache from the crystalline cold.

It can be a challenge to find joy and beauty in the cold and bleakness, even death, of Winter. I am thoroughly wrapped. Only my eyes, nose, and cheekbones expose themselves to the fundamental icy reminder that the sun brings warmth and life—only the sun. The frigid air nips at my cheeks and stings as I draw it in through my nose, to be warmed and utilized, then offered back to our common atmosphere, a puff of foggy warmth. Globules of frost pock my scarf, the cold jealously pulling the moisture from my breath as it passes through the yarn. I wonder that the surfaces of my eyeballs do not freeze over, and I blink more rapidly at the thought.

The coldest winter days help me to recognize the miracle of the sun's rising. The sun's sphere suddenly peaks over the mountain tops, like the crown of a brilliant child playing a game of "peak-a-boo" with planet earth. My hands, painfully cold in the frigid air, immediately feel relieving warmth from the first rays beaming down from over the mountain peaks. Over the next few minutes, the sun reveals its full, unrestrained glory, a glory we cannot fully witness for the degree of heat and brightness, and that we can only weakly describe with words like *amazing*, *beautiful*, and *bright*.

Rabbit Lane is covered with several inches of snow, crusted over with ice from yesterday's melting, now frozen. Truck tires moving slowly down the road have compressed the white snow-ice into white hard-pack as hard as concrete. Places in the ruts show themselves brown, where the mud from a sub-surface pot hole has oozed up to penetrate the ruts, and then has itself frozen, dark and solid. Walking is difficult, as every surface is slippery. I half walk half slide my boots across the icy surfaces. I step on a spot of dark mud, knowing it will be frozen hard. Before I can think the word *slippery* I find myself lying on my back gazing into heaven and thinking many thoughts in rapid succession, much more quickly than can be read:

> *What just happened?*
>
> *The stars are so beautiful.*

Is anything broken?

There's the Big Dipper.

What if I can't get up or crawl?

Look at the Milky Way.

My butt hurts.

Will I freeze to death before someone realizes I should be home by now?

Is that an owl?

Will someone find me lying neatly in a tractor tire rut, stiff as a post?

The stars are so beautiful!

Maybe I should try to move, just a little?

My fingers and toes are working!

One Autumn I read in the newspaper of a coming night during which we might see many shooting stars. The children asked eagerly if they could stay up late to watch for them.

"It's not supposed to start until 3 a.m.," I explained.

All the better, they thought—any excuse to stay up late. After dinner we laid out blankets and sleeping bags on the back lawn with a clear view to the western sky. We crawled in and huddled together under the shadow of the house cast by the crescent moon rising in the east. Panther and Bagheera (Baggy) rubbed against us, purring. Wispy clouds drifted occasionally across the otherwise clear sky, empty but for thousands of points of light.

"What are shooting stars?" one child asked.

"As amazing as they are," I explained, "shooting stars are not stars at all. They are tiny bits of dust and rock called meteorites that fall into the earth's atmosphere. They travel so fast and the air creates so much friction and heat that they burn up with a bright flair. Very few are big enough to make it all the way through and crash into the earth."

"Oh," they said simply, with new understanding.

Lying under the stars, we identified the few constellations we knew, like the Big Dipper (part of Ursa Major). I showed them how to find the faint but immovable North Star by following the line made by the Dipper's last two stars. Then I pointed out the soft band of lighter colored sky stretching from horizon to horizon.

"That," I announced, "is the Milky Way."

They gazed upward in awe as I explained that when we look at the Milky Way, we are looking in upon our vast galaxy from the outer reaches of the wispy galactic arm where we live. Rather than looking down from space, we are looking in at the plane of the galaxy, through its edge.

"How does a star get born, Dad?" one child asked. "Does it have a Mommy?"

"Well, sort of," I ventured, "but not the sort of Mommy that holds you and loves you and reads to you at night."

The universe is full of stuff we call matter, I explained. Slowly, over billions of years, that matter comes together and begins to squeeze down upon itself in a tight ball. When the ball gets big enough and tight enough and hot enough, it ignites into a newborn star.

"So stars are alive, like us?" another child asked.

"Yes, they are alive. But unlike us, stars live for billions of years, giving us light and warmth and beauty, even from millions of miles away."

We talked about Einstein and relativity and the speed of light, about the size of the universe, about black holes and singularities, about neutron stars and pulsars and quasars, about quarks and muons and bosons, and about how for all the stars we could see, our galaxy contains hundreds of billions of stars, and as large and as vast as our galaxy is, the universe contains hundreds of billions of galaxies.

Suddenly, just after midnight, dozens of shooting stars began to flare up, tiny bright fireballs streaking green and red and yellow across the black sky, leaving glowing trails that quickly faded. The science lecture was over, but the real lesson had begun. The only words the children said now were "Oh" and "Ah." Shivering but deeply satisfied, we staggered to our beds long before 3:00 a.m.

Of Ducks and Geese

Away I must fly.

From over a hundred yards away, I hear the enormous sound of what surely is a hundred geese cackling dissonantly. I cannot see them in the pre-dawn darkness. But in the growing light of my return walk, I make out the small gaggle of only a dozen very loud domesticated white geese as they mill under the venerable Cottonwood in Craig's pasture, making its only-as-a-goose-can-do honking.

An acquaintance of ours called to say that he was moving, and would we take his three ducks.

"Sure," I said enthusiastically, "they'll fit in nicely with our ducks."

He brought his ducks over the next day: three big white ducks with creamy yellow bills. We were happy to add these beautiful birds to our aviary. But the moment our friend drove away, the big whites began to chase and attack our smaller blues and greens, tearing at them viciously. Seeing one white grab onto the neck of a terrified Swedish blue, I hurriedly picked up a stick and ran to the rescue. Swinging to strike the white duck's behind, my swing reached farther than I had intended, and the stick struck the white duck on the neck. Its head flopped over on its broken neck, and the duck began to flop erratically around. While I felt sad at having killed the white duck, the indignant part of me felt a sense of justice at having rescued the blue from a bully.

September's first morning frost foretells the coming of Winter. Birds of many species begin to flock southward. At the strange sound of trilled honks, I look up from walking on Rabbit Lane to see three Great Blue Herons fly not 20 feet overhead with broad, powerful wing strokes, their dagger beaks piercing the air. Minutes later a flock of 30 Canada Geese approaches from the Great Salt Lake in the familiar triangular formation. The leader turns rather suddenly, throwing the flock into the momentary chaos of a long single-file line with a bulb of birds in the rear. Within seconds they find their form again. Following their leader, this larger flock of birds also flies directly over me, in quacking cacophony. They fly so low that I can see their soft gray undersides and dark underwing feathers, and I can hear their wings beating, can hear the air whistling through their feathers with a light, breathy sound as they push strongly but smoothly upon the air. Their heads and necks extend fully forward, stretched like graceful fuselages, unlike the Herons, who, gorgeous in their own right, fly with their necks curved back and then forward again in a tight "S" shape led by the beak and followed by the beautiful body and long dangling legs. In iconic fashion, the flying Geese honk noisily to each other. Every few seconds, a single member rolls radically to one side or the other, dropping momentarily out of formation only to immediately rejoin the formation farther back.

Another gaggle flies over me in a gentle arc, not a hard-angled "V", and lands in a cow pasture, where the geese waddle serenely. The echoing blast of a shotgun startles me, and the geese rise in a frightened flush to more gunfire. While I know the farmer has a right to shoot the birds on his own farm, and to serve them up for his dinner, still, irritation seeps into my hot face at this unnecessary disruption of peaceful natural life.

In some places the irrigation ditch flows four to six feet below the banked edge of Rabbit Lane. The trickling water is choked with Watercress and obscured by four-foot tall grass growing thickly in the steep banks and bending over the open ditch. On some cold mornings, a mist hovers over the ditch, rising from the warmer waters.

As I approach one of these deep areas on a morning walk, a small Mallard rises vertically from the depths of the steamy ditch, in complete silence, like a remote control helicopter, its short wings a fluttering blur. Several feet above the ground, it tilts forward and to the side, flying low and away over the ripening alfalfa. Picking a spot to its liking, it comes to a hover and drops, disappearing into the alfalfa.

Had the little duck remained where it was, perfectly concealed in the deep ditch, I would have walked past it, never knowing it was there. It had been safe in its concealment. Something about my approach, however, caused the bird to panic, to reveal itself, and to seek what it perceived to be a safer hiding spot.

One winter day an unsuspecting driver inched his wheel off the edge of the icy road and slid his car into a deep section of the ditch, leaving the back wheel suspended and spinning several feet off the ground. It remained perched on the precipice for several days.

Walking with Erin (11) one morning on Rabbit Lane, I heard a wary quack in the irrigation ditch ahead and stopped her suddenly.

"Ssh. Do you hear that?" I asked in an excited whisper.

"It's just a duck, Dad," she replied with disdain.

"Ah," I whispered, "but do you know what species?"

"No," she answered, looking at me with the mixture of awe and boredom that only she can produce.

"Well," I lied playfully, "neither do I!" Growing quiet and serious, I continued, "But the quacking of a common duck is as precious to me as the mournful cry of a Common Loon, which is anything but common."

We walked in silence then, attentive to whatever would reveal itself.

As Brian (12) and I walked along Rabbit Lane one evening, small creatures made spooky, rustling noises in the ditch-side bushes and willows. We could not see them in the darkness, and our flashlight only served to accentuate the shadows and add to the mystery. Mist moved sensuously over the murmuring water. A small Mallard jumped from the water, captured in the flashlight beam, and hovered for a moment, seeming unable to decide what to do or where to go. Then it pivoted like a miniature harrier jet and eased off over the fields toward an unseen wetland.

I think that the happiest days of Laura's life were the days I brought chicks or ducklings home from the feed store. She begged to let her first yellow duckling swim, so I filled a five-gallon bucket from the mud room sink, and she plopped the little duckling in to swim around. The duckling swam happily for a few minutes. Although only a day or two old, it somehow knew how to be a duck, dunking its head in the water and letting the droplets run down its back. But soon the duckling began to founder and sink. While the danger had not occurred to me before, I suddenly realized what was happening. The water from the mud-room sink was cold, being drawn directly from our 200-foot deep well. The duckling was so new that its little body could not keep itself warm against the pervasive cold of the well water. The frigid water was sucking the warmth right out of the duck—it would be dead within seconds. I hurriedly scooped the ducking out of the cold water, rubbed it dry with a towel, and tucked it inside my shirt against my bare body. By this time, Laura (9) had figured out what was happening, and was in tears. For the sakes of both the duckling and my daughter, I did not want this duckling to die, and uttered a silent prayer. I sighed with relief as the duckling began to move against its dark confinement under my shirt. Hearing its protesting peeps, I drew the living duckling from the darkness and handed it to Laura, who now cried tears of joy.

The next year we brought home a newborn duckling with black plumage. Laura raised it in a rabbit cage in her room for several days, until its incessant night peeping, not to mention its incessant pooping, drove us to move the duckling to an empty pen in the chicken coop, under a heat lamp. Laura and I sat in the yard one day holding her new duckling. Suddenly it stopped moving, its legs straightened and slacked, and its head fell back on a limp neck. I watched its black eyes, gazing wide into the bright sky, literally glaze over. For some reason we could not fathom, the duckling had suddenly died while cradled in Laura's ten-year-old hands. The poor child began to sob. I took the duckling from her and tenderly manipulated the dead duckling's winglets, legs, and head, not knowing what I was doing but wanting to look like I knew what I was doing. A strange premonition popped into my mind, instructing me that the duckling's heart had stopped, and that I needed to restart it. Almost without thinking, I thumped the duckling's tiny chest with my open index finger, once, then again. Without warning, the duckling's eyes cleared, it picked up its hanging head, and it began kicking its webbed feet. Incredulous, I handed the wriggling duckling back to the still-crying girl. This duck lived to become Laura's dear friend, following her around the yard like a puppy. She named it Wingers. I cannot explain the inspiration that compelled me to revive the baby duck. I choose to believe that someone who knew and cared about the tender depths of Laura's heart urged me into life-saving action. She needed her duckling to live, to not die in her hands, and I had been allowed to doctor it back to life. Laura enjoys telling about the time her Dad successfully performed CPR on a baby duck.

A year or so later, a neighbor's marauding dogs killed all of our ducks, breaking one duck's neck with a bite and a shake before moving on to the next duck. Hearing strange noises from my bedroom, I ventured outside with a flashlight, dressed in my bathrobe. Finding the dead and dying ducks, including Laura's Wingers, in the midnight dark, and the tame but bloodthirsty dogs still in my yard, I hauled the dogs by their collars to the neighbor's front porch and banged angrily on the door. Shouting in uncharacteristic rage, I dumped a bucket full of dead and bloody ducks at the neighbor's feet. I am not proud of my outburst; it was a measure of mine and my family's grief combined with fury at the neighbor's carelessness and irresponsibility.

HERE COME THE GEESE

Here come the geese
in noisy, rough formation,
beaks pointed and necks outstretched
in determined expectation,
pushed on by shorter days and cooler nights,
singing their single purpose,
to flee the north for warmer climes.

Canoe Trip

Being accomplishes more than doing.

Our fast-paced society places so much emphasis on getting things done. We often base our self-esteem on the completion of routine tasks. I say to myself, "I had a good day: I got *so* much done." But what did I really accomplish? Did I make a meaningful contribution to the world? Crossing off the tasks on my to-do list is not a true measure of my abilities, virtues, worth, achievements, or contributions. My challenge is this: after frantically chasing down one task after another, to try sitting quietly for a moment, resisting the addiction to do, and to just be. Think. Ponder. Feel. Notice. Because of our inherent mental and spiritual qualities, these moments of quiet being will provide motivation, focus, and meaning to our doing.

We keep our red 17-foot Coleman canoe on the ground, up-side-down, against the side of the shed. We bought it from a cousin, and paid too much for it. But at the time he needed money and we wanted a canoe, so I suppose it was a fair exchange. The canoe looks sadly at me as I arrive home from my morning walks, lamenting its condition, asking to be repaired. I left the canoe one Winter by the edge of the driveway, where it had been buried by deep snow. Cordale, our thoughtful neighbor, drove his trusty, rusty John Deere over to plow the snow from the cul-de-sac and my driveway. Not seeing the canoe for the snow, he rammed it and bent the aluminum frame. I'm sure an auto body shop could straighten out the frame, but I have not yet taken the time, effort, and money to make it happen.

The canoe's other injury, a crack in the thick plastic caused by a boy's skateboard on a cold day, I fixed with some clear epoxy, except that I rolled the canoe onto the grass while the epoxy on the outside was still soft in order to smear some epoxy on the inside. I hurried and rolled the canoe back, but the epoxy had already hardened, lumpy and with grass in it. So I sanded it until I grew tired of sanding, and rationalized, "Well, it's better than it was before; it's good enough." Laura had been after me for two years to fix it so we could paddle around buoyantly in the Great Salt Lake. Having finally fixed the crack, we canoed the Jordan River instead.

Cordale's tractor, and Cordale, first made their impression as they tilled our yard in preparation for planting grass. I scampered about in the dust, picking up stones and sticks so they would not get caught in the tiller tines and damage the tractor bearings. Soon he stopped the tractor and called me over, a serious look in his eye. I wondered if I had missed a stick and broken his tractor.

"Brother Baker," he said in the traditional church greeting. "You're missin' out on an opportunity here. Look at you, runnin' around like a chicken with no head while your children are over there playin' in the dirt. Get 'em on over here to help you. Show 'em what it means to work, to help their dad, to be a part, and to make somethin' happen. Don't you jest let 'em play while you do all the work. Come on now."

With that he nodded his head, grinned, and started up the John Deere. Unable to resist such good-natured chastening, I called Brian (8) and Erin (5) over to help me clear the way for the tractor by picking up debris. After short weeks we had a beautiful lawn, to which they had contributed, and on which they have enjoyed years of play.

Just weeks after prepping the yard, Cordale tilled our garden plot. Being already late Spring, he also offered to plant our garden, with sweet corn, using his tractor-pulled seed planter. That Fall, mother and children often found me sitting in a lawn chair, amidst the rows of tall, obscuring corn husks, munching ear after ear of the sweetest raw corn-on-the-cob.

Seeing the injured canoe reminds me of the wonderful canoeing adventures of my youth. One particularly memorable canoe trip—five days of paddling and portaging from lake to lake in the Adirondack mountains of New York—began in an old 12-passenger Econoline van driving north, before dawn, on the Garden State Parkway in New Jersey.

Joe remarked proudly about his old van, "I love to sit up high in this van and look down at the other cars as I drive by."

As he finished his observation, a giant, new, red 18-wheel diesel tractor-trailer passed the van. Joe looked up at the truck driver, who looked down at him, then Joe looked ahead, mute. I laughed, inside, so as not to embarrass him. Joe was actually a humble man who did not look down on others. He just liked the simple pleasure of sitting high up in his vehicle so he could survey the territory.

Sixteen years old, I sat in the back seat, on the driver side, with our scout troop's backpacks and gear stowed behind me, and with the aluminum canoes on a trailer behind the van. Excited but sleepy, I gazed out the window at the jersey barriers blurring rapidly by in the darkness. Gradually, my consciousness awakened to a faint orange glow that seemed to emanate from the barriers. As the glow slowly brightened, the rational side of my brain began to seek an explanation for the source of the glow. Pushing my face against the glass, I strained to look down the side of the van and saw flames shooting out from beneath me. Hardly believing what I was seeing, I stammered a few indecipherable sounds.

"On fire! The van's on fire!" I finally managed to blurt out.

Joe looked back at me through the rearview mirror, alarmed but also disbelieving, and cried out "What?!" It was part question, part surprised ejaculation. When I shouted again, "The van is on fire!" he confirmed it with a quick look in his side mirror, then sprang into action. Quickly he cut across three lanes of early morning commuter traffic and came to a stop on the sloping highway shoulder.

We all poured out of the van, quickly formed a fire line, and moved the gear out of the van in a matter of seconds. The last kid in the line threw the gear down the slope towards the woods behind him.

My principal thought at this time was that the van would surely explode and kill us all. Immediately upon the last piece of gear being removed, we all dove down the slope that descended from the highway into the forest. Lying prone, we watching the fire spread, and I waited for the explosion. With sudden horror I saw Joe still with the van. He was frantically grabbing every little thing he could find inside the van and throwing it wildly away from the van. Pencils, maps, soda cups, baseball caps. I thought that Joe, my friend and scout leader, was going to die. The last thing I saw before Joe himself dove away from the flaming van was him flinging a box of chocolate donuts, each of which left the box to fly its own path through the air, each catching the glow of the fire on its dark underside as it flew.

Frightened, my blood pumping adrenaline, my heart pounding in my ears, I waited for the explosion I knew would come, wondering if we were all still too close. But the explosion never came. I lied there and watched the flames engulf the van, burn everything that would burn, then die out to leave a smoldering wreck. Amazingly, the tires were unscathed. Just as the last flame turned to smoke, the fire trucks arrived. (We had no cell phones then.) Firemen deluged what used to be Joe's van, and left it a smoking hulk.

Our parents and leaders graciously salvaged our trip, finding new vehicles in which to transport us, our gear, and our canoes. As much as we enjoyed five days of canoeing, that fateful drive became the most memorable part of the trip. I felt sad that Joe had lost his old van with the high seat that he so much enjoyed. But he bought a new old van, a van with a high seat that allowed him to fully survey the territory.

Shirley and Lucille

Please help us to not be mean.
(Hannah-3 to God)

Lucille, in her 80s, still lived in the tiny clapboard shack in which she had birthed her children, surrounded by her family's historic grain fields, next to the small brick house in which she herself had been born. The shack's facilities were to be found in a one-seater outhouse 30 feet behind the house. One very cold morning after an even colder night, a neighbor found her sprawled on the icy ground, her body frozen. She must have slipped or tripped returning from the outhouse, was unable to get herself up from the ground, and slowly went to sleep as the overpowering cold seeped into her warm body. Her sister, Shirley, wasted away in a nearby rest home with crippling rheumatoid arthritis. I wrote this poem to honor their humble yet meaningful lives.

Shirley's House

SUNFLOWERS FOR SHIRLEY

I have brought you sunflowers,
those that grow small and many
on tall and tangled plants.
"You'll want your vase back, surely,"
you mutter, looking elsewhere, while
the others all watch the glowing screen.
I whisper close to your old ear,
"I'll collect the vase when these have wilted
and I've brought you fresh blooms."
You stare at the linoleum.

In your room one month before
I sat on your bed and we spoke
of the house where you live, the same house
where you were born, where you
fry your eggs on an iron stove

burning sticks in its belly,
where you snuff out the lamp at sundown.
You asked me then, "I'll be home next week.
Might I pay you to cut the grass?
Once the summer heat settles in,
the grass won't do much; but
it grows long in springtime. Only,
don't mow on the mound back of the house—
the cesspool. It's only old planks,
and I'm in no condition to pull you out
if you fall through!"

Your brother and his son still farm the old farm
around your house, and will keep farming, you said,
until they cannot make a living at it anymore.
"The town is changing, changing so fast now,"
you reflected. "New subdivisions popping up,
spreading like weeds, plowing under
fertile farms and pastures.
England and Norris have sold their farms
for houses. So have Gordon and Blake.
The buyers care only for profit.
They know not nor care
about the apple trees and the plum trees
or the English black currant bushes
or the hollyhocks or Concord grapes
or the ever-bearing raspberries
we coaxed from the clay 60 years ago.
Beyond them
                    are the generations
of planters and harvesters
of oats and wheat and barley and alfalfa,
and our backbreak and our heartache,
and the life we gave the land,
and the life the land gave us in return.
Dear Lord, how everything has changed."

But today, you stare at the linoleum,
gnarled feet nudging your chair
toward room #5,
clutching your sunflowers with twisted clumpy hands.
"I'll come again, Shirley, to collect the vase."

Virginia Creeper vines climb through the Russian Olive trees, scarlet serrated leaves mixing with powdery olive-white. In late Autumn, the red leaves fall to line the weed-choked ditch, like red confetti in the gutter the morning after a parade.

In a wildflower field guide I found instructions for making a flower press. The press looked so simple that the children and I decided to try making one. First we cut two 12x12-inch squares from some old pressed-board shelving. Next we clamped the wood together and drilled a ¼-inch hole in each corner. (Number the corners so that you can match up the holes later.) We found four bolts and wing nuts in the bolt box to tighten down the press. Erin had some leftover sheets of watercolor parchment, which would absorb the moisture from the fresh flower petals and leaves. (Any absorbent paper will work, even newspaper.) The parchment was fairly rough, so we slipped a sheet of regular copy paper between the rough paper and the specimens. Squares of cardboard between the paper layers would separate and protect the sheets of specimens. All we needed now was our specimens, and we struck out for Rabbit Lane to gather them.

It was too late in the season to press Bitter Nightshade blossoms. The purple flowers with yellow centers had turned to toxic red fruits too lumpy for a flower press. But the scarlet Virginia Creeper leaves were perfect for pressing. Some were still transitioning from Summer's mid-green, deepening to a green-black before shedding this morose color to burst into sunset scarlet. The Russian Olive trees still bore their stiff, powdery green leaves. We left the thick Milkweed leaves alone because of the white sticky sap that drips from the base of the plucked leaves. We would come back next Summer for pink

Milkweed blooms, yellow Russian Olive blossoms, Bitter Nightshade flowers, and deep yellow Sunflower petals.

At home with our leaves, the children carefully positioned them on the clean paper one layer at a time until the paper, cardboard, and specimens rose to two inches thick between the boards. Each of the children took turns arranging their specimens on a sheet of paper. I clamped the boards down on the leaves and flowers, making a couple of turns on each corner wing nut so that the boards would be pulled evenly together. With the leaves and petals tightly clamped, the children looked to me for an answer to their unvocalized question: What next?

"Now," I said, "we wait for a month for the leaves to fully dry."

The process felt anti-climactic to the children—a month!—similar to planting rows of corn seeds and then waiting weeks for the shoots to finally poke through the soil. But after a quick month I brought out the press to unveil the children's pressings. The children eagerly unwound the wing nuts, pulled off the top board and cardboard, and carefully peeled away the sheets of paper. The dried Virginia Creeper leaves were stiff and dry but brilliantly red.

"Those are mine!" one child would call, then another, each proud of the beautiful leaves and petals they had so crisply preserved.

The next Summer we took the press on a mountain campout and gathered a single specimen of every species of wildflower we could find. I had to gently discourage the younger children from picking armfuls of wildflowers.

"Leave them," I encouraged, "for the bees and hummingbirds to harvest and drink from; leave them where they clothe the mountain with breathtaking beauty for all to see. Except for the few we press, the flowers will lose their life's beauty soon after we pick them."

At the insistence of the youngest, I allowed them to pick a small bouquet for their mother.

In Winter, we gathered all the dried specimens from their temporary shoebox and glued them to white paper with spots of rubber cement. We researched the name of each flower and leaf in the field guides and wrote the names on the paper under the specimens. With the glue fully dried and each specimen labeled, we slipped the sheets into plastic sheet protectors. We placed each page in a binder, which we occasionally pull off the shelf and browse through, admiring the unique color, shape, and beauty of each leaf and flower.

For decades my grandmother Dorothy pressed leaves and flower petals between the pages of her encyclopedias, using the pressings to make homemade cards. On my visits to her brick bungalow, built in 1935 by my grandfather Wallace as a wedding gift, I always saw stacks of heavy books in the corners of the rooms. The book at the bottom of each stack contained flower petals and leaves between its pages. Our scrapbooks are filled with Grandma's homemade birthday cards sent to us over the course of several decades. She carefully arranged the leaves and petals, and the occasional butterfly wing found in the yard, to make beautiful cards. I asked her to teach me her craft years ago, and I taught my own children. Laura particularly enjoys making cards like her great-grandmother's.

Begin card-making by cutting a piece of wax paper that when folded will fit into the envelope of your choosing. Cut writing paper to a matching size for your message insert, and set it aside. Water down white glue 1:1 and brush it on the wax paper. Position your petals and leaves as you wish on only one-half of the wax paper (i.e., the right side, which becomes the front of the card when folded), then dab additional glue to wet the petals and leaves. Top your creation with a single layer of tissue paper, white or colored depending on the effect you want. Because the watery glue likes to puddle on the wax paper, you may need to dab additional glue on dry areas of the tissue. Be careful, though, because the wet tissue easily tears (if it does, mush it back or patch it). You can use your fingers to gently press out air bubbles. When the cards are completely dry, slip one card inside a folded paper grocery sack, place it on an ironing board, and pass a hot iron over the sack a few times. The heat melts the wax into the dried tissue paper around the petals and leaves. Trim the wax paper to the size of the envelope. Insert your message paper; you can tape it in if you want. Then fold and insert your card into its envelope. (Grandma discovered that she loved the effect of glitter amply sprinkled onto the wet tissue paper. I recommend against this because the glitter breaks loose inside the envelope and makes a mess at the recipient's house.)

Both the flower press and the homemade flower cards are easy to make. Each activity is educational, brings contact with nature, provides a conversation piece, and makes for individual and family fun.

On numerous occasions I have taken troops of Boys Scouts walking on Rabbit Lane to fulfill their First Class rank requirement to identify ten plants native to their communities (whether endemic or exotic). It takes only minutes of walking to find: Virginia Creeper, Bitter Nightshade, Russian Olive, Cottonwood, Sunflower, Parsnip, Milkweed, Watercress, Willow, Poplar, Alfalfa, various grasses, Evening Primrose, and many other plant species.

Lucille's House

LUCILLE

Her cottage sits small
in the big shade of three
old cottonwoods that now, late
Spring, release bushels of cottony
seeds that ride the breeze,
settling in wispy blanketings
on roads and lawns, houses, and fields.
churned up by cars
in swirling white clouds
that float off to land where they will:
on the ground again,
on trees and flowers,
on barbed wire prongs,
and in my hair.

In the shade
the cottage's weathered clapboards
glower dark, as if soaked
in creosote, matching the nearby privy
planks. A lifetime of bundling
up, kicking through feet
of newly-fallen snow, to sit
on the icy privy seat.
Firewood leans tired
against the cottage clapboards,
log ends covered in dusty spider webs.
The blackened chimney top
misses Winter's fires.
New grass covers
the privy pathway.

Lucille did have running water.
I saw the chipped enamel sink once,
from the porch,
when she answered the door.
Water dripped steadily
from the rusted faucet head.

Rabbit Lane

Her bed huddled in the corner,
a thin mattress pressing rusty coils,
opposite the sink
in the two-room shack.

Lucille hunched in the doorway,
against the frame,
her unkempt hair streaked gray and white,
matted from undisturbed sleep.

"We're having a meeting tonight, about
the road.
You're welcome to come,
if you want.
I wanted you to know."

"Are these your children?"
Her hairy chin-mole moved
a little as she smiled,
revealing toothless gums.

"Yes, ma'am, these are my children."

"You have beautiful children," she crooned.

"Thank you, ma'am," I offered meekly.

"Thank you," she softly offered in-kind,
withdrawing gingerly,
with my letter and maps,
into the shadows of her home.

The new state road, I feared,
would destroy her old cottage,
would tear through the oat fields
that her nephews farm.

I regret
never visiting Lucille before.

Rabbit Lane

I regret
listening to the neighbors
about how ornery and crotchety she was,
about how curmudgeonly she was
toward visitors.

We knocked on her door
and asked if she wanted to
buy some Girl Scout cookies
and she practically chased us
away scolding, 'I don't want any
cookies' they had said.

As it turns out,
Lucille was just as nice as could be,
simply old and tired and lonely.
Perhaps she wished that someone
would come visit her,
someone that didn't want
anything,
someone that might say,
Hello, Lucille.
It's a beautiful day.
And how are you getting along?
I regret
that I never saw Lucille again.
She died and was buried before I knew.

We held the community meeting about
the road,
at my house.
Most of the neighbors came
and talked for hours.

"The road
will desecrate
an unmarked pioneer cemetery,"
one neighbor asserted.
"My grand-daddy told me once

where he thought it was."

"The environmental assessment for
the road
is totally inadequate and entirely suspect,"
a man declared.
"It fails to account for wetlands and species mitigation,
and fails to identify potential alternate routes."

"This is Erda!"
bemoaned an old farmer's wife.
"We've been cultivating our ground
for generations.
The road
will take that all away."

"It's no use bickerin',"
cranked a cynical old rancher.
"The State will put
the highway
where the State damn well wants to,
and there aint nothin' we can do about it."

The old ranchers and farmers,
and the new-comers, too,
designated me their voice,
to write to the Governor about
the road.
He had proclaimed, after all,
this year to be
the year of the Utah farmer.
The new road,
as planned, would decimate
some of Erda's best farmland.

I received no gubernatorial reply—
but Lucille's cottage still hides
in the cottonwood shadows.
Some kin replaced

the weathered wooden door
with a new door painted white,
like a gaudy, too-big bandage
on a fairly minor bruise.
Otherwise, the cottage withstands time.
The little *No Trespassing* sign clings
crookedly to the rusty field fence;
the house gate long since fell off.
Artesian water squirts feebly
from the rusty yellow sprinkler,
lying always in the same spot,
growing a circle of lush green
against the adjacent dormant brown.
In the front lawn,
the finned '56 Ford station wagon
has kept patient watch for decades.
Weeds climb past its flat, cracked whitewalls
and faded blue-sky paint.
The rear window is shattered still;
the others remain intact.
And after every Spring thaw,
the crocuses, daffodils, and tulips
rise through the turf by the thousands,
waiving yellow, red, pink, and purple,
perfuming the air and
bringing life and color
to the empty cottage
where Lucille lived.

Of Caterpillars and Birds

The Goldfinch is a splash of brilliant yellow against
the white snow and brown earth.

The ant hill is the sign of a delicate and sophisticated society,
mostly unseen for its largely underground order. The individual ant
is tiny but far from delicate. It is both formidable worker and fearsome
warrior, taking on burdens and adversaries many times its size. Yet
its civilization is vulnerable to destruction by the careless shuffle of a
shoe.

Every year we find Tomato Hornworms on our tomato plants.
The surest worm signs are bare branch stubs, stripped of leaves, and
large, black, barrel-shaped droppings. Whenever I find a fat, green
caterpillar, I call the children over to see. Because of their tomato-
leaf-green color and subtle yellow markings, the hornworms are very
difficult to see, even though they grow fatter and longer than my index

finger. Tracking them by dung and denuded branch is the quickest way to find them.

My grandfather Wallace, a part-time tomato farmer, detested these pests and hunted them doggedly. Not needing to make a living from my tomatoes, I can afford to not mind a bare twig here and there. In my garden, a bare branch is an occasion for excitement: a hornworm hides nearby. The hornworms, earning their name from the stiff pointed horn on their tail end, do not eat the tomatoes. The children think the "callerpitters" are amazing, otherworldly creatures. John (3) bravely held one in his open palm for a moment, then suddenly exclaimed, "He loves me!"

Unlike many moth and butterfly larvae, tomato hornworms dig into the earth to pupate. They lie in the ground all Winter long and emerge in Spring as Five-spotted Hawk Moths, a species of Sphinx Month. Upon finding a hornworm, I have the children help me to prepare a shoe box with about two inches of loose, moist soil in the bottom. We feed the caterpillars tomato leaves until their swelling, green bodies disappeared, to become dark-brown pupae in the soil. We leave the box outside in a sheltered spot (where the cats will not dig). Occasionally we drip a little water on the soil to keep it from totally drying out. In Spring, with the appearance of the first flowers, we put the box where it can warm in the sunlight, and we watch every day for the hawk moth to emerge. To escape its pupa shell, the moth emits a liquid that dissolves a hole in the shell. The new moth crawls out and spreads its wet, wrinkled wings and vibrates them rapidly in the sun's warmth. The vibrations pump blood from the moth's body into the wing veins, causing them to spread open and smooth. The wings quickly dry. If this procedure is not completed successfully, the moth will never fly.

Hawk Moths flit from flower to flower, sometimes chasing each other. Their wings beat so fast that you see only the vague blur of wings. The large moths look much like small hummingbirds. They feed while flying, like hummingbirds, uncoiling their long, tubular, hollow proboscis to suck nectar from flowers. Hawk Moths are particularly striking, with soft red bands on their underwings.

We found a Hawk Moth floating in the children's little wading pool. We thought for sure that it was dead. Putting a hand under it and lifting it from the cold water, I found that it moved its legs weakly. We placed it on the sidewalk in full sunlight. After a few moments, its wings dried and began to vibrate, circulating blood through the wing veins and warming the body. The moth was a miniature, self-contained solar heating unit. It suddenly rose from the sidewalk and flew away in search of nourishment. We felt a hint of happiness at helping to revivify the moth.

I once gave a large Tomato Hornworm larvae, and a box with soil, to my nephew, Thomas (3). Months later, he reported to me sadly that his moth had hatched. Asking him why he was unhappy, he said, "I like the moth, but I miss my caterpillar."

The children came running to me with alarm in their faces.

"A hummingbird . . . in the garage!" they gasped, trying to catch their breath. Following them, I found the double-wide door up, the garage entirely open, yet the Black-chinned Hummingbird confounded and trapped inside. Apparently, instinct drove the tiny bird to fly always upward. It buzzed around the garage with its beak to the ceiling, and could not see the obvious way out. It stopped frequently to rest on the highest object it could find. The bird looked at us nervously as we paced around the garage, but still could not discern the way to freedom.

I could see the hummingbird's fatigue and hoped that, if I could catch it, it would have sufficient strength to fly away to find food and not fall easy prey to an opportunistic cat. I grabbed the long-handled butterfly net that stood in the corner of the garage. The net was new enough to have survived active children chasing chickens and cats with it. I raised the net and cautiously approached the hummingbird. It leapt from its perch and flew to another resting place. I quickly followed. After repeating this for several minutes, I began to get a sense of its evasion pattern, remembering my old butterfly catching days. Anticipating its next jump, I swung the net ahead of the bird, flipped the net to prevent the bird's escape, and brought the net quickly but carefully to the floor.

Reaching my hand into the net, I wrapped my fingers around the bird tightly enough to keep it from flying away but loosely enough to avoid injuring the delicate creature. The terrified bird peeped weakly and tried to flutter its trapped wings. Bringing the tiny bird out from the net, I held it up for the children to see.

"That's so cool!" one child exclaimed. Then they all began to clamor, "I want to hold it! I want to hold it!"

"Go ahead, touch it," I invited, instructing them how to carefully stroke the iridescent, green feathers and to touch the wiry, black feet.

We walked out of the garage into the Summer sun. Each child placed their hands under mine, and on the count of three we released the little Hummingbird. It hovered erratically for a moment, and then, gathering its bearings and new strength, it flew off to the south. The Hummingbird stopped for a moment at the feeder hanging from the arbor, full of sweet liquid, then flew high into the sky until we could no longer see it. The children (and I) were thrilled at having touched and seen up close such a tiny, wild, beautiful creature. We felt happiness inside knowing that we had rescued it and set it free.

An injured Western Kingbird flopped wildly on the pavement of Church Road near the intersection of Rabbit Lane. It must have been struck by a passing car. As I bent to pick it up, it opened its black beak wide and squawked in terror in a desperate but feeble attempt to protect itself from what it could only perceive as the attack of a giant predator. I carefully folded the injured wing and cradled the bird inside my jacket as I carried it home.

I awoke Laura (9) and invited her help to dress the bird's injuries. We swabbed the wounds with disinfecting peroxide. The bird still pointed its open beak at our awkward fingers, but had stopped verbalizing its protests. We then wrapped the bird so that both wings were gently pinned against its body. When the bindings were removed, we reasoned, the strength in the mended wing would match the strength of the good wing. The wings would gather new strength in concert. Satisfied that this was the best chance the bird had to heal, we carried it outside to a small, protected pen and set it down upon its feet in the straw. We hoped we would be able feed and water the bird long enough for it to recover. We would have to catch bugs, since its diet did not include seeds.

Releasing the bound bird, it immediately fell over onto its face. The bindings had rendered it completely helpless, like you or I would be if wrapped from head to toe with only our toes exposed for mobility. It needed its wings for balance as well as for flight. Discouraged, Laura and I removed all of our careful wrappings and did our best to splint the broken wing. This less invasive treatment allowed the bird to stand and walk about, but the bandage would not stay on for the difficulty of attaching it to the wing feathers.

Despite our well-intentioned but fumbling efforts, the Kingbird died after three days. Still, I was glad we had rescued the bird and attempted to nurse it back to health. The thought of leaving the frightened bird in the roadway to be smashed by the next passing car saddened me. Also, handling the small but proud creature, and working to heal it, had worked some magic in us. We felt a greater awe in nature's wild things and a deeper grief at their loss.

An old Warbler nest hangs, swaying, from a low willow branch like a balled up, gray woolen sock. It clings to the branch through the strongest of winds. Gusts topping 80 miles per hour have neither torn it apart nor pulled it from its suspending branch.

A lone Crow flies south behind a V-formation of Canada Geese. It caws loudly despite a large parcel in its beak, defiant toward the fable of the fox and the crow. This seems to be a savvy, more talented Crow. Is this Crow lonely or content in its aloneness? Do the Geese communicate, or do they merely find comfort in their raucous propinquity?

A cock Ring-necked Pheasant croaks unseen in the tall grass, nervous at my approach. When I stop to search with my eyes, he seems to suspect me of bad intentions, and flaps inelegantly into a tree, landing clumsily in its top branches, his feathers thrashing against leafy twigs. On Rabbit Lane, feathers from a Pheasant hen lay scattered about, chestnut brown barred with beige. Nearby sits a pile of spent red plastic shotgun shells with brass caps.

When the American Robin appears, pulling at worms, I know that Spring is near. Hummingbirds whir and zoom looking for early flowers. They light in me a tiny spark of joy that has lain smoldering all Winter.

The Killdeer scream at me, draw me away from their spare nests that lie hidden in the rocks and gravel, flapping their striped wings as if injured.

In a chaotic, white cloud of winged, shrieking voices, whirling and churning around me, charging my senses, thousands of California Gulls descend upon a newly ploughed field next to Rabbit Lane. I perceive no order in their loose, gregarious grouping, unlike flocks of geese following a leader in formation. Milling around in search of upturned earthworms, the flock calls raucously, sounding like a thousand tuneless New Year's Eve noisemakers. Despite their awful sound, the birds are beautiful: sleek white feathers with gray tips, a red dot on each side of the creamy yellow beak. In flight, their streamlined bodies and powerful wing beats propel them through the air, with their black webbed feet tucked into their downy white undersides.

A Mourning Dove coos in the morning mist, sounding oh so sad.

At Boy Scout camp at Lake Seneca, New York, the older boys sent me to ask another troop for a left-handed smoke-shifter, then took me on a snipe hunt. I found neither the device nor the creature. Only after moving to Erda did I learn that the Snipe is a real creature, a water bird, and not just a fictional Boy Scout bird. Smaller than an Avocet, the Snipe roams the ditches and wetlands, poking its beak into the mud for insects and small crayfish.

On many an evening I strained to discern the source of a soft, ghostly, reverberating sound moving over the farm fields. But I never found it. Explaining this mystery to Harvey one afternoon, he told me to look high into the sky whenever I heard the sound. There, I would see a small dot, the ventriloquistic Snipe. Flying high, the Snipe turns to dive and roll at breakneck speeds toward the ground. Wind rushing through its slightly open wings creates the haunting sound. The Snipe throws the sound somehow from those heights to hover foggily over the fields. I hear it less and less as the years pass.

The water from Rabbit Lane's ditch crosses Charley's pasture diagonally, bogging at the northwest corner. Twenty or more striped Wilson's Phalaropes cackle harshly at me as I walk by, their long legs sunk in the bog and their long beaks searching for insects and worms.

Birds twitter in the willow bushes by the irrigation ditch. Birds sing from the Russian Olive trees. Birds call and screech and chirp from bushes and branches, from the tops of cedar fence posts and in flight. How does one describe the song of a bird? My National Geographic field guide to North American birds assigns all manner of syllabic writing to bird songs and calls, none of which words approach a satisfactory description of the music. In English, the Crow is synonymous with the *caw*. These meager descriptions are like saying a note played on the piano sounds like *plink*, like a Model-T horn shouts *ba-OO-ga*, like a baby's cry is *waaaa*. No euphemistic reduction does justice to the genuine song. Thanks to Cornell University's ornithology lab, some bird books allow the reader to push a button and hear each bird's unique song, sometimes a humble peep, sometimes a glorious, frenetic melody.

The Western Kingbird's song resembles chaotic, unpatterned electronica. A Bullock's Oriole splashes its ember-orange on a canvas of blue-green Russian Olive.

The Western Meadowlark sings frequently from the tops of cedar fence posts. Even driving at 60 miles per hour with the window cracked, I can hear its piercing but beautifully melodious song. Attempts to whistle the tune bog it terribly down and omit half the notes, each critical, resulting in a sometimes recognizable but always shabby imitation.

A Black-chinned Hummingbird perches on a strand of stiff barbed wire, surveying vast fields of grass. Its black beak points as straight and as sharp as the silver barbs, yet the bird possesses a softness and a beauty incongruous with the hard wire stretched tight.

A Field Crescent butterfly flits from place to place on Rabbit Lane's asphalt, flying a low dance around my walking feet, making momentary spots of brightness against the ubiquitous gray.

LISTEN

Listen!

A robin! A robin!
Chirping on the branch.

A king bird! A king bird!
Whistling on the fence post.

A finch! A finch!
Twittering on the feeder.

A lark! A lark!
Singing in the meadow.

A dove! A dove!
Cooing in the morning.

A snipe! A snipe!
Tumbling through the evening sky.

An owl! An owl!
Screeching from the snag.

SONGS OF SPRING

Ice and snow begin
to yield to a longer sun.

Meadowlarks have returned
singing melodies:
> *sogladwearetobeback!*
> *arentyouhappytohearus?*
> *sogladwearetobesingingandsingingandback!*

A hundred little blackbirds
in a bare tree top prattle,
> *zippatappazaptap!*
> *zikkatikkazakkatat!*

Robin hops quietly
in the greening grass,
stops to reconnoiter,
searching,
one eye for juicy brown earthworms,
the other for the cat.

Black-Oil Pavement

Hold on by letting go.

Toward the north end of Rabbit Lane, the ditch crosses the road through a 36-inch culvert pipe, where the water flows diagonally across Charley's pasture in a shallow channel. Charley was losing too much water through the informal channel and decided to install a new culvert a hundred yards or so further south. He cut a new crossing in Rabbit Lane with his backhoe, dropped in a new section of black pipe, and backfilled around the pipe, restoring the road. The water now flowed directly west in a deeper channel following a fence line.

The ditch banks in this area were thick with willow bushes and Siberian Elm trees, and a whole section of the ditch vegetation was now deprived completely of water. I watched every day for these bushes and trees to begin to turn brown, for their growth to stunt. I was sure they would die. But as the weeks passed, I noticed no change in the vegetation. It seemed just as verdant and vibrant as it had before. The bed of dark, moist clay in the abandoned portion of the old irrigation ditch began to dry and crack, forming a string of small island mesas in the bottom of a deep, dry ditch-bank canyon. Still the bushes thrived.

I knew that one day Rabbit Lane would be paved with black-oil asphalt. I suppose it was inevitable. Though I dreaded that day, it finally came. The county government, in its wisdom, decided that my little country farm lane needed to be paved. Of course, the lane was not mine at all. But I had claimed it and loved it and hoped for it. Over my rutted and pocked hard-pack gravel and dirt now stretched a ribbon of black. It began from Church Road and continued northward, meandering slightly, until it faded from sight. To me the pavement seemed an unending ribbon of blackness, weighing heavily upon the world of nature and of my imagination, fouling the aromas of my romanticism, and covering the worm tracks and raccoon prints and aspiring greenery. It catapulted me from my attachment to things past and slammed me into the ever-insistent present of progress and change.

With every step along the new road, the darkness of disappointment pressed in upon me, reminding me of the other black lines and splotches in my life, in all lives. I did not appreciate the reminder. Such reminders are ubiquitous in the comings and goings of life. I needed Rabbit Lane to help me slowly lighten the dark things, to gently heal the wounded places, to fill my eyes and nose and ears with the simple delights of the natural world. I hoped, with utter naiveté, that Rabbit Lane would stay the same, forever. Like everything else in life, Rabbit Lane had changed.

Unlike most new roads, the pavement left Rabbit Lane anything but new. The asphalt, instead of a freshly-blended oil-infused hot mix, evenly and smoothly laid, consisted of rough regurgitated remnants from some other county road demolition project. The asphalt on that other road had been roto-milled, trucked out, and dumped into a heap somewhere, then brought to Rabbit Lane, spread out, and steam rolled, what they call a cold mix road. The new road consisted of the other road's bony remains over which bicycles bounce and cars bump and upon which my booted toe is stubbed.

Hardly a resurrection, Rabbit Lane now resembled a mass grave. Angular pieces poked up everywhere, making the road rougher than the gravel washboard had ever been. Lengthy sections were so dry and devoid of oil that they quickly crumbled into brown asphalt dust. In some areas, lane-line yellow rose to the surface, small yellow patches pointing in all directions at odds with their former life of guiding travelers safely to their destinations. The county had found a cheap, convenient use for its mountains of road waste in covering up the old-fashioned, perhaps out-of-fashion, dirt and gravel of Rabbit Lane. Laying down the old asphalt would spare the county the cost of maintaining the dirt road; perhaps that was the rationale.

I knew better: the cost of an occasional grader and a few dump truck loads of fresh gravel would be far less than the cost of crack sealing, slurry sealing, and chip sealing the new road. The county, however, found an easy way to save money by simply not maintaining the asphalted Rabbit Lane at all.

Like the "new" asphalt, my feelings settled somewhat with the passing weeks and months. Not that time was healing any wounds. I'm not convinced that time heals wounds at all; rather, time merely dims their pain with the buffering and diluting effect of the emotions and impressions of relentless streams of life experience. Healing is a mystery that involves the inner power of personal choice together with the subtle influences of the Divine.

Beneath the ragged pavement, I began to sense a faint stirring, as if the soft breathing of untroubled sleep. Water still trickled in the ditch. Passerines still flitted through the willow bushes. Virginia Creeper still climbed Russian Olive trunks, turning deep scarlet in Fall. The sun still rose and set, while the foot travelled dirt remained faithfully beneath a shallow covering of old asphalt. Rabbit Lane was still there, and I needed to be, too.

After nearly a week in bed, I had to get out of the house. The infection in my lungs, throat, and sinuses had left me weak and despondent. The February weather was obliging, but I still wore a winter coat against lingering chills. Four of the children came with me, Laura (12), John (10), Caleb (8), and Hyrum (6).

The three boys wanted to ride their bicycles. But Hyrum's flat tire first needed repair. John had tried, but one axle nut was stuck. I showed him the vice grips, and we had the tire off quickly. Hyrum helped me pump up the inner tube, immerse it in water, and spot the two bubble fountains. We circled each hole with blue ball-point pen, dried the tube, drained the air, and applied the rubber cement and patches. In minutes we were on the road.

We stopped at Ron's old place to hunt for rusty treasures. Ron had moved away, and had told us we could take whatever we found lying around. The children found an old file, a pulley wheel, a cattle brand handle, and a blue powerline insulator. Caching their treasures behind a tree, we resumed our walk.

I dragged myself down Rabbit Lane, feeling so tired. Infection had sapped my strength. The "new" asphalt was showing signs of heavy wear. Muddy pot holes had appeared where the asphalt was thinnest. I imagined the American pioneers pulling their wooden handcarts laden with meager belongings and scarce provisions. They pulled their carts across much rougher terrain, in much colder temperatures. What happened to their men when they contracted lung infections, when their coughing stabbed their chests with pain, when they would have preferred to rest on the couch until feeling a little stronger? They died, that's what they did. Or they pressed on. My weakened condition, transported to their harsh conditions, would probably have seen my own death. But I live, thinking and writing about it, shuffling down the lane, and resting on the couch.

At Witch's Tree we turned back for home. Laura talked excitedly about the Cecropia cocoons she had ordered and that had just arrived, by mail. Seeing them, I remembered the first Cecropia cocoon I found in a New Jersey woods. Laura's package included two fat dark-brown pupae sealed expertly inside silky dry leaves. She hoped they would be male and female so they could mate and lay eggs that she could raise into more larvae, more pupae, more moths. She laid them carefully inside a dry aquarium, with strips of cloth the moths could climb up to reach the wire-screen cover. Hanging there, they would pump blood into the veins of their crumpled wet wings to stretch them out into their full, glorious size and decoration. She needn't worry about feeding them—the moths do not eat. They mate, lay eggs, fly around for a week or two, then die, having fulfilled their purpose. All the eating gets done by the thick green caterpillars. The adult moths emerge from metamorphosis to display their beauty and to ensure the next generation.

As part of Erin's (8) home school work for the day, Mom had asked Erin to choose a Psalm from the Bible and copy a verse or two from it. Erin was angry at the assignment. When she finally gave in and did it, she picked a verse that mirrored her feelings: "O God whose vengeance. . . ."

For many years I have avoided using the word *hate*. I gradually came to notice that each time I exclaimed "I *hate* this!" came an accompanying momentary unpleasant sensation, as if sucking on candy dipped in vinegar. I began to wonder if hating something, or even just expressing hatred, might be a hurtful thing. I have come to believe that to hate something is to condemn it, to consign it to certain failure, to deprive it of any goodness or merit. So, while I allow myself to express distaste for something, I no longer condemn it with my hatred. Some things, I suppose, deserve to be hated. Perhaps murderers, or molesters, or mosquitoes. But hatred is a feeling that I create, that I hold on to, that I radiate. Hatred hurts me and those around me without changing the character of the thing hated.

Why is it so hard to fulfill the hopes and dreams that pull at our hearts and occupy our minds? Aspiration seems to have opposition as its companion. Hopes and dreams imply a becoming, a process of moving from here to there across rough spiritual terrain that seems to have no care for the traveler. The bigger the dream, the longer and rougher the journey. The longer and rougher the journey, the more fatiguing the effort. It is the dream, perhaps, that determines the roughness of the road. And it is the roughness of the road, likely, that shapes the dream. As we walk and climb and struggle, the dream shifts and morphs. Upon achieving and embracing the destination— the dream—we discover that the dream is in fact a mere milestone along a much longer path, with more glorious objectives ahead, a path that ends only at life's end. And then we will discover that the road has not ended at the opaque wall of death, but that the wall has faded into a cloudy curtain, and that the road continues beyond this fragile barrier to new adventures and new achievements.

I asked Erin (10) on a Saturday afternoon if we could talk. She agreed, and we began walking together toward Rabbit Lane. We talked about things she was learning and feeling, the ways she was growing and struggling, the things she wanted to do and dreamed about doing, her hopes and her fears. She wanted so badly to grow up, to be 12 years old and to do what 12-year-olds do. Arriving at home, we sat on an old 2x12 lumber bench spanning two log stumps. I suggested that if she were to become 12 right now, she would miss being 10 and 11 and all the wonderful things that go along with being 10 and 11. I promised her that being 12 years old would come very soon, as would 13, and 14, and 18, and 25. She just could not see it yet. I encouraged her to try her best to not look too far into the future, but to enjoy her present life, the age she was, and the things she was doing.

All too often in my life I have found myself thinking too far into the future. For example, I rationalize that life will be simpler when the children are grown and on their own, or when I retire. You fill in the blank: *if I could just . . . then I'd be happier*. But fantasizing about the future, or "futuring," only increases the disparity between what we want and what we have, between who we want to be and who we are. Futuring adds to our distress and unhappiness. I am not saying that we should not dream. We should look into the future to see where we want to be, and make a plan for getting there. But while we aim for the future, we must live in the present. We must be, here and now. While we can build upon the past and plan for the future, the present is our reality.

Our country house near Rabbit Lane was our dream come true. We had worked for it, saved for it, searched for it, longed for it. Not many weeks after moving in, however, the smell of new paint faded, the carpet suffered its first stains, and we all became accustomed to our rooms. It seemed that in the move to the new house our personal struggles had stowed away and also made the journey. I woke up one morning to find that our dream home was just a house.

It may feel disappointing, but I believe there is no such thing as a dream home. There is no perfect physique. There is no ideal climate. The dream house never has enough storage space or a big enough laundry room, and the closets are always too small. The perfect physique yields to age and illness and DNA, every time. The ideal climate still presents days that are too cold or too hot or too humid, and always brings bugs.

We may think that we have achieved the ideal something-or-other. But soon after capturing it, we realize that it has faded from its idyllic quality to become mere routine, sometimes monotonous and even boring.

I once believed that dreams were better left unrealized. It seemed to me that in accomplishing a dream, it ceased to be a dream, a thing of the future, becoming instead a reality of the present, flowing quickly into the past. The fulfilled dream would have disappeared, leaving in its place a sense of emptiness and disappointment rather than fulfillment.

But some years later I decided to abandon this cynical view, realizing the importance of having a dream. To be complete and fulfilled individuals, we absolutely must dream. Dreams are what enable and ennoble us to increase our capacities and to improve ourselves and our communities. I say that we must dream. We must strive to be better tomorrow than we were today. At the same time, we must balance that striving for tomorrow with a contentment for today. We can make a better tomorrow without condemning today.

Caleb (3) ran into our room late one night, crying, "A crocodile is chasing me!" I sat up in bed, bleary-eyed, and pulled him to me.

"Don't worry," I pronounced, "I'll catch him, and bite him."

He looked at me wide-eyed and asked, "On the tail?"

"Yea," I bragged, sleepily. "On the tail!"

He rejoined, "And I'll bite him on the toe!"

Suddenly equals in the same cause, I said, "OK. We'll get him. No more crocs."

Then I pulled him into bed with us and he went right to sleep.

Angie learned one night in July that a friend and neighbor was pregnant, the baby due in November. Angie's baby was also to have been born in November, but the May miscarriage destroyed that hope. With the neighbor's news, her heartache and emptiness returned with full force, and she lay in bed weeping by my side.

Earlier in the day, Caleb (4) had said to her, "Your baby is in heaven, huh Mamma. I'm sorry your baby died, Mamma."

Mom responded, "It sounds like you're sad about it, too, Caleb."

"Yea," Caleb nodded, "because if it had been a boy we could have named him Archimedes."

This brought a smile to Angie's grieving face. She had read to the children earlier in the week about Archimedes, the Greek scientist and mathematician after whom Caleb had hoped to name a little brother.

A dead Katydid lies on the desiccated asphalt, a puddle of faded green in a hard gray world. Robin's egg fell from its high Cottonwood nest, a splash of cracked sky-blue on black.

PAVEMENT

It happened sooner than I expected.
ROAD CLOSED barricades appeared at either end.
They had paved Rabbit Lane.
They had paved Rabbit Lane with roto-mill from some other road's temporary demise,
mixed the black rubbish with new oil
and plastered it flat upon the hard, living earth.
Now, after rain, Rabbit Lane reveals nothing,
no tracks of the earthworm pushing perilously slowly across the road,
no paw or claw prints of raccoons or pheasants.
No more wet pot holes for the children to ride their bicycles through
  with a whoop.
Instead, oil leaches invisibly into the ditch
to water cattle and crops some place too far away for accountability.
Pink-flowered milkweed and wispy willow bush cling to the asphalt
  fringe.
They had transformed Rabbit Lane from a dirt farm road with country
  appeal
to another icon of the American Nowhere, with all the charm of a
  parking lot.
Rabbit Lane, of course, neither knows nor cares about the change.
But I know, and I am saddened.

Erda

Erda: the good earth.

The weekend cowboy had neglected to secure the trailer gate as he drove down Church Road. Arriving at Russell's arena, he put his truck in park and hopped out, stopping stunned at the horror of what he saw behind. His horse had slipped off the back of the open horse trailer, its head still tied to the trailer bars by the halter rope, and had been dragged on its haunches for half a mile down the road. A long skid mark of hide and flesh and blood reached back down the road from where the terrified animal lay in agony. The animal had lain bleeding until the vet arrived to put it down. My children were very quiet that night. The next morning, with the truck and trailer gone, the road as it passed our house was stained a rusty red.

Joe was reared in the old, grand clapboard house that stood until the late 1990s on the country road bearing the family name: Liddell Lane. Born in 1923, Joe as a teenage boy delivered newspapers on horseback to Erda's farmers six days a week, traveling 15-20 miles every day. His rounds completed, he and his horse cantered home every evening by way of Rabbit Lane. Water flowed freely in the adjacent ditch from the Isgreen wells. One night, the sudden sound of a startled Muskrat diving from the ditch bank into the water in turn startled Joe's horse. From its quick canter, it stopped on a dime. Joe's inertia sent him flying over the horse's head into the four-strand barbed wire fence on the side of the road. Suffering lacerations on his forearm and thigh, he unwound himself from the wire, remounted his horse, and trotted home. The cuts healed, without stitches, leaving respectable scars, which he was glad to show us as we sat around the Sunday dinner table. With no anesthesia, stitches may well have hurt worse than the barb cuts.

During the Great Depression, Joe trapped the Rabbit Lane muskrats and sold their pelts for $1.20 to $1.65 each, depending on the volatile market for such commodities. This provided the family with a rare source of cash during hard times. The family also harvested Watercress from the flowing ditch to flavor their salads and soups—slightly sweet and slightly bitter. Many times I have been tempted to harvest the lush weed for my own meals, but refrained for fear of salmonella.

Dempsey's property at the north end of Liddell Lane supports an assemblage of odd out-buildings and pens. He boasts imported Bull Frogs in his spring-fed pond, and he keeps bison, cattle, horses, chickens, ducks, geese, and one milk goat. The poor mammy's teats hang so heavy and low that she walks with difficulty, the teats tangling with her hind legs.

Nina, born in 1924, often traveled Rabbit Lane in her youth. As she walked down Rabbit Lane, Jack Rabbits jumped out from the brush to run across the road and scurry about. Her husband, Keith, and their sons hunted Jack Rabbit so that the family had meat on the dinner table. Today, their family grazes hundreds of beef cattle on their sprawling Erda acres. But in the days before big beef, Jack Rabbit was the staple meat, and Rabbit Lane had an abundance of them. If the settlers had a cow, it was usually one milk cow. In the days of her youth, frogs sang from the irrigation ponds and ditches and the soggy areas where springs percolated up in the fields. Now the rabbits and frogs are all gone.

"I think it was DDT," she guessed.

Nina's son, Charley, attributes the disappearance of the animals to the loss of their habitat through urbanization. The Tooele valley floor was once covered with Greasewood, ideal Jack Rabbit habitat. Greasewood made way for grass pasture and cultivated farms. The valley is dotted with natural springs, which the settlers diverted into ponds and control-released into irrigation ditches. The ditches were often collocated with cedar post fence lines, where the native grasses grew tall, forming perfect habitat for Ring-necked Pheasants. The grasses formed ideal year-round cover for pheasants, perfect for nesting, and protecting against Winter's harshness, when heavy snows would bend the grasses over, forming insulating lodges.

"Me and the boys would catch our limits, and then some, every hunting season, sometimes 20 pheasants a day each," Charley reported.

Mallard ducks throve in the ditches. Although Erda remains a rural area in many respects, the spring-fed ponds and irrigation ditches that once proliferated have vanished in favor of the piped ditch, the pressurized irrigation system, and the rural home lot. With them have gone most of the wildlife. I have never seen a Jack Rabbit in Erda.

On a Sunday morning as I sat reading scripture and enjoying the quiet, I was suddenly startled by the too-close reports of shotgun blasts. Jumping to the living room window, I observed a hunter in camouflage standing in the tall grass not more than 150 feet from our house, his shotgun at the ready, following a pheasant as it flew past the house. "Bang!" he fired again, practically pointing at the house. I rushed out the front door and shouted, "What the hell do you think you're doing? You are way too close to our house, and you don't have permission to hunt here!" Not waiting for his answer, I hurried back inside to call the Sheriff. I felt both angry and dumbstruck that this hunter would be so careless as to hunt this close to a house, even aiming toward the house as his bird flew by. Angie was furious, too. The Sheriff's deputy soon arrived, took my report, and had me sign the citation as the witness. County ordinance prohibits hunting any closer than 600 feet from a building. I noticed that the hunter was allowed to take his pheasant, and I never heard from the court, the same court in which I prosecuted crimes occurring in nearby Tooele.

A few weeks later Charley shot a pheasant in his field, from where it flew across Church Road and landed in the tall grass near our house. Charley strode into the grass, with his shotgun on his shoulder, looking for the injured bird. Angie, not realizing he was Charley, and with the memory of the reckless hunter still fresh, flew out the door shouting, "Hey! Take your gun and get out of there, away from our house! You're too close! There are children here!"

"It's okay, Angie," Charley chuckled. "I shot the pheasant in my field and it managed to fly over here somewhere. I'm just looking. I won't be doing any shooting, I promise."

Angie was too upset to recover her calm and chit-chat with the neighbor. She just turned her back and stormed back into the house, leaving Charley to wonder at her distress.

Charley and Judy have been sweethearts since the third grade. As a young boy, Charley's church primary teacher, Margie, sometimes took the weekday primary class children to the neighborhood ponds to catch Bull Frogs. Margie took the children to her home, dressed the frogs, and fried up the plump frog legs.

"We *loved* eating frog legs," Charley reminisced.

Charley's great-grandfather Charlie was the father of nine sons. They hitched horses to the family wagon early in the morning and hunted about 15 miles from Erda to South Mountain, then 15 miles back, filling the wagon with Jack Rabbits and ducks. At the end of each hunt, they dressed their catch and hauled it to the train station, from where it was shipped to the Salt Lake valley markets. Rabbits and Mallard ducks each brought $1.50 a dozen, while the lesser ducks brought only $1.00 a dozen (Blue-wing Teal, Green-wing Teal, Gladwell, Norwegian, Bal Paint).

Joe and Charley both told me proudly that Erda, the name of Rabbit Lane's home town since 1880, means "the good earth" in German. I respected their love for their roots, but secretly wondered if the German word "erda" did not translate simply to "dirt." My admiration for these men has caused me to reflect that the quality of a community's soil is comprised not only of the ingredients of its dirt, but is enriched by the labor, the sacrifice, the contributions, and the love of the people that work the soil and raise their crops and rear their families. So, even if *erda* means simply *dirt*, or whether *Erda* hearkens back to the name of the Anglo-Saxon earth goddess, I believe that Charley and Joe are right. Erda is in fact the earth that surrounds and sustains and nurtures: the good earth.

Wind

I know what makes the wind. Trees!
(Laura-3)

The big wind came in the night. I awoke suddenly to hear the chicken coop's sheets of corrugated metal roofing flapping and grinding as if under torture, while asphalt shingles beat on the roof over my head with the steady staccato of automatic weapons fire. It felt like an earthquake, not mere air, shook my bed even as it shook the house. Violent gusts of wind flung buckets of rain against my bedroom windows. The house shuddered as each new gale struck, lashing it with rain. Sleep was impossible.

A sudden tapping on my shoulder combined with the night's frightful hours to make me start, my heart beating hard against my ribs. The low silhouette at my bedside seemed a dark specter for a moment, then resolved itself into a small, scared boy.

"If you want, you can make a bed on the floor," I offered to Caleb (2), perceiving his unuttered question.

I rose to help him fold his jumbled quilt in two, half for a cushion, half for a cover, and to find a spare pillow. I would have found the floor hard, but he found it soft and soothing. Sooner than mine, his breath lengthened into the calm breathing of a serene and guiltless sleep. The wind and I kept company for another hour, until I would normally have awoken to venture out under the early-morning sky. But not this morning. On this morning, I stayed under the covers, insulating myself from the wrath of the sky's tantrum but still hearing its screams and sighs and gnashings.

Late the next morning, I ventured forth, under calm and sunny skies, to find sheets of mangled metal strewn about the lawn. Sections of Charley's wheel line lay twisted and broken, having been blown downhill across his fallow winter fields.

In the afternoon, ominous clouds, charcoal black, formed quickly in the west, obscuring the mountains. The wind began to blow hard, with sharp bursts like shock waves that knocked me off balance. The dark sky suddenly descended to the ground, like a raptor swooping down to claw the earth and its prey, then rising with clutched talons to scatter furious dust in the wild wind. The wind blasted through the trees, whipping them meanly, bending and straining them almost to breaking. Thunder followed close on the heels of the lighting, shaking us with its too-close sonic booms.

From where I stood on the front porch, the wind drove the hurting rain like pins into my sensitive skin. To the boys, however, the squall was a great adventure. Brian (12) ran unrestrained over the grass, wearing his Roswell alien Halloween mask, partly to shield his face from the rain, but also to participate in a phenomenon so strange and alien, so electric and exciting. John (4) ran the length of the porch and leapt high and arcing into the wind and rain, then ran and rolled somersaults and cartwheels in the wet grass, giggling and shrieking with the sensory thrill of the storm. Caleb stood by me on the porch, his arms clutching my leg.

"I don't like it when the sky burps," he complained. "I don't like it when the clouds bump heads."

From an angry, lowering sky, clouds hurled lightning at the obscured mountain peaks, and thunder enveloped all with its deep, echoing booms. Pea-sized hail suddenly inundated Erda, as if poured from some celestial bucket. It bounced off the grass and appeared as a school of thousands of tiny white fish jumping up through the surface of a vast green sea.

Gusts blowing down through mountain passes through the Tooele valley can top 85 miles per hour. One storm blew a section of vinyl siding off the chimney, 30 feet high. The warranty had lapsed, and an insurance claim would barely clear the deductible. I called a few contractors, but the job was too small for them to bother with given the active construction market. I sure did not know how to fix it.

I looked up at the bare spot every evening driving home from work. I could see it from walking on Rabbit Lane. On Saturdays, working around the yard, I looked up frequently to see the patch of exposed plywood. It bothered me to have my house scarred.

One day I announced, "I have figured out how to fix the siding on the chimney!"

I tied all the siding pieces together with a timber hitch, and tied the two parts of the extension ladder together so they would not slip when pulled from the top. I climbed up onto the porch roof, pulling my bundle of siding pieces behind me. From the porch roof, I pulled the ladder up by the top rungs. My knots kept the ladder from sliding apart into two useless pieces that would leave me stranded on the roof. A two-by-four scrap nailed into the porch roof kept the ladder from sliding off. From there, I climbed the ladder onto the steep gable roof above my bedroom. I pulled the siding and ladder up behind me again. Nailing another two-by-four to the roof, I leaned the ladder against the chimney. I snapped each piece of siding into the other, pulling nails from my utility belt to secure them against other blasts of wind sure to come.

When I told Angie, "I'm going to fix the siding today," she replied softly "Okay" without looking at me and without saying another word. She began working madly about the house, appearing to pay no mind to the nail pounding. She mostly vacuumed. When I walked into the house two hours later, the siding project done, she rushed over to me and hugged me tight. She half-whispered half-sobbed, "I was too scared to go outside. I did not want to see you fall off the roof. I was frantic inside."

"Sweetheart," I replied with a little less feeling than I should have shown, "I had planned it all out, down to the nail. And it worked out just as I planned."

Of course, it could have turned out tragically, not just as I planned, had any little thing gone awry. I know several people who have injured themselves terribly from falling off their roofs. Remembering that, I just held her for a while, then moved on to the next project. When the next big storms blew off large sections of siding, I hired a contractor.

We know the familiar, iconic image of a breeze caressing golden wheat fields into "endless waves of grain." The ripe wheat ebbs and flows in swirls and waves as if alive and dancing in a liquid sea. Less familiar is the effect of a strong wind blowing across a field of harvested grain. I witnessed this one morning as the wind ripped around and through millions of short, stiff stalks, rustling and whipping their tattered and peeling layers with the sound of a heavy rain on the road, though the sky was dry. It frightened me to hear this enormous sound emanating from a flat field that held only wheat stalk stubble. As I walked nearby, the wind blew in frenetic, jumbled gusts so that no matter which direction I walked the biting winter wind buffeted my face.

Walking on a calmer winter day, the wind whistled dissonantly over and around live power lines stretched between antique blue glass insulators bolted to wooden cross-members mounted on tree poles soaked in pungent creosote.

In Summer, the wind blows frequently and for days, hot and dry from the south, at times blowing in great, house-shaking gusts. It does no good to open the windows for air. The air conditioner whines all night, moving the air a little, but bringing scant relief from the heat. I cannot sleep. Fine brown dust appears mysteriously in the corners of the closed windows, as if sprinkled by a Brownie in the night.

WIND

Nothing frightens me like
Wind.
A million whispers rushing
through a million forest leaves,
coalescing to crescendo and
a horrifying howl,
a gusty, sibilant scream,
a prolonged and violent accusation.
Wind
rattles my home,
shakes my bed,
shivers my nerves.
Wind
disturbs my well-gelled image,
exposing me: unkempt and scattered.
Wind
bellows dirt into my eyes and nose and throat;
I squint and cough and curse.
Wind
batters and tears as
I fight for footing.
Wind
whips up the storms
that stir the deep and hidden things,
monsters that slink mysteriously about,
revealing themselves in
cursings and covetings, in
lashings and lustings.
Give me
Driving Rain,
Booming Thunder,
Sizzling Lightning,
Desiccating Sun:
I embrace them.
But keep away the
Wind.

Of Marriage, Lies, and Promises

Marriage is a long, clumsy dance, with frequent stepping on toes.

I sat on the couch next to Angie while she held baby Hyrum over her shoulder. Feeling romantic, I put my arm around her neck and shoulders. My hand alighted upon a cold, wet spot of vomited breast-milk on the burp cloth draped over her shoulder. She laughed at how "romantic" it was. I joined in the chuckle after a momentary shiver of "ew."

Angie and I both speak Portuguese, which has come in handy when we want to talk without the children knowing what we are talking about. For example, "fazer marmelada" (to make jam) is continental Portuguese slang for "to make love." The children have heard some words like "filme" or "video" so often, associated with the ensuing entertainment decision, to know that their parents are talking about whether to watch a movie tonight. They no sooner hear the word than they clamor, "Yea, let's watch a movie!" Fortunately, the children have not caught on to the meaning of "marmelada."

One particular word has saved Mom and Dad significant embarrassment during church services. The Portuguese slang "chi-chi" (pronounced "she-she") is the equivalent of the English "pee-pee." So, during church, when a young child needs to go to the bathroom and calls out unabashedly in the middle of the sermon, "I need to go chi-chi!" no one but us knows what is going on. By logical extension, "chi-chi" has also become the code word for penis. I have no idea why a little boy would choose a church sermon as the time to loudly announce "my chi-chi itches!" This code word has kept my face from flushing numerous times.

Another code word—a favorite for its embarrassment-saving quality—is the English word "this." Angie has breast-fed our children for up to two years each, much longer than Western modernism finds fashionable, and past the time when some children can speak quite well. When one of our infants was hungry, Mom would ask, "Do you want this?" and hold the child's face to her breast, where the child would suckle and satisfy both physical hunger and the desire for comfort and closeness with a loving mother. The word "this" came to mean the opportunity for an infant's meal at mother's breast. Eventually, the word "this" came to be equated simply with the word "breast" in the child's mind, and "thises" meant "breasts."

"I want thises, Mom," became a frequent toddler's petition echoing throughout the house, and meant "I'm hungry, Mom." Church can be a chore for young children, trying their patience and causing them to raise their impatient little voices with their various wants and discomforts. More than one of our tired and hungry toddlers has been known to yell during church services, "I want thises!" And no one knew.

Abraham Lincoln once described that attitude that furthers slavery and oppression with these words: "You grow the food, and I'll eat it." Too often I see his words replayed in American homes: "You cook the food and I'll eat it. You wash the clothes and I'll wear them. You tend the children and I'll hang out with my buddies." Partners in marriage are not partners unless they share their burdens as well as their pleasures. Each must uphold the other, not live off the other's labors without contributing their own. Living in ease while our partner toils under his or her loads is no partnership, no marriage, but a mockery of that partner and of the relationship.

I often take the garbage out as I begin my walk on Rabbit Lane. I first open the door a crack so that I can easily pull it open with gloved hands each holding bulging bags. This way I can minimize my effort, grabbing the bags and leaving through the door with one fluid motion. As I reach for the door knob, however, the bulky bag pushes the door shut at the very instant that my hand seizes the door knob. My repeated attempts to use minimal effort in making a single trip to the garbage can end consistently with this result. Every time, in fact. I have tried reaching slowly for the door knob, as if to grab hold of the door knob before the door awoke to the pressuring bag and swung shut. I have tried the sudden approach, as if to surprise the door, thinking that perhaps the momentary backswing of the bag would give my hand a split-second advantage. Always the result is the same: the click of the latch as my hand touches metal. I laughed the first time, but soon succumbed to cursing. It would have been better to put one bag down, open the door, pick up the bag, walk through the door, put the same (or another) bag down, close the door, then take both bags to the can. Not fluid, perhaps, but still simple, efficient, and methodical. Nonetheless, I keep reaching for the door with the bag in my hand, only to have the bag push the door shut and stymie my plan. Why do I think the result will change merely by virtue of repeated vain attempts? Albert Einstein said something about that. Anymore, I follow the multi-step approach, with consistent success. But I find myself still fighting the urge to see if I can win the contest.

Another night of chasing after children to brush their teeth and get to bed.
"Brush your teeth," I commanded Brian (10).
He looked up at me sincerely: "I did."

I knew he had not, and asked him, "Are you telling me the truth?"

"Yes," he replied innocently.

I deliberated for a moment about my response. Should I confront and accuse? Should I teach? Should I just walk away in disgust or exasperation?

"Good," I said, "because I believe you, and I would not want to believe a lie, especially from my son."

I told him that I knew when someone was lying, like when Carli had told him about the rabbit that had killed their cow, or the witch that lived under Witch's Tree, or the piranhas that infested the irrigation ditch on Rabbit Lane.

Brian turned his eyes to the floor, then shuffled off to the bathroom where he brushed his teeth. I worried that I had hurt his feelings, and hoped I had not been too harsh. His lie had been less about his honesty than about his independence. At least I had not labeled him a liar. I had just tried to teach him that it was important to be honest, especially with his dad. After he brushed his teeth, I thanked him for being honest with me and tucked him into bed.

"Good night, son," I said. "I love you."

The older our house becomes, the more frequently the toilets back up. I have wondered if the sewer pipes might be slowly gathering a collection of hair clips, Band-Aids, dental floss, and toothpaste caps flushed by curious children who enjoy seeing the objects swirl around noisily and disappear. One afternoon as I talked with Angie in the kitchen, an indignant Laura (14) marched in and reported,

"The toilet is *plugged*! And *I* didn't do it. By the awful smell it must have been plugged all day."

I knew that the offending toilet was in the "family bathroom" shared by Laura with her three younger brothers. Laura clearly believed that because she had not plugged the toilet, the unplugging of the toilet was not her job, but ours. Her duty was merely to inform us, and she had discharged it. I reinforced her belief by reporting to the malodorous bathroom and plunging out the toilet. (I did not know for years that Laura had tried to plunge the toilet, without success, before reporting it to me.)

Sometimes I feel like all I do is walk around unplugging other people's plugged toilets. Metaphorical toilets are plugging all day every day at my work, where people seem to line up at my office door to report toilets backing up and overflowing, and to suggest that I should do something about it. All too often I thank them and run for the plunger (in the shape of a phone call or a demand letter or a hastily called meeting). If we each plunged the clogs we make or find as soon as we make or find them, the world might smell a lot better. We would all share often unpleasant duties, no one carrying disproportionate burdens or unpleasantness.

Angie took the children to the Deseret Industries (DI) thrift store to shop for children's clothing. John (7) came home with a bag full of clothes that looked good and fit him well. But Angie had found nothing for Caleb (5). His husky build was difficult to shop for.

"We'll have to get you some clothes somewhere else; maybe some overalls," his mom reassured him.

"Can you get me some on your way home from your date tonight?" Caleb inquired hopefully.

"Maybe," Mom said noncommittally.

On the way home from our date later that night, Angie suggested, "Why don't we stop and see what Cal-Ranch has."

We stewed and debated over prices and styles, but finally chose a pair of denim overalls.

The moment we walked in the kitchen door at home, Caleb came running to the kitchen, calling hopefully, "Did you keep your promise, Mom?"

Mom certainly had not promised him anything, but he had taken her noncommittal "maybe" as a promise. Excitedly Caleb pulled on the overalls.

Standing very proud, he showed them to everybody and exclaimed happily, "Mom kept her promise!"

How relieved we felt that we had stopped at least to look, that we had managed to not disappoint our small child, and that we had kept our "promise."

Birdhouses

There is no sweeter sound than raindrops on the rooftop.

I love birdhouses and birdfeeders. Probably because I love birds. Their often sweet, sometimes cacophonic twittering and chirping brings me happiness. Providing them with an endless supply of seeds brings me happiness. They gather at the feeders on my grape trellis by the hundreds: House Finch, House Sparrow, Pine Siskin, Redwing Blackbird, Mourning Dove, and on occasion some less-often-seen species like Brown Cow Bird, Indigo Bunting, Black-headed Grosbeak, Bullock's Oriole, and Towhee. One Common Sparrow shares the same general markings as its hundred cousins, but appears to be an albino morph, nearly white. The Western Meadowlark, Western King Bird, and American Robin sing, fly, and hop around nearby, but do not come to the trellis, being mostly insect and worm eaters.

Beyond the birds, I enjoy the sight of the little wooden birdhouses mounted on the beams of my grape trellis. I call it a grape trellis not because it grows grape vines, but because I built it for grape vines and wish it grew grape vines. For reasons peculiar to the Erda soil, or to my cultivation of that soil, grapes have never grown up my grape trellis, though I have tried many times with several varieties. After ten years of false starts, the only thing growing on my grape trellis is bird houses. Each of my children has assembled one or more birdhouses and attached them to the trellis.

I decided one year to make large bird houses and mount them on poles throughout the yard. Not content to purchase plastic models from Wal-Mart, and unwilling to pay for more expensive wooden models, I resolved to construct my own. I drew out several designs that departed from the standard models. In other words, no squares or rectangles, but unusual trapezoids and even a circle. I constructed interior frames on the workbench in my shed, then attached gray, weather-worn siding harvested from discarded pallets. No master woodworker, I awkwardly attached the siding to the frame, and the roof to the house. Before attaching the roof, I drilled a hole in a bottom frame cross member, inserted a 4-inch-long bolt-head screw, and with a ratchet secured the house frame to a post.

The posts came in various forms from several places. We found one while on a drive by Black Rock, on the shore of the Great Salt Lake. The post had washed up on the rocks, worn smooth by years of buffeting by wind, sand, and salt water. (The salt content of the Great Salt Lake exceeds 25%, while the oceans average about 5%.) We tied the post to the top of our car and brought it home. Another was an old cedar fence post I found lying broken and discarded in a ditch by the side of the road. Four-by-four lumber also makes excellent posts. I made a post for each of my four birdhouse models, cementing three of the posts in a cluster in the bird house garden, with the fourth nearby behind the picket fence. The fence runs 40 feet from the grape trellis along the garden border to the birdhouse garden. I made the pickets from old pallets, too. I seem never interested in building the same thing twice, and built only one of each birdhouse model. But seeing them each morning on their tall posts as I begin and end my walks on Rabbit Lane brings to me a simple satisfaction. I would be happier were they inhabited by more birds and fewer yellow jackets.

Trees

Boogers are sticky!
(Hannah-3)

Dead and dying poplars stand along the ditch bank on Rabbit Lane, like sentries propped up against battles long ago lost and won. Many branches, devoid of leaves, poke absently out and up like ten thousand fingers on stubby arms. On the oldest, the only leaves huddle close to the trunk, near the base. Finches and sparrows hop happily amidst the morass for some purpose unknown to me, or for no purpose. Their nests lie hidden somewhere in dense bushes; no seeds or insects can be found in the spiky tree stubble. But safety from cats and falcons the branches certainly provide.

Many of these soldiers that stood for so long have fallen, in their last battle, to the chainsaw. The track-hoe needed to straddle both ditch banks in order to dredge the ditch, to clear the way for the pipe that now encases the water forever, and the trees were in the way.

The water will still flow, but undrunk by the birds, unswum by the muskrats, uncluttered by watercress, and unheard and unseen by me.

Certain trees sprout up spontaneously in Erda, most notably the Siberian Elm, but also the Boxelder, the Silver Maple, the Cottonwood, and the Russian Olive. The elms, growing several feet each year, even with no water but the occasional scant rain, quickly reach the height of the power lines on Church Road, Erda Way, and other local roads. The power company cannot countenance this conflict, and periodically appears with its boom trucks to cut the trees back. The word "prune" would unduly dignify their work. With little thought for the structural integrity of the trees, or for their aesthetic value as roadside amenities, the company arborists slice away all interior limbs nearing the lines, leaving behind huge V-shaped gaps through which the lines pass unencumbered. A tree slightly off-center from the power lines avoids the V-cut in favor of the total side slough, in which all limbs on one side of the tree are cut away. The resulting trees, planted by prior generations of farmers or sprouting spontaneously in decades past, are both ugly and ridiculous in appearance and impotent in aesthetic quality. Staring at the butchered trees, I wonder what holds them together, how the massive trunks do not split down the middle, away from the repulsive presence of the power lines. Public complaints against this practice are met with the company's stock answer: *We have a franchise.* They deal with tree conflicts in whatever manner they see fit, which means cheap and easy. Also, the company provides no advanced notice of its arrival on a given day to perform its rough, hasty operations. The tall, rounded canopies become gaping Vs or Us before one has a chance to utter one's feeble protest.

The property we purchased was devoid of vegetation but tall, wild grass and a lone old apple tree. Just before the deer hunt during our first year in Erda, a woman stopped her car on Church Road by the apple tree and started picking its red delicious apples. Angie called for me to come and see, which meant that I was to do something about it.

I waded through the tall grass toward the tree, greeted the woman, and stated politely, "Um, you're picking apples from my apple tree."

Surprised and a little embarrassed, she looked up at me, then toward my house, and replied, "You own this land?"

"Yes," I said patiently, "this is my land, that is my house, and this is my apple tree."

She looked worriedly down at the paper shopping sac full of apples. "What should I do with all of these apples I picked?" she asked.

"We're so used to picking apples off the old church tree to take on the hunt, it didn't occur to me that someone else owned it now."

Appreciative of Mayla's humility, I was happy to respond, "You should keep those apples and pick more so you can fill the bag. Enjoy them, and good luck on the deer hunt."

My response seemed to surprise her even more than my initial approach. She thanked me, picked a few more apples, and drove away. Mayla turned out to be a neighbor, married into a family of other neighbors with whom I would become close friends and who, in the coming years, would fill my empty sac many times over.

When we moved to Erda, the venerable apple tree was suffering from years of neglect, and badly needed pruning. Suckers had grown ten feet or more straight up from the fruit-bearing branches. The Utah State University extension literature said that, when dealing with a neglected tree, it was unhealthy to prune more than one-third of the tree in any one year. Pruning more than one-third of the tree would trigger a shock reaction, and the tree would redirect its energy away from producing fruit toward recovering from the aggressive pruning. Following the pruning instructions, I cut off the small branches growing up from the lateral limbs, so that the branches and buds growing out and down would bear the fruit. Still, I could not resist climbing high in the tree and removing some of the excessive top growth. I also removed some interior limbs that crowded the tree and made it nearly impossible to climb. The children were happy to have a climbing tree, and called frequently to me from its highest branches, "Look at me, Daddy!" The tree accepted my pruning without noticeable distress.

Like the children, I myself enjoyed the view from 20 feet up in the tree. I could see for 12 miles from the blue-gray waters of the Great Salt Lake to the tops of the Oquirrh mountains near Tooele. These views from the top of the old apple tree worked their way into one of the songs that came to me, slowly over the course of weeks and months, during my walks on Rabbit Lane.

When I first approached the task of pruning the apple tree, it was so tall and choked that I could not reach the highest branches. So I purchased a telescoping pruner with both pruning and saw blades at the end. The pruning blades worked by pulling on a long rope that brought the blades against the branch being pruned. Standing on a ten-foot step ladder with the pruner extended another 15 feet, I managed to reach the highest suckers and cut them off. The strain on my back, neck, shoulders, arms, and legs from leaning against the ladder and pulling on the rope and craning my neck kept me from pruning for more than an hour at a time.

During my walks on Rabbit Lane after pruning the apple tree, I began to ponder the concept of pruning a tree's growth so as to produce the tastiest, biggest, most accessible fruit. Was there a principle here? Certainly an agricultural principle. But what about a human principle? Of course, the principle of knowing people by their fruits, or deeds, is millennia old. Was it through good pruning practices that people produced the best personal fruits? I began to consider what traits, tendencies, and weaknesses I might prune from my own personality, to consider ways in which I had grown that did not produce the most pleasant fruit. I began to perceive that my fruit was sometimes shriveled and bitter, unpleasant to those with whom I shared myself. I needed to prune my soul of anger, of jealously, of selfishness, of pride, of fear, of shame—of many other qualities that did not bring joy to those partaking of me.

Changing the human soul is not easy or quick work. I cannot prune my entire self-tree at once without harmful shock to my core systems, without regression and failure. Some branches I would not be able to reach by myself, and would need the assistance of trained self-tree therapists. I would have to learn what tools were available for pruning, and learn how to use them. I would have to take care not to leave torn branches, open wounds, dripping sap, or stripped bark. And pruning for too long would leave me fatigued and in pain. But I could identify one or two errant branches at a time and lop them off, beginning to make way for the sun to nourish the rest of the tree and begin to fill its fruit with swelling sweetness. When those cuts healed, I could identify a few more branches ready for pruning. With regular, enlightened pruning, my self-tree might someday become more shapely, and my fruit more sweet. While this analogy may seem cliché to some, it was a new insight to me.

Our experiment with goats was hard on the old apple tree. Tiring of the wiry grass, and liking the smell and taste of the apple bark, they began to nibble at it. One day they discovered that they could grasp a loose shred of bark at the tree's base between their teeth and gums and yank upwards, pulling off long strips of juicy bark. In one day, within only a few minutes, they managed to strip nearly all the bark off the first four feet of the old tree's trunk. I ran to the tree and shooed the goats angrily away with sticks, painted the bare wood with black sealing pitch, and wrapped the trunk with old chain link fence. But the damage had been irretrievably done. The tree made a valiant effort the following Spring, putting out a few leaves and blossoms, but I am sad to say that the old apple tree died. Though it would not help the tree, I decided I had had enough of the full-grown goats that seemed capable of jumping any fence, pushing their way through any hole, and stripping the bark off my fruit trees. I gave them away. Later, we brought home some baby pygmy goats: much sweeter creatures.

APPLE TREE

The tree has grown
unpruned
for some seasons now. Golden
apples hang unpicked,
falling one by one
as breezes blow
and neighbors jostle, to cider
in the soil, enriching
first yellow jackets,
then slugs and worms and grass
still green in Fall.

The old brick bungalow,
white paint peeling,
has gone unlived in
for many years now. The smoke
is stilled, and the chimney soot
is old and cold. She was
born here, birthed
in her mama's brass bed.
She played in the ditch,
munched raw oats, picked
nosegays of daisies and asters,
and planted pips
from a golden apple
in a secret spot of soil.

The misted vase has sat
empty upon the table
for so very long now. Dust has settled
into stem and petal etchings, caught
upon dry, white mineral rings. Outside,
beside bungalow brick,
hyacinths, daffodils, tulips,
irises rise in rows
to bloom each Spring,
bidden only
by sun and warm soil.

Wandering

Roger Baker

1.I oft-en go wan-der-ing in - to the gar - den to

climb in - to ap - ple tree tops where I feel safe from the world be -

low. From high in my ap - ple tree I can see the

2

Wandering

sun - rise, the mist - y mount - ains far a - way, and taste the salt - y

o - cean breeze.

Pno.

2. I wander throuth city streets, noisy and crowded.
The church welcomes me into its calm and silence, where I kneel to pray.
A rainbow light streams from a brilliant sun through stained-glass rose,
Down on people everywhere, kneeling in their search for truth.

3. I often lay wondering: "What is my purpose?"
This I know: I will be kind and show respect to all who come my way.
For love is a power that opens minds and softens hearts,
Nurtures children, makes a home, beautifies and sweetens.

4. I lie in the cool Autumn grass gazing at Heaven.
The night sky, a sea of stars, rests like a blanket on the world below.
From under the starry sky, I can see the crescent moon,
Hear the owl call from its tree, feel the dew upon my face.

Of Death, Swords, and a Bear Hunt

Wow, Caleb, you have lots of brains.
No, I don't! I only have one brain!
I mean, you have lots of sense.
I don't have any cents, only three pennies.
(Caleb-3 with Laura)

"I hate it when things die!" Erin (7) sobbed bitterly.

I have tried to teach the children not to hate because hating makes you feel hateful. But I understood her sentiment: her pet goat had died. She did not want to feel the deep grief of the loss of things loved.

"We never even gave him a name," she lamented. "We just called him Goatie."

Goatie was a cute kid, with white and black and brown splotches, and almost no ears: a La Mancha. The floppy-eared goats are Nubians. Goatie had seemed alright, although he coughed a lot. One Saturday Erin found him lying on the ground, too weak to get up or even move his head. She ran to me, crying that Goatie was sick and that I needed to call Harvey or the vet. I looked at Goatie helplessly; I called Harvey, but he was not home. Erin got some paper towels and held the kid while I gently wiped slimy mucous from his nose. I rubbed his side hard and told Erin and Laura (4) to rub too, to help Goatie warm up. After all we could do, we laid Goatie in the warm sun and put hay and water by his head.

An hour later Goatie was dead. We watched him kick weakly into the air, in the death throws I had only heard about. Then he collapsed and lay still. Erin screamed and sobbed. I picked Goatie up and held him on my lap, rocking. The girls stood by, crying, and I put my arms around them and pulled them close to me and to Goatie.

"I'm sad, too," I whispered sincerely. "I'm awfully sad."

We cried and rubbed his fur and head.

"Why did Goatie have to get sick and die?" Erin asked accusingly. "Why did he have to go away?"

I did not try to answer her questions. I did not have the answers. I just held her close and said, "It's ok to cry. Goatie was special, and now he's gone and we miss him and are sad. So it's ok to cry. I'm sad, too."

After a few minutes, I ventured, "We need to take care of him. We need to bury him in the earth. That's where his body needs to rest."

Erin nodded her head, her face red and swollen from sobbing.

"Would you like to have a funeral?" I asked.

The children all nodded their heads.

I stood, gently lifting Goatie. Brian (10) joined the girls and followed me to the garden. Brian and I dug a deep hole while the girls watched over Goatie so no flies would land on him.

"It's time," I said, sadly but firmly. "Say good-bye one more time."

The children petted him again, then I laid Goatie in the hole, on a bed of straw the children had made. Erin would not let me put dirt on Goatie. She asked her mom for an old sheet and used it to cover the animal. She said it would keep him warm and clean. Erin and Laura placed beautiful little roses on Goatie's blanket, roses that Angie let them pick from her new rose garden that we had planted for our anniversary.

"Goatie will like to eat them, huh?" Laura asked hopefully.

I offered a simple funereal prayer. Brian took a shovel and lightly placed dirt over Goatie's blanket until it was covered. He filled the hole, leaving a mound above the grave. Erin had saved the most beautiful rose, a crimson bud, to place on top of the grave. Somehow, the funeral had helped us all feel better. But we will miss Goatie. He was our friend.

Soon after, Erin found a little bird dead in the grass. She was amazed and grateful that the cats had not found it and torn it to pieces, leaving its feathers scattered across the lawn. She scooped up the little bird and determined to find a peaceful resting place. Even if the cats never found it, she did not want it to just lay there and turn into bones with nobody caring. Erin had a feeling that the little bird was somehow still alive and still had feelings, that it would still want to be cared for. She laid the bird against the forked trunk of one of our trees, made it a blanket of fresh, cool grass, and placed a flat rock over it, leaning against the tree. She showed me how she had taken care of the dead little bird.

"It's resting, sort of like Jesus, under his blanket behind the stone."

I could not suppress a smile. "Thank you for taking care of the little bird, sweetie. Little birds are special creatures, to be taken care of." I knelt down and hugged her softly, hoping she knew I loved her.

My children have seen many animals die. Some of their kittens have died, and the children have cried and buried the kittens with roses and blankets of grass. Guinea pigs and gerbils. Another goat.

And Teancum killed more chickens. We always take care of them, and we always feel sad. I mentioned to the children that my grandmother Dora had died because she was very old. Laura (4) became frightened that she would die soon, too. But I reassured her that she would not die: she would live a long, happy life. Laura appeared relieved and happy.

For a short time, Brian (11) kept Firebelly Newts in a ten-gallon aquarium. Their glossy black bodies were striped with scarlet. They paddled lazily around the plants and rocks, rising when necessary to breathe. Floating plants and wooden disks allowed the newts to rest with their heads above water when it suited them. After several weeks, Brian was distressed to find that the newts were disappearing, one at a time. They must have climbed up the water circulation tube and dropped from the aquarium tank onto the floor. We found a few newts in time to save them from drying out. While cleaning his room weeks later, Brian and his mother found the missing newts shriveled up and dead in the corners of his room.

When I returned from my walk one morning, Angie told me that she had screamed with a terrible start after almost stepping on a newt slowly crawling across the dark kitchen floor, forty feet and one floor away from Brian's room. Somehow it had made its way down the carpeted hall and stairs, then across the tiled den to the kitchen. Quivering, she had hesitantly picked up the slimy animal and dropped it back into the aquarium. She screamed again upon finding another live newt in the children's bathroom amongst the bath toys scattered on the floor.

"Why am *I* the one that always finds these disgusting creatures dead and dying around the house?" she complained with a grin.

We did our best to block all the aquarium escape routes, to no avail. All the newts found their way out, to their demise.

Caleb (3) engaged me in a playful duel with his plastic cutlass after work one evening. Jabbing me with the point, he declared, "I keeled you!"

"Oh yeah?" I responded.

"Yeah," he challenged.

"Well, take that!" I said as I thrust with my plastic coat hanger.

We hacked and wacked at each other, then Caleb declared, "I keeled you again!"

"Oh yeah, well I keeled you!" I parried.

Caleb laughed and put down his sword, suddenly aware of the irony, "We *both* keeled!"

Even when our game was over, Caleb kept "keeling" everybody, and everything, including chairs, walls, couches, bookshelves, and the wood stove: "I keeled you, chair!"

Working at City Hall ten or more hours a day during the week, Saturday was my day to mow and edge the lawn, weed and tend the garden, fix a broken door knob or sprinkler or chicken coop door, and perhaps make something like a birdhouse or a section of picket fence. It seemed to become a weekly occurrence for John (7), Caleb (5), and Hyrum (2) to approach me with a humble, pleading, "Daddy, can you make me a sword?" I could swear that I had just made a sword last week for one child or the other.

"Why do you need a *new* sword?" I would ask.

"Well," the child would respond. "The one you made last week is broked, and the one you made before that is losted."

I would grit my teeth and breathe deep, then, unable to resist their boyish requests, finally relent: "Sure, I'll help you make a sword."

We would march off to the shed, cut an appropriate length of one-by-two, cut one end to a point, and nail on a hilt.

While sometimes resenting these childish intrusions on my grown-up chores, I had nonetheless kept a supply of one-by-two lumber and box nails on hand so that I could respond to their frequent requests. Each boy's eyes and smile would widen with gratitude and admiration as I handed him the new sword. Running from the shed, he would call his brothers to see his new sword, then begin a three-way sparring match. Sometimes big brother Brian would join in. Often one of the boys would come to me in tears, explaining that his brother had hit him on the knuckles with his sword—*on purpose*. I would listen and sympathize, and he would run away to spar again, his knuckles still smarting but his wound healed.

We were reading the *Redwall* series at the time. As the boys ran and sparred, they yelled, "Redwall!" as their charging battle cry. They added to each sword thrust and parry a vocal "ching! ching!" of steel clanking on steel. Caleb swung with a loud "ching!" John and Hyrum responded with their own swings and "ching! ching!" Caleb had taken to sleeping with his sword. At night, lying in his bed, Caleb more than once suddenly burst out with, "I am Mathias!" or "Long live the King!"

Those little boys soon grew up enough to make their own swords. They did not ask me to make new swords any more. They still had a frequent need for new swords, and I kept lumber and nails on hand for that purpose. As I prepare to mow the lawn on a Saturday morning, I first must clear the yard of the variety of weapons: swords, spears, axes, daggers, machine guns, pistols, and Star Wars light sabers. Picking up these weapons, I find that part of me is glad that the boys no longer bother me weekly to make their new swords, while another part of me misses helping them make the tools of their imagination and play. Perhaps my feelings will always be mixed as the passage of time relieves me of both my old burdens and my old pleasures, invariably to be replaced with new ones.

Play comes hard to me. Play is not my natural mode of operation or expression. But one day I decided to play, to take the children on a pretend journey through the forest and into the mountains, on a bear hunt. Shod in work boots and armed with knife and staff, I became Big Chief Daddy. Caleb (3), perceiving some fanciful change in the air, became suddenly serious, and donned his wooden dagger and a rough-sewn pouch in which to collect treasures.

Caleb stated solemnly to Laura (7), "Squaws can't hunt; only braves."

Only mildly annoyed, Laura shot back, "I'm coming anyway."

Of course, she was invited. All in a line and ready for adventure, we began our march through the tall grass of the Great

Plains. The grass grew to over four feet, taller than all of the children. We chanted impromptu marching songs as we blazed our trail through the grass, stopping every so often to look for bears.

I placed John (5) in charge of finding water, vital for any expedition. He brought a water bottle. He also brought some nuts and crackers in case the hunt was unsuccessful. Caleb was to use his dagger to cut meat for roasting, when we caught it. Laura was the fire master, with tinder and flint. She would roast our meat to perfection.

Meandering through the grassy plains, we arrived at Clay Hill, and started our mountain climb, resting at the top to admire the mountain top view. The Great Salt Lake shone distantly as a glistening gray-blue ribbon on the horizon where the grass met the sky. The tall weeds on the clay mound became a pine forest. Resuming our trek, we climbed down the mountain into the tall grass again, searching for our prey.

I halted suddenly and crouched, stopping our song and motioning for the children to be still and silent.

"There," I whispered. "Can you see? It's an enormous bear. Follow me, but be very quiet, and very careful."

We stalked through the grass like cats after voles. Without warning I jumped up, yelled, and hurled my staff, spear-like, toward the invisible giant bear. Cheering, I directed the wide-eyed Caleb to dress the bear.

"I'm famished," I told him.

He charged off through the grass while Laura cleared a fire ring, and we settled down to our feast.

That was our only bear hunt. Since then, we have searched instead for pretty leaves and berries, for striped Monarch caterpillars that elicit sighs of wonder, for Hawk Moths flying frenetically between Mimosa blossoms, for the occasional bright Western Tanager and the ubiquitous House Finch and House Sparrow, for the beautifully marked American Kestrel and the proud Red-tailed Hawk, for cattails that look like hot dogs on skewers, and for rocks with crystals or odd dimples that our fancy hoped were fossils millions of years old. Let the bears alone, magnificent creatures of the great American wild. We will be content with crackers and nuts and the view of nature around us. We will hunt only with our eyes. Our neighbor, Charley, can do the real hunting for all of us.

Of Light and Love

I need the light on to keep my eyes warm. (Caleb-3)
I need the light on to go to sleep because I can't see. (Hannah-3)

Early one morning I notice a light in the Weyland wheat field next to Rabbit Lane. The soft circle of lantern light bobs around over the newly-sprouted wheat, magically, as if without a master, seeming unattached to a farmer. The night sky begins to lighten, and I can see the dim outlines of a man checking the sprinkler heads on a wheel line.

Ron starts his big John Deere early, headlights blaring, before I can see its trademark green and yellow. The tractor pulls behind a homemade harrow: creosoted railroad ties loosely chained together with railroad spikes pounded through. The harrow tears at the rooted wheat chaff, spewing up dust that creeps over Rabbit Lane like a heavy, brown fog.

The day after Thanksgiving is a favorite day for the children and me, not because of bringing home a Christmas tree or putting up Christmas lights. Rather, it is because the "tree" of lights appears on Little Mountain in Tooele. The tree is a 30-foot-tall pole from which strings of over 300 incandescent light bulbs, circling the pole, are stretched at 45-degree angles and anchored to the ground. The lighted tree offers a steady beacon to the entire valley from Thanksgiving to New Year's Day. From the moment we round the point of the mountain after a jaunt to Salt Lake we see the tree, ten miles distant. "There it is!" the children shout upon first sighting it on our way home from Thanksgiving dinner. Walking on Rabbit Lane, I see the tree seemingly suspended in the dark sky, whether in the rain or snow or fog or cloudless sky. The tree has become a local icon. We look forward to seeing it, count on seeing it, every day, as part of our traditional holiday celebrations. As property owners and power company policies change, I hope the tree remains.

Wherever the sun and the earth come together, there is light and shadow. Light both dispels and creates darkness. Darkness both yields to and softens the effects of light. Neither light nor darkness exist alone. Each has an indispensable part in the creation and the qualities of the other. Each are perceived and measured in relation to the other. But light does not create shadow directly. The creation of a darkening shadow requires an intervening object, like a house, a tree, or a cloud. Light is dimmed only when something gets in the way.

We are all beings of relative light. To keep ourselves from dimming, we must choose to use our energies to keep objects and issues from intervening to cast their shadows. Ours is the choice not to darken others by imposing our wills, thus darkening ourselves. Be a light to others through kindness and service, by listening with empathy and without judgment, and with music and art.

The common Pill Bug, often called Potato Bug, is tank, infantry, and command center all in one. Bands of flexible armor enclose it from head to toe. Dozens of legs carry it along in a smooth glide. When threatened, it rolls up into an armor-plated sphere, protected from most predators (except those like me, a million times its size and weight). No other bug elicits such joyful cries from children with curious little fingers that pluck up the bugs and roll them around in the palms of their hands. No other bug is so successful at escaping its child captors, rolling easily out of palms into concealing grass.

As I put John (5) and Caleb (3) to bed, they each asked me plaintively, "Will you lay by me?" Their faces took on such dejected, mournful aspects, inducing increasingly severe pangs of guilt, until I relented, giving up my big-person plans. I laid myself down for a minute with one and then the other, arising from each bed with a whispered, "I love you." At the end of my evening, I retired to my own bed and found myself wishing that my wife would come and lie by me—she was with the baby. Don't we all want the comfort of having a friend to be with us and to show us tenderness? Unlike my sons, I did not ask for what I wanted.

At 13 months, Hyrum's first intelligible word was: "Daddy!" I derived special pleasure from his pronouncement, and reserved a special place in my heart for Hyrum, my sixth child. Though the older children clamored for the opportunity, I insisted on pushing little Hyrum in the jogger on Rabbit Lane. Wrapped in blankets against the cold, his little head bounced around from the roughness of the hard-packed washboard. Of course, I had a special place in my heart for each of my children, not just Hyrum. But Hyrum's place was his, occupied by no other.

When Angie became pregnant with our second child, Erin, I did not know if I would be able to find a place in my heart for her. Brian, our firstborn, was the only child I knew, and he filled my heart. How could I possibly make room in my heart for another child when I had given my whole heart to Brian? I found, however, that the moment Erin entered the world my heart grew to make plenty of room for her. I did not have to do anything but see her and hold her. The space in my heart that I had reserved for Brian did not diminish. Rather, my capacity to love suddenly expanded to include Erin.

It has been so with the birth of each of my seven children. I take no credit for it. It simply happened. I believe it is the nature of human parenthood to love and make room for our children as they come along. And there is no need to stop there. Despite a world filled with suffering and despair, we can make room in our hearts for neighbors, friends, congregants, and colleagues. We can make room for strangers and even enemies by granting that they were all newborn children once, loved tenderly by their mothers. They are all human beings that deserve a measure of respect. Perhaps the downtrodden deserve a greater portion of our kindness and respect, because for so long it has been denied them by so many. As a prosecutor, I found no strength or advantage in diminishing the humanity of the accused, and found no weakness in offering them my polite respect. I can loath acts of betrayal and injury without despising the person of the perpetrator. However generous you believe your heart should be, find someone that needs a friend and let your heart grow enough to make room for them.

We walked as a family on Rabbit Lane one Winter afternoon. Caleb (3) and John (5) ran ahead, whooping, kicking in the snow, thrilled to be alive. Erin (10) walked quietly beside me, and I reached down to take her gloved hand. She looked up at me and surprised me with a sincere smile and moist eyes. Something caused me to reflect that I do not reach for my daughter's hand often enough. She needs to know that her dad loves her and that she can safely anchor herself to me in the swelling, churning waters of her youth.

Hannah Joy, my youngest, continued to share the master bedroom with Angie and me long after she turned four. With six older brothers and sisters, the other bedrooms were cramped, and personalities sometimes clashed. Besides, Mom was not quite ready to send her last baby away. So Hannah slept on a mattress in a corner of our room, surrounded by her clothes and books and toys. With the passing weeks and months, Hannah's clothes and books and toys left their tidy places to join growing heaps rippling out from her bed into space that I considered mine, not hers. We tried to help her organize her things, but a small girl who changes outfits for entertainment is not easily contained. As the piles spread, my annoyance grew. I lie on my bed one night, in dim lamplight, looking around the room. Hannah's presence was everywhere: her scattered things. After several moments, I began to sense another presence, a subtle but clear awareness of my young daughter's life inside mine. She came from me. She was a part of me. I realized how sweet she was, with her pink pajamas and her pigtails, and her picture books on her pillow. My heart changed, and I fell asleep to the sound of her soft snoring.

Caleb's chubby cheeks were flushed red and streaked with new tears. Eighteen months old, he had been crying, again, over who knows what, and whining, again, in a language no one understood but him, if even him. He had been whining and crying much more frequently in recent months than he ever had during his first year. I felt frustrated by the nightly emotional breakdowns. It occurred to me as I walked on Rabbit Lane one morning that perhaps Caleb was complaining because he was growing old enough to want to communicate, that he was attempting to communicate, but that no one understood him. Perhaps he felt as frustrated as I did, if not more. That evening, as soon as he began to blubber nonsensical words, I turned toward him and listened with my eyes looking into his. While I did not understand a word he said, I showed him my genuine interest by listening. I also talked to him, not thinking he would understand, saying things like, "You sure are a cute little boy," or "It's been a long day; you must be tired." To my amazement, I found that he could understand much of what I said, and responded with nods and smiles and more babbles.

Caleb's fits began to decrease as Angie and I engaged him, giving him the courtesy and attention he deserved, validating his need and ability to communicate with us. How often do we give other people the courtesy of really listening to what they have to say, or of sincerely trying to understand how a person is feeling? We devalue people when we deny them this courtesy. We communicate to them in subtle ways that they are not worth our time and attention. Even my one-year-old comprehended my disengagement and protested by complaining and crying. For weeks my frustrated reactions only reinforced a disconnecting and devaluing message, causing him to react with his own increased frustration in a cycle that threatened our infant relationship. Fortunately for us both, the insight helped me to change my perspective and caused me to return to him and listen. Communication is most powerful in the listening. This lesson, however, is one I have struggled, repeatedly, to learn and relearn, to apply and reapply.

I played Backgammon with John for the first time when he was five. He had often watched Brian and me play, and he had badly wanted to play. There came a point in our game where John could not safely move two checkers. I hit his blot, then he mine. He came to see that he would lose his first game against me, and that he would lose badly. But he wanted to win in the worst way. He suddenly burst into tears and gave in to absolute defeat.

"Okay," I declared. "End of the game."

His sobbing intensified.

"Look," I suggested, "we're just learning how to play. If we can't learn and have fun, then we're not going to play."

I was not harsh, just matter-of-fact. He stopped crying and rolled the dice. A double six! I ended up winning the game, but only by one point. I congratulated him for how well he had played his first game.

"Thanks, Dad," he replied, beaming.

I felt happy, humble, and grateful for how the experience had ended.

"See!" I said. "Never give up. Keep pushing forward until the game is over, even if you don't win. Never give up!"

Engineers at the Erda Airport, owned and operated by Salt Lake City, saw fit to change the lighthouse beacon fixtures and bulbs. The new lights flash quick pulses of green and white as they turn, barely visible on my bedroom walls. The slow, sweeping beams of the old lighthouse now lighten only the insides of my memory.

I WAITED FOR YOU

I waited for you:
waited for you to come to me.
But you did not.
I waited for you
like the crimson clouds after the tired sun drops behind the mountains.
When you came to me at last,
I had faded and gone.

I waited for you:
waited for you to touch me.
But you did not.
I waited for you
like a dry, dusty leaf under a charcoal sky when the soothing rain will
    not fall.
When you reached for me at last,
I had withered and gone.

I waited for you:
waited for you to smile at me.
But you did not.
I waited for you
like a famished infant yearning to suck from her mother's ripe, fragrant
    breast.
When you smiled at me at last,
I had drifted and gone.

Of Boys, Pigeons, and an Evil Rooster

You're my big, bald buddy-boo.
(John-3 to Dad)

As I readied to leave for my Rabbit Lane walk, I noticed a pungent odor from the little boy that hugged my leg.

"I'll change him," his mom offered. "You go ahead."

Little John (2) responded, "NO! Dadda!" and I felt the dubious honor of being chosen by my son for this special duty.

Two years later, Caleb (3) wandered around the kitchen whining and crying for no apparent cause. As I approached him to see what was the matter, a powerful aroma quickly revealed the cause of his complaining: he needed a diaper change. I retrieved a diaper from the linen closet. Holding the diaper flat on one palm, I placed the other palm on top, and moved the diaper folds up and down like a set of jaws.

"I'm going to bite your bum!" I said with a mad scientist laugh.

Caleb froze for a moment, then began to squeal in mixed delight and anxiety, running in circles in the kitchen, holding his buttocks with protecting hands as I chased him slowly enough to not quite catch him.

With seven children, Angie and I changed diapers through at least 15 of the prime years of our lives. In my evening house wanderings, I often found neatly folded but soiled diapers on banisters, stair cases, and countertops, waiting expectantly to be conveyed to a more appropriate final resting place. Having addressed the immediate need to replace a dirty diaper with a clean one, Angie sometimes quickly moved on to other demands without discarding the dirty diapers in the outside trash. Those diapers that were not immediately apparent to my sight revealed themselves to my nose rather forcefully, sometimes after a day or two, as I walked by their hiding places. Often the hiding place was the kitchen garbage can. One garbage-day morning before leaving the house to walk, I lifted the bag out of its can intent on taking it to the curbside can before the garbage truck came. Bending over the bag, I inhaled deeply as I gathered up the bag's loose plastic to better tie the top. Up from the bag's bowels came a malicious odor that elicited a regurgitating gag. As I took what was supposed to be a replenishing breath, the foul vapors spewed into my unsuspecting face and followed my nasal passages deep into my lungs. My stomach turned all the way to Witch's Tree. I have never repeated that mistake. Instead, I take a deep breath and hold it while I complete the whole process of removing, twisting, and tying the bag. Thereafter, I forbade anyone to throw a dirty diaper into an inside garbage can. I held my breath just the same, in case of accident, disobedience, or treachery, and from memory-induced self-protection.

We have no more diapers to change, for now. Someday our children will bring their children . . .

The city animal control officer knew that I raised chickens and other birds from chicks that I purchased at the local feed store. She called me at the office one day and offered me two very young pigeon chicks that a resident had discovered on the ground near her house. I was happy to say yes, and scrounged up an empty box from the basement of city hall. When she brought them to my office, I was shocked at their appearance. The chicks were, frankly, ugly. Their feathers more closely resembled porcupine quills, sticking out from wrinkly, gray skin. Their heads were too large for their bodies, and boasted large bony knobs beside their beaks, beneath their eyes.

Still, I pitied the ugly pigeon-lings, doomed to death without human intervention, and took them home to nurse. I shaped a small bowl in the straw in a vacant pen, and placed them in it, under a heat lamp. They bobbled their too-big heads and stumbled clumsily in the straw, pecking at mashed grains. The pheasant chicks in the adjoining pen, by contrast, were petite and well-proportioned, each displaying a full dress of downy striped feathers. Half the size of the pigeon chicks, the pheasant chicks chased each other nimbly around their pen, peeping happily.

As the pigeon chicks grew, their spines sprouted gray and white feathers, some with a metallic green and blue sheen. The knobby protrusions receded as their beaks lengthened, and their bald skulls sprouted soft head feathers. In two months' time, the ugly chicks had grown into dignified birds. When they fledged and began to fly around the pen, I removed the wire mesh from their window and allowed them to leave the coop. The now-adult pigeons flew in graceful circles around the house and garden with crisp, muscled wing beats. They seemed joyful in the knowledge of their new ability, coupled with their new freedom.

Though pigeons are capable of strong flight, the two birds spent much of their time mingling with the free-range hens, pecking at specks of seed on the garden ground. Still, every day they flew up from the hens and circled the yards, as fast and powerful as falcons. One hot day a flock of wild pigeons descended upon the fields to feed upon wild weed-seed. Moving on to graze elsewhere, the flock coaxed my pigeons to join, and they all flew away together. I missed my two pigeons when they were gone. But I took pleasure in knowing that I had raised them from chicks, watching them grow from their ugly-duckling stage until they were fully fledged fliers.

Growing up in New Jersey and often visiting the Big Apple of New York City, I had come to perceive pigeons as junk birds that polluted bridge bellies and building cornices by the millions, soiling sidewalks and crowding plazas, swarming like mosquitoes, taking aim at unsuspecting pedestrians from marquee-top perches. My opinion of pigeons softened at the Praça de Rossio in Lisbon, where Brian (2) fed and chased thousands of tame pigeons, some of which would perch on his head and eat out of his hand. Now, my two little pigeons had shown me a more exalted view of the species. I have come to admire pigeons as strong fliers and survivors of harsh urban environments, purring with confidence from their perches, their feather patterns as unique and beautiful as sparkling snowflakes.

Walking on Rabbit Lane one evening after dinner, Caleb (5) said to me: "Dad, you'll know this because you're an attorney."

I sucked in some air and prepared to give an intelligent answer to a boy with high expectations of his father. His question caught me completely off guard.

"Dad," he said, after an ominous pause. "How do airplanes fly?"

Caleb believed that I, his father, was an intelligent, informed man, and apparently assumed that this was because I was an attorney. In fact, the sweet boy thought his dad knew everything. My legal training and law practice, however, did nothing to prepare me for this question. Luckily I knew the rudiments of aerodynamics and explained to him how the shape of a wing in motion causes the air coursing over the curved part of the wing to travel at a different speed than the air passing under the wing. These different air velocities cause a higher pressure to exist under the wing, creating a condition called lift. The higher pressure pushes up on the wing. With fast enough speeds, the lift is sufficient to raise the plane into the air despite its enormous weight.

Caleb did his best to take in this explanation, nodding seriously with his new knowledge. I believe he was convinced that there was no question his dad could not answer. I was glad he did not ask me anything difficult, such as, "What do I do if I'm bullied at the playground?" or "What is pornography?" or "What can I do to be happy?" Actually, though, these questions are much more important than "How does an airplane fly?" and I need to be ready to intelligently discuss these and other life questions with my children when they are ready to ask them, as they work to navigate life's pathways.

There came a time when we moved John (4) into Brian's (12) bedroom, where they shared a bunk bed. John felt proud to have been promoted to part ownership in his big brother's room. One evening I heard John calling repeatedly for Brian.

"Brian, Brian, Brian, Brian"—over and over.

Finally, I called, with some irritation, "Brian, will you *please* answer your brother!"

So, Brian answered, "What?" with some irritation of his own.

John answered, "Don't come into *my* room—I'm changing."

I rolled my eyes with exasperation. It had taken longer for John to get Brian's attention about changing his clothes than to just change his clothes. Of course, the situation was not about changing his clothes so much as it was about asserting himself in his new surroundings. A few years later, I overheard an older John (10) say to his little brother, Caleb (8), at bedtime, "I'm going to tell you a story."

Two types of doves grace Erda, the native Mourning Dove and the imported Eurasian Collared Dove. Upon taking flight, the Eurasian Dove spreads its tail feathers into a broad fan. The Mourning Dove's tail forms the iconic "dove tail" where the feathers begin to spread wide, then curve back in upon themselves to form a rounded diamond shape. The Eurasian sports a black collar around its neck. The Mourning Dove softly calls, a sad, haunting sound, while the

Eurasian utters a harsh sneer that often startles. During hunting season, the Eurasian is fair game: kill all you can kill. To take the Mourning Dove, however, the hunter must have a state permit. Then he can kill all he can kill. To me, both are beautiful. In the dawn of misty mornings, the Mourning Dove coos softly, sounding so very sad, its cry floating low over the ground with the mist.

The Doves occasionally pecked at the seeds in the flat-dish bird feeder, but most often pecked in the grass, cleaning up seeds spewed by finicky House Sparrows. Watching the birds with fascination from the living room, Hyrum (7) determined to catch his very own Dove. He schemed and planned and consulted. Having made his plans, he placed a large shoebox up-side-down on the grass, propped up one end with a stick, and spread seeds under and around the box. It took several days, but the Doves finally began to peck at the seeds despite the presence of the raised box. Seeing that the Doves would eat even under his trap, Hyrum tied a kite string to the prop stick and ran the string across the grass, over the porch, and through a small hole in a living room window screen. Kneeling on the couch, he waited and waited, watching for just the right moment. As a Dove finally stepped beneath the box to peck at seeds, Hyrum pulled the string and dropped the box on top of his prey.

"I caught one! I caught one!" he cried with delight, slamming the front door behind him as he ran to the box, the rest of the family close behind.

Reaching a hand under the box, Hyrum carefully grasped the Dove and pulled it out of the trap. I helped him cradle the Dove gently so as not to hurt its wings or legs. Hyrum held the bird proudly, a huge gap-tooth smile on his face. I watched Hyrum watch his bird, and saw the boy's look slowly change from one of triumph to one of awe at the soft beauty of the bird. After proudly showing his prize to all of his siblings, he opened his hands to release his catch. The Dove's wings whirred musically as it rose into the air, brushing past Hyrum's face.

I sat next to Brian (12) on his bed one night. Without talking, we gazed westward out his window, watching the alternating white and green flashes of the airport lighthouse.

After several minutes of silence, I asked sincerely, "How ya' doin' son?"

"I'm alright," he said.

"Are your friends treating you good?" I inquired.

"Oh, sure."

"Are they asking you to smoke, or drink, or do drugs, or look at porn?" I asked.

"Oh, no."

"Good," I said, "because real, true friends wouldn't push you to do things you don't want to do."

He did not respond. I could sense a touch of sadness in his brief responses, as if maybe he had some friends that were not true. Maybe he felt that he had no real friends. But he did not volunteer, and I did not pry. Instead, I put my arm around his slender shoulders and he snuggled into my side, each of us looking silently out the window into the night.

In the dark evening after work and dinner, I carried a flashlight to the chicken coop to gather the eggs. Reaching into a nesting box in the dim light of the coop, I was startled to notice in the box a small, furry, gray face, with tiny, black beads for eyes. It sat unalarmed under the beam of light, probably unable to see me for the glare. It turned its head to show me its profile, and its pointed nose resembled a short bird's beak. The mouse seemed to have transformed into a little mouse-bird.

Caleb (5) had been struggling. Thinking it might help, I invited him to go for an evening walk with me. Just the two of us. He responded enthusiastically. I asked him where he would like to walk.

"Rabbit Lane," he said matter-of-factly, as if there were no other place to walk.

John (7) wanted to go, too, but I told him that this walk was just for Caleb and me. Hyrum (2) begged to go, also, and received the same answer.

Caleb looked up into my face and asked, "Am I in charge of the walk?"

"You bet!" I answered.

Then Caleb spoke to his little brother, "Hyrum, you can come on my walk if you want to."

Caleb's generosity of heart touched me. Sharing candy or toys is hard enough, but to share his time alone with dad was downright magnanimous. He quickly found that inviting Hyrum to share his walk gave him positive power over the situation, not to mention the good feelings that come from living generously. Had I invited Hyrum, or encouraged Caleb to invite Hyrum, I would have taken away Caleb's power and may have created resentments.

With his new awareness, Caleb then invited John to go, too.

"That's fine," I explained, bolstering Caleb's empowering invitations. "But I need everyone to understand that Caleb is still in charge of this walk."

And out the door we went.

Harvey had told me about the "Easter Egg" chickens that lay pastel blue and green eggs. It was hard for me to believe him, but I could not think of why the old man would lie to me.

"The real name of the breed is Araucana," he told me.

I took the children to the feed store where we looked in the catalogue at pictures of the many breeds. Sure enough, the Araucana breed was pictured there. I still wondered about the eggs. We decided to give it a try, and ordered one rooster and several hens. Eight months or so after we brought the chicks home, the fully-grown hens began laying eggs. Not white. Not brown. But pastel blues and greens! We gathered and fondled the eggs carefully, gawking. Even holding the marvels, it was difficult to believe that the eggs had naturally come that way. Seeing our first success in the egg effort, Harvey joked with me, "You don't even need to dye them at Easter time; they come pre-dyed!"

The male Araucana chick we bought grew into an enormous rooster, twice the bulk of the hens, with long, curved tail feathers colored dark brown, black, and red, contrasting with the rest of the light-colored bird. As the hens were taking naturally to laying and brooding, the Araucana rooster began to show aggression towards nearly every moving creature, regardless of species or size. He began to charge at me, each time backing off, but becoming more and more bold with the passing days. He soon charged me so close that I put a boot hard in his breast. He seemed to fly backwards at the impact, with nearly six-foot wings flapping and voice box squawking alarm. Upon landing, he came right back at me, unphased. The children named the rooster Hitmonle, after an evil cartoon character.

One afternoon, Caleb, only 18 months old, came toddling into the garden with a wide smile as he approached his dad. I thought of the threat too late. Before I could act to prevent the attack, Hitmonle charged Caleb, propelling himself in the air with wings spread and claws bared, the long, deadly spurs flung forward like quarrels from a crossbow. The flying fury struck the stocky toddler in the face, knocking him to the ground. I moved quickly to prevent another attack, and found that one three-inch spur had punctured the skin only a millimeter from Caleb's eye. That moment decided Hitmonle's fate. He clearly had no place at my home with my family. I carried Caleb crying into the house. Armored with leather gloves and long sleeves, and wielding an ax, I cornered the monster, pinning him against the chicken coop wall. With both feet clamped in one hand, and the wings clamped under my arm, I laid his neck on a board and hacked off his ornery head with the ax. I have never raised another rooster.

Caleb, almost five, became indignant with me for parking my truck in *his* bicycle parking spot in the garage.

Hyrum, almost two, came to me with a piece of white paper on which he had drawn random swirls and loops and circles. His free hand had circled round and round, as if chasing his toddler thoughts. He pronounced, "I drew a poem for you, Dad."

I worked with John (9) Saturday teaching him to fix broken and bent hoses with connectors and new ends.

"I'm a good worker, huh Dad?" he said to me.

I saw his question as an expression of his young hopes: a hope that he is good enough; a hope that his dad thinks he is good enough; a hope that he has value and that his dad will validate his value. I don't do it often enough.

I carved a walking staff from two-by-two pine lumber. It stands seven feet tall, rounded on the top, with a screw and washer in the bottom to keep it from splitting and curling with heavy use. Rubbing in mineral oil gave it a rich but humble shine. It makes a straight, stout, smooth staff. A leather patch glued and tacked to the staff forms the grip. I tied waxed cotton string every inch of the top one-foot, leaving tiny knotted loops, then wrapped the same top one-foot with strips of various colored leathers, gluing and tacking the ends with decorative upholstery tacks.

The little loops were for feathers. Harvey showed me how to attach feathers to the staff through the loops, as the Indians do.

Holding a banded pheasant feather with the quill pointed inward, I drew my sharp knife toward me, carefully slicing away the top half of the unfeathered portion of the hollow quill. I slipped the cut end through one of the tiny loops and folded the end over itself, thrusting the cut quill end into the hollow, round, uncut portion of the quill. I added a dab of glue for strength. In this manner, I attached the bright orange feather of a Red-shafted Northern Flicker, the blue-black feather of a Steller's Jay, the white-dot-on-black feather of a Downy Woodpecker, a light- and dark-banded tail feather of a Ring-necked Pheasant, a long iridescent tail feather of the departed Hitmonle, and the feather of a wild turkey that resembles an Osprey feather I found on the rocky shore of a high mountain lake.

I sometimes carry the staff on Rabbit Lane, even though I do not need the staff on the level-flat road, just because I made the staff, and I like it. I like the feel of the stick striking the ground to give strength and stability to my legs and feet. I like the grip of the leather patch in my hand, and the swing of the weighty staff. I stop and raise the staff for the morning breeze to catch the feathers fluttering loosely like small kites or ship sails, to speak to the spirits that soar, and to express my wish for my own spirit's flight.

AWAY I MUST FLY

Away
I must fly,
sang the restless little bird,
Away
I must fly.
Away.
Only for a moment.
Only for a day.
Only for a season.
Then back I'll fly,
to stay.
But today,
sang the restless little bird,
I must fly
Away.
Away.

AT MIDNIGHT

I lay on my back
at midnight
and wondered if I should
go to his room,
where his light still shone,
and talk to my son,
a young man.
I lay on my back and wondered.
I lay on my back and thought.
When I at last arose,
I found his light too soon turned off.

Big-Wheel Ecosystem

Rabbit Lane is a short nothing of a dirt road in Erda, USA.

The air was crisp but warmer than a typical January day. The sky hung gray, and pockets of darker clouds dropped round, soft pellets of dry snow. Shades of orange accented the western mountaintops. Feathers of unseen Sparrows rustled from inside Wild Rose and Willow bushes. The scene made for an idyllic late Sunday afternoon walk on Rabbit Lane. Idyllic and peaceful . . . except for Hannah (3) riding her big-wheel tricycle behind me. The wide, hollow, pink plastic wheels ground over the disintegrating asphalt, radiating into the peacefulness the racket of an ore crusher. I could not hear anyone talk or myself think.

"I'm tired. You can pull me now," Hannah announced magnanimously, as if bestowing upon me some privilege. I unwound the rope leash from the handle bars and yoked myself, the family ox, to pull the big-wheel past Witch's Tree. A few minutes later, she interrupted her own rendition of *Puff the Magic Dragon* to inform me, "I don't need the rope now, Daddy." Stopping, I wound it again around the handle bars. (I had thought that bringing the rope would be preferable to carrying the big-wheel.) She wheeled past me, her long blond hair flowing out from under the cap Laura (14) had crocheted as a Christmas gift: white, pink, and purple, studded all over with purple crocheted knobs. Hannah wore the cap proudly, even though it had slipped forward to all but cover her eyes. Turning her head back, she lightly patted the tricycle's flank as if to urge it forward.

The boys were busy searching for treasures. Hyrum (8) held a barred pheasant feather. Caleb (10) carried a walking stick fallen from a dead Cottonwood. John (12) discovered a mouse skull complete with long incisors.

Rabbit Lane today—recycled asphalt pressed cold onto rutted, hard-pack dirt and gravel—has deteriorated seriously in just a few years' time. Large patches have become bowls of pulverized asphalt dust, devoid of oil from their old life somewhere else in the county. Large chunks of pavement break loose and grind to gravel and dust under high chassis. Where the chunks break clean off from somewhat cohesive pavement, vehicle tires fall in suddenly with a clang and a clunk, jolting the occupants severely, at odds with the pastoral serenity on either side. Children on bicycles seem to fall into the holes, whereas they used to roll into and roll out of smoother wok holes with a gleeful whoop. Whole sections of the asphalt road stretch out in a worse condition than the previous gravel washboard and mud-puddled chuck holes. Again, now with some hindsight, I question the wisdom of the county officials who ordered the lonely farm road paved in the first place.

Rabbit Lane, in its present helpless and neglected condition, seems to me a symbol of the deterioration of other things that Rabbit Lane knows so well. Our tender memories of the land, our visceral connection to the land, our fond feelings for the land: the crop land and the pasture land and the tree-lined ditch banks, the ducks and muskrats and pheasants. Once we felt the need to preserve and nurture the land as it preserved and nurtured us. We loved it as if it were our own offspring, in whom we both found heritage and left legacy. More and more these values are considered quaint, hardly relevant to our plugged-in modernity. We put them behind us in favor of the developer's dollar, arguing the sacrosanct nature of private property rights while we turn away from the land's inherent virtues, both corporeal and metaphysical. *How much can I get for it?* is the only question we regard, to the exclusion of the paramount questions of a more balanced, georgic age. Old Cottonwood is slowly dying, dropping its thick bark onto the road to be ground up, its dry dust mixing in to brown the gray of the oil-less asphalt dust.

Rabbit Lane forms its own linear ecosystem, vertically from the ditch bottom six feet below the road to the tops of the Cottonwood trees, and about 20 feet wide. Yes, an ecosystem—with a dirt road at its heart. So, what is the relative value of the Rabbit Lane ecosystem to this planet of ours? Is it great, or even noteworthy? Is it *de minimis*? In truth, it does not matter what *our* answer is. Every ecosystem is of vital value to those who comprise it, who eat and are eaten, who drink up water and breathe in carbon dioxide and exhale oxygen, who wriggle through mud and swoop down from the trees and trot across on all fours.

Many, perhaps most, would say that the world would not mourn the loss of such an insignificant ecosystem. It would not be missed. But I know that I would mourn. I would mourn the loss of the barely audible trickle of the water through Watercress, the splashing of a surprised Muskrat as it submerges in sudden escape, the yellow and black stripes of the Monarch larva winding its way through fragrant pink Milkweed blossoms, the Mule Deer peering at me from behind Russian Olive trunks in the early-morning mist, the Great-horned Owl springing noiselessly from its tree-top perch. Pipe the water, slab over with asphalt, rip out the trees, and you have lost something. You have lost the whispering memories of the Jack Rabbit that fed the farmer's family a century ago, the echoing hoof beats of old Moses carrying the 1930s paperboy, the delight of laughing boys riding bicycles through mud puddles, and the paw prints of the Raccoon in the ditch-bank mud. A living part of us will have departed.

Every night, it seems, new lights appear on the bench lands that sit at the feet of the Oquirrh mountains and look over the valley farms and subdivisions. The lights appear to advance like an army of glowing insects conquering the higher ground. We have always coveted the high ground. It invariably fetches a higher price in our speculations over land. I suppose we prize the views. Yet for every foothill house that sighs over its valley views, thousands of other houses look up to see the natural foothills disappearing. Vinyl siding replaces Gambel Oak. Better to preserve the high ground as a natural asset for the enjoyment of the commonwealth.

Climbing up out of the valleys has created new divisions of class. The Contour Class finds its prestige in a map's contour lines and elevation numbers, in ridiculous driveway slopes, and in the profusion of retaining walls. It is as if by buying tighter lines and higher numbers, we purchase a license to look down upon the valley dwellers. Instead, we should gaze gratefully at those that grow the corn and the wheat and the beef that sustain them and us. We should acknowledge that the inhabitants of both foothill and valley share the same generous heritage and together lay a common legacy.

During the hours of daylight, front-end loaders, earth scrapers, track-hoes, and back-hoes gnaw their way across the land, the same land that is grazed less and less by cattle, the same land that once housed the stick-and-mud huts of the Goshute Indians, the same land that hides the bed and bank of the ancient Lake Bonneville. The land itself is a living fossil of prehistoric ocean beds thrust up into mountain spines fleshed with fertile, voluptuous valleys. More and more it is becoming a land of asphalt, concrete, and boxes we call homes, in one of which I live.

Development is ever approaching with its subdivision sprawl, like an engorged caterpillar bulging forward one bloated section at a time, slowly but steadily, always in one direction: toward the green.

Most people around me see it as the positive, undeterred march of opportunity. I built a house, too, didn't I? Is there a place where one can reasonably draw a line and say, "There, that is the right place for the line"?

"If we build enough houses to reach a population of 50,000," one public official told me, "we can get our own Costco." Perhaps the Costco line is the magic line.

My surroundings seem to be always changing their proportions, like an amoeba that changes shape as suits it. The weight inevitably changes, tipping the scales, the balance changing between people and nature. In more and more places, one end of the scale has hit the table, to rest there, flat.

I may have to face the likelihood that the loss of Rabbit Lane, at least its wildness, is inevitable. The new high school opened its doors at the road's northern end; the marching band's drum beats and horn toots drift over the fields. At Rabbit Lane's south end, a new *One Way* sign attempts to alter old habits. Historic farms have been scraped off for new roads and one-acre-lot subdivisions. Roadside trees that used to form a verdant tunnel have been felled. The ditch is dry: the water than ran openly for a century and a half has disappeared into a 12-inch-diameter pipe.

Others easily accommodate such changes. I, on the other hand, cannot seem to appreciate the future for my overwhelming sense of loss of the past. But the Canada Geese still fly, honking, overhead. The Red-tailed Hawk still shrieks on the wing, searching for field mice. The Milkweed still blooms roadside, fragrant and pink. The Mule Deer still hide in the copse. The cock Ring-necked Pheasant continues to crow. And I can still feel the leaves of the Russian Olive trees pass through my fingers as I walk down the lane with my arms stretched out to the sides.

Russian Olive tree

If it is not already apparent, I will confess that I sometimes feel I own Rabbit Lane, as if it were mine and no one else's. The presence of others—cars, joggers, even other walkers—can feel threatening. Why should I feel this way? Perhaps it is because on Rabbit Lane I find the peace of solitude like nowhere else, and I do not want to lose it. On Rabbit Lane no one can demand anything of me (if I leave my phone at home). No one can pull me back or prod me onward or knock me off course. I can simply be. To be sure, my movements remain linear, together with the movement of time: always forward. But life does not rush by in a drowning torrent on Rabbit Lane. Rather, life cradles and caresses, gently turning and rocking as if in a streamside eddy, helping me to see life more calmly, more clearly, from new points of view. When I rush through my walk—like the mother instructing her child to "hurry up and play!"—I have launched myself into the torrent, and risk missing whatever Rabbit Lane would teach me that day.

So, is Rabbit Lane just a short nothing of a doomed country road? Or is it something more? You can decide. As for me, Rabbit

Lane is everything. Rabbit Lane enlightens. Rabbit Lane teaches. Rabbit Lane soothes. Rabbit Lane strengthens. Rabbit Lane heals.

On a Sunday morning walk on Rabbit Lane before church, I discovered what I had searched for thousands of times and rarely found, a large Monarch larvae feeding openly on a Milkweed leaf. I left it alone, but told Hannah (8) about it upon my return, gauging her reply.

"Can I raise it into a butterfly?" she asked excitedly.

Short on time, we drove to the spot, carefully picked the leaf upon which the caterpillar fed, and placed them together inside a screen-walled bug box.

"Which end is the head?" Hannah asked, seeing the faux horns on both ends of the worm. "Oh. I see," she answered her own question as the caterpillar began to move.

"You'll have to feed it fresh Milkweed leaves every day. Every day," I enjoined.

"Oh I will," she promised.

Hannah faithfully fed her new tiger-striped friend. Within a week, it formed a beautiful powder-green hanging chrysalis with a black-and-gold band and gold spots. We used the jeweler's loop to examine up close the exquisite chrysalis. Its gold spots and band glimmered like real gold leaf in the sun. We checked the chrysalis frequently for any change in color that might signal the butterfly's imminent emergence, though I suspected it to be weeks or months away. To our surprise, less than two weeks after pupating, a beautiful male Monarch emerged. He hung on the clear skin of the spent chrysalis, slowly opening and closing his large orange-and-black wings.

Inserting my hand into the box, I coaxed the creature to step onto my index finder, then slowly withdrew him for Hannah to see. Holding Hannah's finger with my other hand, I encouraged the butterfly to walk from my hand to Hannah's. Hannah watched, elated, in wonderment, as the Monarch crept up her finger, onto her palm, and slowly up her forearm.

"It tickles!" she giggled.

Although the Monarch's wings were fully extended, they flopped flimsily. I knew that, in the sun, the wing veins would harden into flight-worthy sails.

"Let's take him out into the sun," I suggested.

Hannah carefully walked with her butterfly out the front door, and allowed him to step onto a Milkweed flower cluster that waved in the hot July breeze. Within minutes, the Monarch lifted himself upon new wings into the wind. We watched him fly around and fly away. A longing sadness began to settle onto Hannah's face.

"You did it!" I burst out. "You raised a beautiful Monarch butterfly from a caterpillar. You're amazing!"

"Yes. I did it," Hannah agreed quietly, beginning to realize that she had cared for, and raised to maturity, one of planet Earth's beautiful, miraculous creatures.

What Is To Come

Wherever you live, find your Rabbit Lane.

Christmas day. A warm south wind had begun to howl in the early morning hours, the kind of wind that tears off siding and rips at shingles. A particular set of vulnerable shingles had flapped irritatingly above my bed all night long, as if under the sticks of a novice but indefatigable drummer. All day long the wind had blown, with frequent gusts that shook the house and trembled the floor under my chair. The bird feeders swung wildly on their wires, like marionettes under the hand of a demented puppeteer. We knew the pattern: the wind would blow and blow until the climactic dissonance resolved in a downpour of driving rain or sleet or snow. At nine o'clock in the evening, Angie called us to where she stood by the front door opened wide to a world covered with new whiteness. The south wind had stopped, replaced by a steady northern breeze bringing the snow from over the lake. Brian, home from his first semester of college, announced happily that he was going for a walk. He bounded away with enthusiasm.

Weary from Christmas chaos, I nonetheless determined to venture forth. A walk down Rabbit Lane, at night, under the falling snow, is enchanting and not to be missed. Proceeding down Church Road toward Rabbit Lane, I followed Brian's footprints. At the intersection, I saw that Brian's tracks turned north onto Rabbit Lane. I felt contented to see that his spirit had chosen the path that I have so often taken. Now my boots followed his. He had chosen to walk in the fresh snow, avoiding the twin tire ruts of a recently passed truck. I followed suit. The northern wind blew the soft snow into my face and eyes, so that I kept them pointed downward to the road. The crumbling black asphalt had disappeared under six inches of fresh white powder. In addition to the snow, the north wind brought with it a hint of salt from the great lake, like the winds of my childhood once brought to me the scent of the great ocean to the east.

A mile from home, I met my son on his return trip. We greeted each other simply, as father and son often do, and I turned to accompany him. The breeze had abated. We walked together under a softly glowing sky, neither saying a word to the other, both taking in the magic of the snowflakes settling upon the grassy fields, upon the black cattle, upon the tree branches, and upon us.

I looked up as we walked to see in the distance the icicle lights Angie had bought a few weeks before and hung from the rain gutter across the line of the front porch. She had not previously ventured to hang holiday lights herself, and now enjoyed them doubly for her successful effort. I contemplated how that house sits on my small square inch of planet Earth. In that small space we have loved, worried, worked, hurt, and made love. On that small space we have conceived and nursed our children, taught our children how to live in this world and how to love and respect nature and other people. On that small space we have grieved over illness and death, sat with good books and good movies, worked pulling weeds, cutting firewood, and tending to animals. We have prayed together, fought together, cried together, sung together, cooked and eaten of the earth's bounty together, cuddled kittens and puppies and buried sundry pets together. And we have walked down Rabbit Lane together.

My grandparents lived on a little dirt lane now known ignominiously as 4200 West. A bermed irrigation ditch ran alongside the lane. Every few years my family traveled 2,200 miles to visit. As a child in the early 1970s I loved to run down the dirt lane and walk along the slowly moving water beside my leaf and bark boats. The dusty strip possessed a subtle but real power to kindle the imagination and to incite healthy play. As the area developed, the ditch was piped, the land was paved, and the house my grandfather built in the 1930s was torn down to make way for a car dealership's overflow parking lot. My grandparents are dead now, as is the lane, the ditch, the house— and the magic.

I suppose it may be the destiny of Rabbit Lane, and all insignificant country roads like it, to have their ditches piped, their dirt asphalted, their edges curbed, and their fields plowed under to make way for houses and offices and stores and warehouses and parking lots. Millions of such roads have disappeared unnoticed, unlamented. Still, I feel a sadness at the prospect of Rabbit Lane becoming a modern Rabbit Road. I know that I will have lost something, like the quiet, steady presence of a friend that moves away, leaving me lonely, or the finishing of a good novel that must now be closed and put on the shelf. When my Rabbit Lane is gone, might there be another Rabbit Lane remaining somewhere else? Might there always be a Rabbit Lane surviving somewhere? Or will they all disappear, and with them, the magic that we almost did not know was there?

I believe that Rabbit Lanes exist in every community, all over the world: places where history and nature and transcendence converge to create special meaning within us. The importance and meaning of these Rabbit Lanes to individuals, families, and communities, while not screaming for attention, cannot be denied and should not be underestimated. We must find them. We must preserve them, if not literally, then in our lore.

New families have moved into the subdivision that was the old Norris farm, each to claim their share of life's dreams. I do not begrudge them and their impacts on nature, on history, and on Rabbit Lane. After all, I have had my impacts, too. Instead, I rejoice in seeing these families, the parents with their little children, walking and riding together on Rabbit Lane, exploring, feeling, laughing, and soaking in the treasure.

THE END

Appendix:
Round Shells Resting

(Published 2003 in *Tooele Valley Magazine*.)

The weathered hinges creek as I enter my patchwork coop. Its quiet inhabitants, rudely rousted from their roosting, suddenly jabber with a cacophony of clucks, crows, honks, and coos. They run nervously about as I turn over a bucket and occupy a corner of their space.

I sit quiet and motionless, and the chatter calms as their anxiety fades. Soon they ignore me and go about their normal bird business: pecking at mash, scratching through straw, drinking from water they muddied the moment it was poured, brooding on freshly laid eggs, and general roosting.

This is where I come for quiet contemplation. Here I am free from the suit and necktie that pay the mortgage but strangle my dreams. If I sit long enough, I begin to see again a glimmer of who I am.

In the coop, the delicate fragrance of fresh, dry straw soothes my frazzled nerves. An impressive portfolio of molted feathers decorates the room in abstract patterns that appear a mere mess to the unenlightened. Eggs nestle comfortably, softly, in beds of straw—a perfect still life of brown, white, and pastel-green ovals.

I soak in the simplicity and innocence of feathered life. I silently bless the absence of drool and bark and bray. I relish the moment's escape from trivial chatter and from the weight of the world's woes. My birds demand nothing of me. I feed them; they eat. I water them; they drink. I leave them alone; they leave me alone. We are together in a four-walled world of quiet being—no doing allowed— happily minding our own business.

My chicken coop is unique in all the world. It follows no blueprint or pattern. Its configuration is determined wholly by the dimensions of the pallets that previously carried snowmobiles and four-wheelers to the local dealer. The pallets were free, except for one blue fingernail, five stitches in a knuckle, and three dings in my truck. Scrap fiberboard sides the pallets, with old storm windows framed into the south and east corners for winter light and warmth.

The finished product stands twelve by eight, ten feet tall in the front and six in the back, with more pallets nailed together forming the roof. After driving the last nail, I stood back and admired my beginner's handiwork. *Beautiful*, I thought with pride. The chickens seemed pleased, too. A month later, Grandpa offered to cover the mottled scrap wood with exterior wood siding, and the roof with corrugated aluminum. He said it would last longer that way—he was right, of course—but I could tell he was also concerned about preserving my property value.

Chickens and ducks share the coop. Sometimes the billed birds peck at the beaked, but the coop is spacious enough to permit these distant cousins to live together in seeming familial friendship. Maybe they merely tolerate each other. I suppose at any moment an invisible tension could erupt into a flurry of feathers.

Despite both being fowl, however, they are really nothing alike. They eat the same food—grain, mash, bugs—whatever is available. But chickens peck with sudden snaps of the neck that bring whiplash to mind. The hungrier they are the faster they peck. At feeding time their heads lurch toward the grain with such ferocity that my head hurts, and I wonder what cushions their small brains from becoming mush against their skulls. Their hunger satisfied, they meander around the coop, casually scratching and pecking at straw, feathers, grains of sand, but still with the same mechanical whip-snap motion.

Ducks, on the other hand, definitely do not peck. In fact, their heads remain practically motionless while they feed. The head merely points the bill, which opens and shuts with remarkable speed, as if plugged into a vibrator. My slow eyes perceive a vague blur as bills pulverize a strand of straw into straw-dust.

In contrast to whip-snapping chicken heads, chicken feet unfold and flex with a smooth, fluid motion. This fact holds true with all chicken gaits, but becomes obvious to my eyes with the slow, searching gait employed in casual grazing and roost pacing. I notice suddenly that each chicken breed has its own foot color. White Leghorn: yellow. Rhode Island Red: orange. Araucana: steel gray. Golden Sebright Bantam: blue-gray.

Red combs flop around carelessly with the chickens' bobbing heads. Some combs reach over an inch tall; others resemble short, blunt spikes barely protruding from the head. While the height of a chicken's comb depends partly on its breed, the comparative height within a single breed indicates a hen's egg cycle. A tall comb indicates productivity. A short comb tells me she's taking a break for a few weeks.

I wondered one evening, *Just what does a chicken comb feel like?* I had to know. To find out, I employed my practiced chicken-catching technique to apprehend the subject of my curiosity. I cornered a long-combed hen and inched forward slowly, rocking back and forth on wide-planted feet. With a sudden stretch I grabbed her. Terror struck her: she squawked hysterically, struggling to break free. I cupped her head gently in my hand to calm her down. Then I stroked her comb. It was rough and firm, but fleshy, like an old, cracked rubber scraper. I sat on my bucket and smoothed her ruffled feathers. "Don't worry, little one," I whispered. "I won't hurt you." I began to savor this simple moment and to appreciate this creature who lives unfettered by the concerns and dysfunctions of humanity.

One evening, as I sat contemplating nothing, I watched a tiny field mouse skitter along a lateral plank, keeping to the shadowed corners. It paused behind each pallet vertical like a thief slinking behind trees before a caper. Yet I just could not quite make the metaphor work: the tiny black eyes, soft, glossy coat, tissue paper ears, and delicate, bony hands painted a picture of sweetness, not deceit. The tiny creature just wanted a little food, after all—and the chickens' leftovers would do quite nicely. The image of a poor vassal gleaning the fief's fields fitted better. But the chickens' crumbs were far from subsistence: they were a bounty to the contented mouse. Perched on petite haunches, it ate undisturbed from a kernel it turned in its delicate hands.

As long as I sat quietly, the mouse seemed to not be aware of my presence. I noticed that the loud crowing of the big rooster registered not the slightest tremor in the mouse's calm nibbling. Neither did the soft hen clucking or high-pitched Bantam crowing. *Hmmn*, I thought, and whistled a few notes. No sign of rodent distress. A little humming—still no observable trauma. It must have thought I was just a big, motionless chicken, as oblivious as the rest. Then I snapped my fingers with a *crack*. The mouse jumped with a start and disappeared. But my little friend soon peeked its dark bright eyes—small, but huge on its tiny snout—out from behind a board. The mouse blended naturally with the setting: warm straw, yummy grain, lots of places to hide, and freedom from felines.

Not only roosters like to roost. Roosting, among chickens at least, rises almost to the exaltation of eating. Old two-by-fours form their roosts, crossing the coop at different heights and angles. As evening comes, the chickens instinctively return to the coop and hop up to segregated spaces. The full-grown chickens claim the highest roost. This Spring's juveniles take the middle. No one chooses the lowest.

I have never actually witnessed any pecking to this pecking order. But I surmise that, when I am not watching, the mature birds throw off any pubescents who presume to attempt the highest roost, in a sort of king-of-the-roost affair. I engineered some equity in their social order by positioning the roosts so as to protect the younger birds from getting dropped on by their roosting superiors.

Ducks do not roost. They prefer to cuddle comfortably together in the straw. Long necks sway their heads back to settle in a fluff of wing feathers. From this position, the ducks' heads appear bizarrely to rise neck-less from the middle of their backs.

The crowing instinct has recently possessed my daughter's young Bantam. With no one to coach it, it is learning nonetheless. But its attempts require an effort painful for me to watch. Dropping its wings slightly, the young Bantam's crow unfurls from the tip of its tail feathers through its small body, which contorts like a crawling caterpillar, and releases itself as a wheezy little croak, sounding like a leaking old bicycle bulb horn. Between crows, it struts around confidently, like a politician at his election party.

The big Araucana rooster paces inside its rabbit cage, to where it was banished for its summer misdeeds. An amiable young rooster, the adult became arrogant and aggressive. As I gathered eggs one morning, it flew at me, spurs first, like an eagle swooping upon a giant rodent. My denim-clad legs felt like they'd been struck with a willow switch, and I was glad I had not worn shorts. But the unprovoked attack annoyed me more than hurt. A swift boot kick ended the fight, temporarily at least. Each visit to the coop replayed the scene: flying spurs; boot kick; peace.

Pulling weeds in the flower garden one Saturday, my seven-year-old began screaming hysterically. I spun around to witness her racing across the grass with the big Araucana trotting after her like a miniature painted ostrich. Its face devoid of emotion, I nonetheless divined its malicious intent.

With the rooster now securely in the rabbit cage, my children more safely gather eggs from the irritated hens, whose pecks, after the rooster attacks, seem to them friendly taps. I'll someday expand the coop so the Araucana can enjoy life without ruining it for others. It is a beautiful bird, after all, with luminescent blue-black tail feathers and a rich golden mien. In the meantime, it paces endlessly in quarters that cramp its tyrannical style.

For the children, discovering the first egg was as exciting as finding hidden candy, not just because it was our first egg, but also because it was green. Araucanas lay pastel green and blue-green eggs. Some call the breed the Easter egg chicken, for obvious reasons. Pre-died, you might say.

Despite the eight identical nesting boxes that line the rear wall, the hens insist on laying in only one box—the second from the right, to be exact. Even when one hen is brooding a newly-laid egg, another hen, in answer to nature's urge, oozes herself into the same one-foot by one-foot cubbyhole to lay. Although they soon both give up on brooding, they continue to lay their eggs in the same box, day after day, egg upon egg. Left uncollected, the eggs soon form a neat, multicolored pile, with the other seven boxes vacant. The plastic eggs I placed in the other boxes to induce a more even distribution were pecked open and kicked out.

Each day, the children thrill to gather the eggs in their skirts and run to the kitchen. At least one egg inevitably suffers a casualty, cracked or dropped along the way, sometimes before it even leaves the coop. The chickens rush upon the broken egg, devouring its spilled contents in a cannibalistic frenzy.

Each broken egg tempts my irritation. But a moment's reflection reminds me that I love my daughters more than my chicken eggs. Anyway, the majority of eggs usually weathers the trip without incident. I figure we have the chickens not just for the eggs, but for the experience of having chickens and eggs: to earn the rewards of work; to care for something besides ourselves; to nurture life; to find simplicity and peace in the midst of a frantically materialistic world.

Soon to come will be a pallet patchwork addition, with rooms for pheasants, jungle fowl, pigeons, quail, and maybe an exotic breed or two, like the iridescent Japanese golden pheasant. We'll admire their remarkable beauty and diversity. We'll cry when a raccoon spreads feathers and feet through the field. We'll curse as young roosters spur to defend their turf. And we'll witness the process of life as old birds die and new life emerges from thin, round shells resting in the straw.

To Say Thank You

How does one say thank you to a road, to a strip of dirt and gravel? Yet that road is the main character, the protagonist, of *Rabbit Lane: Memoir of a Country Road.* So, I must unequivocally thank Rabbit Lane itself for every gift bestowed to me over the years: calm, insight, resolution, understanding, beauty, history, transcendence, and healing. And, for the gift of this book. I also thank all of the people listed below who are mentioned in, or who contributed to, this book.

Angela Cottle Baker, and our seven remarkable children: Brian, Erin, Laura, John, Caleb, Hyrum, Hannah. My parents Nelson and Lucille Baker. My fifth great-grandmother Susanna Ann Burgess and her daughter Jean Rio Griffiths Baker. My maternal grandparents Wallace and Dorothy Bawden. Jeanette Baker Davis. Thomas Nielson. Darwin Cottle. Sarah Jolley.

Harvey "Two Suns" Russell (pictured above, by Mary Russell). Cloyd Russell. Native American sun-dance chiefs whose names I never knew.

Austin and Mary Barrus. Cordale Gull. Ron and Mary Norris. Carli Gressman. Craig Vorwaller. Evan Coon. Chelsea Parkinson. Don Summit. Ben Court. Ray and Betsy Henninger.

Charley and Judy Warr. Charley's mother Nina Vorwaller Warr. Charley's great-grandfather Charles Warr. Mayla Warr. Joe Liddell. Doyle "Doc" Taylor. Glenn Thompson. Dempsey Prichard (sp?).

Shirley Weyland and Lucille Weyland Rydalch.

Mathew Reza Arbshay. Diba Arabshahi, and her parents Bobak and Anahita. Mrs. Kastanis and her three children. Bob Morgan. Joe McNall.

I want especially to thank my faithful friend Carl Johanson, and his wife Cláudia Giron Johanson, who gave me both a place and a reason to live during the darkest hours of my life. Carl called my writing room my Walden Pond, which compliment greatly lifted my spirits and helped me believe in myself while writing this book.

(All photos by the author, except for the portrait of Harvey.)

About the Author

A Utah post-graduate student couple brought Roger Evans Baker into the world while living in São Paulo, Brazil, in 1964. Nelson and Lucille reared Roger and his five siblings in East Brunswick, New Jersey. Following a second stint in Brazil and one in Portugal, Roger earned his BA in English at Brigham Young University, along with a minor in Portuguese. After law school at BYU, Roger returned to Portugal in 1991, where he studied international law as a Fulbright scholar. In 1993 Roger went to work as a criminal prosecutor for Tooele City, Utah, where in 1995 the Mayor and City Council appointed him to the position of City Attorney. He continues to work there today (2016). In his free time, Roger rears children (7), raises chickens and goats, pulls weeds in the garden, walks Erda's farm-flanked roads, reads, and writes the occasional poem and lullaby.

Enjoy more of Roger's poems and lullabies on his Rabbit Lane blog at www.rabbitlaneutah.com.

CPSIA information can be obtained
at www.ICGtesting.com
Printed in the USA
FSHW02n1941210618
49694FS